PIERCE M. B. YOUNG

The Warwick of the South

PIERCE MANNING BUTLER YOUNG

LYNWOOD M. HOLLAND

PIERCE M. B. YOUNG

The Warwick of the South

UNIVERSITY OF GEORGIA PRESS
ATHENS

To

ELLA *and* LOUISE

LYNWOOD M. HOLLAND grew up in Georgia and attended Emory University for his A.B. and A.M. degrees. For further graduate study he attended the University of Illinois where he earned the Ph.D. After teaching at Middle Georgia College, the University of Illinois, and the University of Arizona, he returned to Emory, and is currently Chairman of the Department of Political Science. He is the author of several books and articles in the field of political science. Dr. Holland's interest in Pierce Young was sparked by his research into grass roots politics in Georgia and nurtured for over nine years by a study of the Milner-Cummings personal collection of Young memorabilia at the family home, Walnut Plantation.

Copyright © 1964
University of Georgia Press
Library of Congress Catalog Card Number: 64-17062
Printed in the United States of America
By Foote & Davies, Atlanta

Contents

Preface

SOMETIMES the story of a minor but representative figure reflects the life of an era. Such a figure is Pierce Manning Butler Young, who is perhaps the most nearly forgotten major general from Georgia in the Confederate army. And there are reasons why he should not be forgotten. His career reflects the history of the South, and in some respects of the nation, from 1865 to 1896. He was a youth in ante-bellum Cartersville, Georgia, an officer in the Confederate army, the first Georgia congressman to be allowed to take his seat in Congress after the Civil War, a gentleman farmer harassed by the economic and political problems of the Reconstruction period, consul-general to St. Petersburg, minister to Nicaragua and Guatemala. A handsome bachelor, he was forever viewed as a desirable catch by romantic daughters and their ambitious mothers.

For the past nine years I have been working with a wonderfully full, original collection of letters, documents, diaries, newspaper clippings, and scrapbooks related to the career and family of Pierce Young. The materials date from 1806 to 1896 and cover phases of Georgia history largely ignored by historians. The correspondence in this collection reveals hitherto unnoted facts about Young's contemporaries, and seldom-noticed undercurrents of the times. The owners of the collection, Miss Louise Milner and Mrs. Ella Cummings, descendants of the Young family, who live at Walnut Plantation, have been most generous in granting use of the materials. In addition they have been most helpful in assisting in my research and in arranging contacts for me with their friends and acquaintances. Their cooperation has been of inestimable value in the writing of the biography.

I have received grants from Emory University and the University Center in Georgia that have made it possible for me to do research in the National Archives in Washington; at West Point; in Richmond, Virginia; in Columbia, Greenville, and Spartanburg, South Carolina; in Henderson and White Oak, North Carolina; and in Rome, Marietta, Athens, Kingston, Cassville, and Cartersville, Georgia. The grants have enabled me to work with special collections at Emory University, Duke University, the University of North Carolina, the University of South Carolina, and the University of Georgia. I have also examined newspapers from Washington, New York, Atlanta, and Athens.

Many long quotations from the letters and materials have been included because they have never been published and because they give an excellent flavor of the feeling and the rhetoric of the period.

All quotes not documented may be taken as coming from the Milner-Cummings collection at Walnut Plantation. Original spellings have been kept, without use of *sic* or explanatory insert except where meaning may not be clear otherwise.

Much credit for the book is due to my wife, Wilma M. Holland, who typed the original manuscript and assisted me in my research. Special thanks are due Mrs. Ann O. Lee and Mrs. Charlotte R. Harris for their careful typing of the final copy and their patience in proofreading, and to Miss Callie McWhirter, of the University of Georgia Press, for her patience, understanding, and kind help. I am also deeply indebted to my colleagues, Dr. Ronald F. Howell and Dr. Floyd Watkins of Emory University, for reading and criticizing the manuscript. Their recommendations have been carefully followed. The author, however, assumes full responsibility for any mistakes or ambiguities in historical interpretation.

LYNWOOD M. HOLLAND

Emory University
Atlanta, Georgia

I

❖❖❖

Southern Heritage

THE DECADE beginning 1820 was a critical period for South Carolina, for the opening of the cotton lands in the West had flooded the market and greatly reduced the price of cotton. Within one year, 1825, the price dropped from twenty-eight cents to eight cents a pound. The effect was to increase the depression in rural areas. The depression was intensified for the farmers in Spartanburg County, South Carolina, by droughts and poor crops of corn and wheat. Thus the story of fortunes to be made in the former Indian lands of Alabama and Mississippi grew into a kind of Midas myth for those in financial need. The reports intrigued Dr. Robert Maxwell Young, a young physician who had received in 1821 his diploma in medicine from the University Medical College in Philadelphia, and also many of his friends and relatives in and around Spartanburg Courthouse.

Robert Maxwell Young, upon receiving his medical diploma, returned to his home county of Spartanburg to practice. On October 26, 1826, he married Caroline Elizabeth Jones, his eighteen-year-old sweetheart, daughter of a wealthy North Carolina planter, George Jones. From his wife Dr. Young received a dowry of several Negro slaves and several horses for carriage and farm use. He built a small wooden building as an office and there saw patients and dispensed medicine as was the custom of his day. By 1833 the doctor was facing, with his neighbors, financial difficulties. The previous year one noted South Carolinian had lamented that "our merchants are bankrupt or driven away, their capital sunk or transferred to other pursuits, our ship yards broken up, our ships all sold," because of the high national tariff.[1]

1

In addition to complications resulting from the low price for his cotton and the inability to collect from the farmers for medical treatment, Dr. Young's family obligations had increased by 1833 with the birth of two sons, George William and Robert Maxwell, and a daughter, Louisa. Then, too, Dr. Young had been made executor of his father's estate, which was heavily involved in debt. The difficult task of trying to collect what was owed the estate and at the same time pay the debts incurred against it was a drain on the doctor's limited finances.

Getting deeper into financial difficulties, he realized that the Indian lands would give him an opportunity to improve his finances, although it meant buying the land on credit. After each session with his neighbors under the trees around his small shop on East Main Street, the young doctor's desire to speculate on western lands increased. The tentative discussions matured into definite plans, and he, his father-in-law, and a friend, William Foster of Spartanburg Courthouse, set out on horseback for Alabama to buy land. Early on Monday, November 20, 1833, the three men arrived at Greenville, where they stayed three days with Dr. Young's mother. Joined here by C. Henderson and William Hubbard, the travelers took up the journey, crossing the Tugaloo River on the Cleveland Ferry and going on to Carnesville, Georgia, where they spent the night of November 23rd.

Three days later the men made their first major stop—at Lawrenceville, Georgia, about a hundred and fifty miles from Spartanburg Courthouse. The weather had been cold and the journey tiresome; dysentery and rheumatism contributed to making traveling slow and difficult. Although the roads had been rough the horses had performed well. During the stop the young husband wrote a letter to his wife, in which he described his traveling companions as "remarcably sober and morrel" and told her that the trip had already proved to him how much he loved her and their three children.

On the morning of November 28 the men set out again, and, according to Dr. Young's account to his wife, stopped at "Allatooney, a small town in the Creek Nation, named from the Creek near which it is cituated—town very rudely built, some small but neat huts, claboard rough, some dirty hovels; stoped with Mjor Dawson, fare very good; the country is very poore, broken and has a remarcable barren apearance; met with no Indians until we arrived here about sunset; distance 35 miles."

After crossing the Coosa River at Childers' Ferry, Henderson and father-in-law Jones left the party to go to Tuscaloosa while Dr. Young and the others went to Asheville where they stopped at the Bishop Hotel. The next stop was at Marion, where upon his arrival Dr. Young found a newsy letter from Caroline, "which [as he wrote back to her] produced sensations easier to be imagined than described" when she told of how much the children missed and called for him. As at previous places where they had stopped, the travelers stayed several days to allow the horses to rest. Dr. Young visited the countryside around Marion and was astonished at the productiveness of the land. He did not think highly of the sandy portions but judged the river lands would be productive in cotton and easy to clear and cultivate. However, he thought that what was available was too expensive at $10 an acre and judged that the best land in this section had already been bought.

Besides the expensive land, Negro slaves were very high, selling from $100 to $800. Dr. Young wrote his wife that he thought it better to rent than to buy, though most of his friends advised him to purchase even at the high prices. "The people do not fear going in debt here as they do in South Carolina; if they have a few hands they do not hesitate to give their notes for one or two thousand dollars to be paid in one year." He could buy the best land around Montgomery on credit, for several of his friends had offered to go as security for five or six thousand dollars, payable in one, two, or three years. But he declined the offer, although he was impressed by the health and wealth of the people around Marion.

Dr. Young did not rent land or buy; he returned to his family. But unhappy and dissatisfied over his first efforts to speculate, in April 1834 he set out once again for Alabama, this time with his father-in-law, two brothers-in-law, and several neighbors, all on horseback, to investigate the land. At their first major stop, Decatur, Georgia, they were discouraged by the rainy, cold weather and the muddy roads. From Decatur they went to "Franklin Courthouse, Herd County; took very bad dinner; Chatahoochee was high; remained until evening." Leaving Franklin, the men rode to Talladega, Alabama, where they separated and explored the surrounding countryside as far as Benton Courthouse before returning home. Although some of the land looked promising, Dr. Young could not get his father-in-law to see its value sufficiently to invest his money; in fact, Jones not only refused to buy any land himself, but he also opposed Young's buying any. Discouraged, Dr. Young wrote disconsolately to his wife, "I have lost all hope of your father getting land here or indeed anywhere and if we have to remain at Spartanburg Court-house, it will doom me and my family to poverty and discontent-ment the balance of our lives." Then he added disheartenedly, "What I am to do, God only knows."

After his second Alabama trip Dr. Young's financial status became worse. Feeling it necessary to have another try at improv-ing his fortunes, he started out with three friends, identified in his diary as Bobo, Webb, and Foster, from Spartanburg Court-house in October 1835 to explore with a view to speculating in the rich agricultural lands of the Chickasaw Nation in Mississippi. However, Young had a presentiment that the trip would not be profitable. His horse began to give out on him before the party arrived at Lawrenceville, Georgia, and he wrote his wife from there that he was discouraged and hoped this trip would be his last. He and Bobo separated from Webb and Foster and on November 9 arrived at Columbus, Mississippi, to look at the land in that area. Eight days later, Dr. Young wrote his wife that it had rained for eight days and the streets were "some three or four inches deep with mud; there are people here from every portion of the United States, all seeking land." He com-plained that rooms were priceless, that the beds were small and mean, and the "table fare is worse than you can possibly conceive of; we have plenty of beef and fresh pork—no vegetables but yams, potatoes, this not half cooked; our bread is half raw, at least three times out of four; indeed everything is horrible bad, and to complete our misfortune, I have strong doubts whether we can get any land on such terms as we will be willing to accede to. . . ."

The speculation trips were physically wearing. One had to search out the good lands and could do so only by taking to the woods and becoming acquainted with the surrounding country. This was "a most laborious and unpleasant business, having to get out many nights, swim creeks, and live on anything or almost nothing." The speculation was also wearing on the nerves, for competition was keen. Many of the rich planters in the lower part of the state wanted to procure settlements of land in the Chickasaw Nation, some not so much for the productiveness of the land as for the prospects of health.

Dr. Young believed the Alabama and Mississippi planters were getting rich faster than the people in any other section of the country. He felt sure that if he had a "tolerable good farm here and ten hands to work it," he would become wealthy from the land investments; however, he expressed to his wife some doubts whether he could "bare great and sudden prosperity or not; one thing I do know, that is, I can bare adversity pretty well, at least as well as the most of men, for I have had a full and thorough trial all my life." He found that the fabulous tales of profit reputedly made by others had attracted to Columbus gamblers and thieves. More than once he wrote that he felt he could not trust any man whom he met, "because the temptations are very great—too powerful for many to resist."

On November 29 Dr. Young wrote his wife that he and Bobo and a third partner, one Henry, had organized themselves into a company and had bought 10,000 acres of land in the Chickasaw Nation. He explained, "Henry and myself are equal in the purchase. Bobo not so much." Although Henry estimated the investment would make a return of $40,000 within three years, Dr. Young figured more cautiously: "I do not estimate them quite so high but I have no doubt but I have done very well. . . . The highest evidence that we have done well is that a rich and experienced land speculator offered, without any hesitation to pay 25 per cent on our purchases." Then he added: "You will think it strange when I tell you that we have not seen one foot of the land which we have purchased, but such is the facts. We purchased from the recommendations of our friends, and we were fortunate enough to get the lands at less than half the amount which were advised to run them; we have determined to let the lands lie for one, two or three years." Despite the amount of time devoted to speculation and financial investment, the doctor wrote weekly to his wife and children. The inadequate mail service brought him news so irregularly that he was in constant anxiety about his family. So as soon as the company had completed transactions for purchase of the 10,000 acres, Dr. Young wrote hastily to his wife that he planned to leave for home in three or four days. By December 20 he had returned to his family at Spartanburg Courthouse. The Mississippi land never made any money for the doctor, and he never went back to Mississippi. He remained in Spartanburg Courthouse and rented out his slaves in an effort to add to what he made by his practice of medicine. His responsibilities were increased when a third son,

Pierce Manning Butler, was born on November 16, 1836. From the very first the child was sickly and after his birth Caroline herself did not regain her health for many years. According to a letter written by the new baby's grandmother Jones his three Christian names were for relatives and friends, although she did not identify the individuals.

Pierce Manning Butler Young's maternal great-grandfather, George Jones, was born in Maryland and later moved to Orange City, Virginia. He served in the Revolutionary War and was at the seige of Yorktown. He married Phoebe Foster of Virginia; they had five sons and four daughters. After the war they moved to Wilkes County, North Carolina. George, their second son, who became the grandfather of Pierce Manning Butler Young, married Elizabeth Caroline Mills in 1806. They lived at White Oak, North Carolina.

Pierce's maternal grandmother, Elizabeth Caroline Mills, was descended from the Cavaliers of England who migrated to Maryland; there one Ambrose Mills married Mourning Stone, massacred by the Indians in 1748. Ambrose moved to Virginia and later to Rutherford County, North Carolina. In the Revolution he was a Royalist; as an officer under the English government he refused to break his oath. When Cornwallis went into South Carolina he made Ambrose Mills's house his headquarters. Cornwallis commissioned him as colonel and he commanded a regiment in the British ranks during the Revolution. Captured by the Americans at Eutaw Springs, he was kept a prisoner till after the Battle of Cowpens. Then the Americans hanged Ambrose Mills as a Tory and seized his lands. His son William escaped and moved into western North Carolina; there he married Eleanor Morris, whose ancestors had moved to South Carolina from Virginia and accumulated a large estate in land and slaves. As one of Pierce's uncles wrote later, the descendants prided themselves on being the progeny of Cavaliers: "The fact that the Mills [sic] formerly were cavaliers is evidence of their respectable origin in England. The cavaliers were of the better classes, the roundheads were made up of the rabble."

Elizabeth Mills Jones, Pierce's grandmother, a daughter of William and Eleanor Morris Mills, imbued her children and grandchildren with pride in their family heritage. She was a matriarch within her own right and from the home place at White Oak, North Carolina, tried to rule her six sons and two daughters. She emphasized continually in her numerous letters to Caroline,

Pierce's mother, the importance of good stock and blood, education, and the fear of God; she did not hesitate to express her
opinion and give advice to her daughter and grandchildren. Her
frontier training in the belief that the husband was the head of
the house prevented her from giving similar advice to her daughter's husband.

On his father's side Pierce was the descendant of the pioneer
Virginia families of Young and Wood, who were among the leaders in the early settlements of Spartanburg District, South Carolina. His grandfather William Young entered the Revolutionary
War at the age of sixteen as a private and rose to the rank of captain of cavalry. He fought at Kings Mountain, at Cowpens, at
Augusta, where he was wounded, and at Savannah, and in all the
major engagements on both sides of the Savannah River. He married Mary Solomons and settled near Greenville Courthouse; they
had a large family of thirteen children—eight sons and five daughters, some of whom emigrated before 1836 to the Indian lands of
Alabama and Mississippi. They were soldiers and the frontier
was a challenge to them. But they too, even as Pierce's family on
the distaff side, believed in education, and in trying to provide
advantages for their children.

Pierce's heritage was indeed a goodly one. His ancestors were
proud aristocrats, leaders in the social and political life of their
communities. They owned large plantations, and many slaves,
whom they treated almost as members of their families. To them
wealth, social position, and dignity were the real tests for success
in life while concomitant factors—fear of God, tolerance, education—were essential because the environment within which they
lived demanded such in order to obtain desirable secular objectives. To obtain these objectives Pierce's ancestors did not hesitate
to migrate to where opportunities were available. Although they
wanted and strove for wealth and social position, they did not
shrink to austerity to attain them, but always managed to live
well. Yet they did not sacrifice dignity, honor, or sense of duty.

II

◇◇◇
◇

Education of a Southern Gentleman

PIERCE did not remember living in South Carolina, for his
family moved to Cassville, Cass County, Georgia, in the summer of 1838 when he was two years old. He heard his mother tell
later of the panic year of 1837, when his father bought five hundred acres of land along the west bank of the Etowah River, north
of the Indian village Allatoona in Cass County, in order to improve the financial condition as well as the health of the family.
Growing up he liked to hear his mother or brother George tell
stories of the long trip from Spartanburg Courthouse to Cassville,
especially the story about the Indians who tried to show their
appreciation for Dr. Young's treatment of an Indian girl by
teaching him where the best wild game and fish could be found.

In later years Pierce remembered how lonely his mother became because of the lack of communication with her family at
White Oak, North Carolina, and because of the lack of society in
the frontier village of Cassville. He remembered how pleased she
was in 1846 when his father employed a contractor from Rome to
build in the walnut grove knoll behind Pettite Creek a two-story
brick house with a portico in front supported by two large white
hand-hewn columns. It was completed in 1850. Mrs. Young, ambitious for her family, felt that the brick mansion would encourage people of high social standing to visit them. Pierce shared
with his mother the love for flowers and shrubbery and together
they planned the formal walks and the carriage drive. Within a
few years "Walnut Plantation," a name given the home, became a
show place and the center of Cass County social life.

The first education Pierce received was from tutors until he convinced his parents of his seriousness to become a soldier. In July 1852 he enrolled at Georgia Military Institute, a popular military preparatory school at Marietta. One reason Mrs. Young consented for her son to enroll was the nearness of the school to Walnut Plantation—only twenty-five miles away.

The boy was homesick at the Institute and remained so throughout his first fall there. In letters to his mother he complained of the food, too much work, and the rigid discipline, and asked that he be allowed to visit home on weekends.

He was just another cadet with no special privileges. He was placed in the fourth class and in a company for daily drill except on Saturdays, Sundays, and during unfavorable weather. He was required to stand guard, regardless of weather; in addition he had to attend a dress parade every evening and inspection every Saturday morning when the weather permitted. Each cadet lived under rigid disciplinary rules of the United States Army regulations and was offered little opportunity for indiscretion. Punishment for infringement of regulations was carefully detailed.

The first three years at Georgia Military Institute were difficult years of adjustment. Pierce was a serious student; he often expressed doubt in his letters home that he was learning as well as he should. But in spite of being discouraged, homesick, and at times resentful of the military discipline, the young cadet began to develop the characteristics that later made him a superior officer and a Southern gentleman. By the end of the first year he had acquired a neatness in his dress that he retained the rest of his life. His carriage was always that of a soldier—straight, with shoulders, back, and head erect. He quickly made friends with other cadets and with members of the staff, especially with the sergeant majors and the first commandant of cadets. By the beginning of his junior year his qualities of leadership were recognized by the administration when he was made captain of a company—an appointment made in merit of grades and leadership. He was affable, friendly, and daring. He possessed a certain sympathetic understanding that attracted cadets to him—a characteristic that was later to endear him to his soldiers.

It was while he was a student at G.M.I. in 1855 that Pierce first manifested an interest in politics. He wrote excitedly to his family about the successful election of the whole Democratic ticket for Cobb County, and the possibility of Herschel V. Johnson's election as governor. He severely criticized the Know-Nothing candidates as inferior.

It was during these early years at G.M.I. that Pierce first
realized that his father was not able to manage his finances and
that the family's need for money was real and constant. The boy
was embarrassed when he discovered that his father had failed to
pay for all of his tuition and books for several seasons. The colonel dunned Pierce himself for the unpaid amount. The young
cadet said in a letter home, "I wish I could be somewhere I would
not be an expense to my parents." Then he again expressed a
definite desire to go to West Point—whether the desire arose because of his financial embarrassment or because of a genuine interest remained to be seen. But he wrote a letter to President Franklin Pierce inquiring about the procedure for applying to the
military academy.

Two persons at G.M.I. influenced Pierce most in his decision
to apply for admission to West Point. One was Captain Samuel
Jones, who attended West Point and afterward served in an
artillery regiment of the United States Army. He obtained a leave
to serve as commandant at Georgia Military Institute in 1855.
Captain Jones's description of his experiences at the military
academy kindled the flames of Pierce's desire to go there.

Captain Thomas R. McConnell, who succeeded Captain Jones
in September 1856, Pierce's senior year, was the second person at
the Institute to have a major influence on Pierce. Also a graduate
of West Point, Captain McConnell saw service with the United
States Infantry in the Mexican War. He organized a cavalry class
at the Institute. Enthusiastic about the new class, Pierce with his
closest friends enjoyed the training and devoted many hours to it.
A few years later as soldiers, some in blue and some in gray, they
were to remember this special cavalry training.

Unsuccessful in getting any information from President Pierce
about an appointment at large, the would-be candidate wrote
Secretary of War Jefferson Davis asking for help and explaining
what he had already done. Then he wrote his father about the
letter to Secretary Davis, and Dr. Young began to write to political friends asking them for assistance in getting an appointment
for his son. On October 14, 1855, Governor Herschel V. Johnson
of Georgia wrote President Pierce a letter recommending the
young man, a "descendant of a Revolutionary Son . . . the grandson of Captain William Young of the Continental Army of '76.
His family connections are of the most respectable character. He
will do honor to the service and his country."

On January 18, 1856, Dr. Young wrote Secretary of War Davis

asking for an appointment to West Point for his son. Meanwhile
Colonel John H. Lumpkin, a good friend of the Young family,
had been elected congressman from the Fifth District. All of the
necessary papers for Pierce's recommendations were placed in
Congressman Lumpkin's hands. A week later Congressmen Lumpkin, Hiram Warner, and Howell Cobb wrote to the President
recommending Pierce as a "cadet at large at the Military Academy
of the United States." They reiterated comments on Pierce's distinguished heritage and added that "the patronage of the President would be most judiciously bestowed by appointing Pierce
Young as a cadet at large. . . ." They expressed confidence that
"he would be an ornament to the army and if occasion should
present itself would distinguish himself in the service of the
country. We take great pleasure in urging this appointment upon
your consideration."

Receiving no reply, and unable to obtain any satisfaction,
Pierce on February 10, 1856, wrote timidly to Alexander
Stephens, asking him to write a recommendation. In his letter he
explained that he was trying to get an appointment at large since
there was no vacancy in his district, and that he had the recommendation of all members of the Democratic delegation from
Georgia in the House except his. Pierce explained that he had
forwarded Governor Johnson's recommendation but had been
told that the recommendation of the Honorable Alex Stephens
would be a great addition to his list. He referred Stephens to
Congressman Lumpkin for his character and concluded his letter
with "I have made the application and now, Sir, I would be under
everlasting obligations if you vouchsafe to consult Mr. Lumpkin
and forward a note of recommendation to the President before it
is too late." On February 29, Stephens in his inimitable, frank
style wrote, "I don't know this young man but recommend his
case to the more favorable consideration of the President."

Meanwhile Pierce's relatives in South Carolina were busy working for his appointment. They wrote close friends in Washington,
D. C., urging them to use their influence to get an appointment
for the young Georgian. They described his training and his
heritage. One of those appealed to was Colonel James L. Orr of
Washington, D. C., who wrote to President Pierce, with the comment that the boy's grandfather was a Revolutionary War soldier,
adding, "I would be much gratified if you could appoint him at
large. His application will be more fully endorsed by a part of
the Georgia delegation." Since Colonel Orr was slated to be

Speaker of the House at the new session of Congress, President
Pierce did not treat the recommendation lightly.

By March Pierce was discouraged and undecided, for he had not
heard anything about his appointment. He wrote his mother, "I
suppose my chances are by this time knocked in the head for
West Point, for I know I shall not get it. Judge Butler wrote as if
he would try and get Lumpkin to give me the appointment from
the district. Why indeed I should think Father had more influence with Lumpkin than the Judge. . . . There is no vacancy
from the dist and I didn't wish the Judge to recommend me [to]
Lumpkin of course, as it would avail nothing so his endeavors are
perfectly worthless; I perhaps may go if I get the appointment
even next year; but I don't know if I should as the time is now
five years; but if I should be so fortunate as to get the apt this
year I shall most certainly avail myself of it." Throughout the
spring Pierce waited and by June realized that he would not get
an appointment for the July class. He hoped very much that an
appointment would come before 1857.

On August 22, 1856, Pierce, now a senior at G.M.I., wrote again
to Secretary of War Davis stating that he was expecting an appointment to West Point next year and wanted some information.
He wanted to know if as a graduate of G.M.I. he could enter
West Point higher than the fifth class. He explained that his class
would graduate on the 20th of June, 1857, and as the plebes had
to report at West Point by June first, "I would like to know if I
would be allowed to remain at this Inst. till I graduated which
would only throw me late about three weeks, and if I cannot enter
higher than the fifth class, I may not wish to go and I would like
to know if I might through the intercession of influential friends
get the appointment at West Point transfered to a commission in
the army." He added, "I would not ask this information but I
have a friend who obtained a commission in the army a short
while since and I think—in fact—I know I can get the recommendations of influential friends in Congress vouching for my capability of holding a commission. I shall have been at this Military
Institution 5 years when I graduate."

Congressman Lumpkin wrote Dr. Young in September to have
his son make application for the vacancy which would occur in
the Military Academy in June 1857. When Pierce received the
news, he could hardly contain himself. He got his commandant
to assist him in writing to Secretary Davis. In making the request
for the appointment, Pierce explained, "I am nineteen years and

seven months old. My height is five ten and a half inches. I hope, Sir, you will duly consider my claim. I already have the highest recommendations of my state. . . ."

It was not, however, until December 17 that Congressman John H. Lumpkin nominated Pierce to Secretary Davis to fill the vacancy at the Military Academy from the Fifth District of Georgia. The following day Lumpkin wrote Pierce that he had nominated him, and had no doubt of his appointment at the proper time. He continued, "and my only desire is that you may do honor and credit to the selection I have made." He explained that there were a number of applicants, all deserving of consideration, but he preferred Pierce because "I believed that you would be most useful in the military service of the United States. I will not permit myself to believe that your unusual friends or myself will be disappointed." Enclosed in the congressman's letter was an acknowledgment of Brigadier General Loften stating that Pierce had been nominated and that it would be brought to the attention of the Secretary of War when cadet appointments were being made for the next year.

The Young family rejoiced with Pierce. Brother George and his family, who were visiting Walnut Plantation during the Christmas season, joined in the celebration. Outwardly his mother rejoiced at the news, but secretly she was in despair at having to give him up for another long stay away from home. In a letter to Pierce written several months earlier she expressed the wish that he would soon be finished with his studies: "I hope you will make a great man some of these days; it will compensate us in some degree for your absence so long from home." But though she longed for Pierce to return to Walnut Plantation, she was unwilling to allow her selfish desires to stand in the way of her child who she believed would make a name for himself and his family. Mrs. Young's life was devoted to the success of her children, and she had a special regard for her baby son. She proudly displayed Pierce's ambrotype which he had made in 1856, and she carefully cherished in her trunk in the attic every letter he wrote to her.

On February 20, 1857, Pierce wrote Secretary of War Davis a letter accepting the appointment and with it he again requested that he be allowed to graduate with his classmates at G.M.I. in June. He explained that he could get a certificate from the officers of the Georgia Military Institute who were graduates of West Point and that "it would be no loss of time for my entrance in the academy to be delayed. . . . If I do not obtain the permis-

sion I shall of course report myself at West Point in the time
specified." This was not a letter of a braggadocio but of a
frightened young man who after sober reflection hated to leave
the Institute he had learned to love without his diploma as a
recognition of five years of study.

Pierce received letters from his two brothers, who wrote their
congratulations and expressed wishes for his success. Both gave
him advice on the importance of receiving an education and admonished him to study hard and to uphold the name of the family. They believed that a diploma from West Point was a passport
into the best society in the world. Brother Robert promised
Pierce that if his business would allow he would try to go to New
York with him. An aunt in Greenville, South Carolina, wrote,
warning him that it was difficult at West Point and that very few
Southern boys had been able to stay any length of time. Her
advice was for him to "stick it out."

Captain McConnell immediately began coaching Pierce on
what courses he should take and how he should act at the "Point."
Pierce's pride knew almost no bounds when Colonel Brumby
congratulated him on being the first cadet of the Institute to
receive the honor of appointment to West Point and wished him
great success. The members of the staff rejoiced with Pierce in his
honor, but they did not relax their insistence on discipline and
scholarship. He was allowed to go home only upon the regular
conditions prescribed in the rules of the Institute. Thus he was
not allowed to have a visit at Walnut Plantation until the second
weekend in April 1857. Upon his return to Marietta he expe-
rienced one of the most exciting incidents in his Institute life.
Fire broke out in Sabel and Tennent Drugstore and burnt half
the town, and "Captain" Young, placed by the major, in charge
of a guard of cadets to stand sentry, proved that he was able to
assume responsibility, show initiative, and demonstrate leadership.

He had become a young man self-assured and certain of himself.
He had gained confidence. He was to demonstrate the rest of
his life the qualities of leadership. He accepted leadership without pomposity, and although he showed signs of vanity and egotism in his letters to his family, he seldom exhibited such characteristics in dealing with his friends and other people with whom
he came in contact. His attitude of friendliness and sympathetic
understanding won for him many friends and supporters.

On April 29, 1857, as a senior Pierce participated in the court-
martial of Cadet L. R. Marshall, who was being tried for "conduct

prejudicial to good order and the discipline of the Institute."
Cadet Marshall had been called upon as a witness before another
court-martial on April 27, and had positively refused to give
testimony either upon oath, by affirmation, or in any other manner. In addition Cadet Marshall had acted in a manner disrespect-
ful to the court. Pierce was impressed with the seriousness of
military offenses and with the strict discipline demanded by competent military officials. As he watched Captain McConnell pre-
side firmly but without prejudice, the efficiency and decorum
with which military matters were executed thrilled him. The
court found Cadet Marshall guilty and sentenced him to be dismissed from the Institute. Superintendent A. V. Brumby approved of the proceedings of the court-martial and directed the
sentence to be carried into effect. Pierce was never to forget this
experience. It made him determined to become the best soldier
possible.

On the day following the court-martial Pierce received a letter
from his father, telling him that he was to set out for West Point
early in June. Secretary Davis had informed the father that Pierce
was ordered to report with other plebes and that no extension of
time could be allowed him. Dr. Young advised his son to make
his plans and to request the faculty as a favor to permit him to
stand his examinations by the 20th or 25th of May, adding, "We
all desire that you should spend a few days at home before you
leave." The staff acquiesced in Dr. Young's request for Pierce to
leave early but questioned whether the diploma would be conferred since the cadet was leaving several weeks before the board
of visitors would arrive to examine the graduating cadets. Captain
McConnell was one of Pierce's chief supporters on the staff.

At Pierce's request Dr. Young sent, on April 23, the amount of
$93 to be credited to his son's account. On May 1, R. A. Johnson,
the Commissary of the Institute, wrote Dr. Young that Pierce had
drawn a draft on his father's credit and asked the commissary to
honor it. Pierce in his last letter to his mother requested twenty
dollars to pay some private debts in town before he left. "I know
Father is hard up and that I am an awful drain on his pockets;
but I hope I shall soon cease to be any expense to him at all."
Cadet Young was humiliated by the financial inability of his
father. He knew that unless the debt was paid at the Institute he
would never receive his diploma even though the staff approved
giving it to him *in absentia*.

Just before Pierce left Georgia Military Institute, he received

from the commissary a dun for $146.88, due on his account for
1855-56. This was the second dun on his account. In fact, Commissary Johnson had written Dr. Young in January that "according to the resolution passed by the board in December last,
[Pierce] ought not to have been allowed to enter his class until all
arrears to the Institute were paid. But Colonel B[rumby] having
full confidence in your promptness and responsibility allowed
him to enter." The financial worries at Walnut Plantation increased, and all Dr. Young was able to do about the overdue account at the Institute was to give a note, which dogged him for
several years before the indebtedness was paid. Realizing the
financial straits of his father, Pierce worried about how to obtain
money to buy a small trunk to carry his clothes to New York. He
wrote Robert seeking a loan, but was unsuccessful in obtaining
it. His mother, who could never refuse her son, came to his rescue
and gave him the money.

Pierce's vacation time at Walnut Plantation was spent in various diversions, entertaining friends from G.M.I., fishing and swimming in the Etowah, riding over the plantation, eating his favorite
food—everything moved too quickly, until he "caught the cars" on
June 9 for Savannah, where he planned to take a boat to New
York. He had not had time to think and to be sorry that Robert
could not go with him. The tight hug and kiss of his mother, the
firm handclasp of his father, the tears of Louisa at the depot—all
made Pierce for the first time understand that he would not see
them again for months. The tears and hugs of the servants, old
Sutton and Phoebe, caused a gloom that he was not able to throw
aside until he had almost reached Savannah. Physically, a handsome, black-haired, properly dressed young plebe was hurrying
toward his future at West Point. At heart a very young boy was
leaving Walnut Plantation, already beginning to feel pangs of
the homesickness that would strike him heavily in his new environment along the Hudson River. But he was daring.

III

❖❖
❖

A Plebe at West Point

AS CADET PIERCE YOUNG took the train in Savannah to Washington, he thought of the circular which had been prepared by Secretary of War Jefferson Davis. It announced that only a third of all those who entered West Point graduated, and advised the appointee that unless he had an aptitude for mathematics, language, etc., it would be better for him not to accept the appointment. Thus he would "escape the mortification of failure for himself and family." Pierce wondered if he was prepared; but he soon cast the worry aside and planned to meet straight on whatever West Point had to offer.

On arriving in Washington Pierce had a new world opened to him. He had never been any farther from Walnut Plantation than to Grandma Jones's plantation at White Oak, North Carolina. He wrote his father that he was getting on well, and that after arriving at Savannah he had decided not to take the steamer for Baltimore, because it took five days to make the trip. He went by train, although the train trip cost more; he had plenty of money, he explained.

He was impressed by the town of Washington. In fact he thought it was worth "twice the fair from home" to see it: "Everything is on a manificant [sic] scale." He thought the city was one of the busiest places he had ever seen, for everything was in "commotion." He enjoyed the boat ride down the Potomac River, and the trip to Mt. Vernon.

By the time he was ready to leave Washington the next day, more than fifty plebes had joined him. He knew only his companion, Plebe Camp from Savannah, and two appointees from

17

South Carolina and Alabama, who had joined them on the trip
to Washington. The young men left by train for New York, and
stayed there a few hours before leaving by boat for West Point,
where they arrived on Tuesday, June 16. In describing the Point
to his mother Pierce wrote that it was the prettiest place he had
ever seen and that the river and mountain sceneries were magnificent.

From the time that Pierce arrived at the hotel as a cadet, he
lost his identity as a citizen, or "cit," and became one of the
group of plebes, trying to fit into the complex life of a new student. From the hotel the plebes were directed to the adjutant's
office in the library building, where one crossed the boundary
between civil and military life. After the adjutant got the perti-
nent personal information about the plebes, he turned them over
to a soldier orderly, who led them to the barracks. Along the way
they were pebbled by buttons saved by plebes of the previous
year, who were now throwing them at the new arrivals from the
cockloft of one of the buildings.

Pierce had been a captain in the corps at G.M.I. only a few
weeks before, and to be treated now as a nonentity offended his
pride and irked him—especially since many of the cadet officers
were Yankees. The most difficult time came when the cadet officers detailed in charge of new cadets yelled "Take off your hat!
Stand at attention!" almost before his registration slip from the
adjutant was in their hands. Finally it was his turn to receive his
record book and he was assigned number 298. As cadet number
93 he paid his sixty dollars to the treasurer's office. His first issue
from the commissary department was for "1 arithmetic @ 55
cents."

In his first letter home he wrote his mother that he was "a
gump to leave home" and if it was not for disappointing folks he
would resign and come home. Letters from Mrs. Young and
Louisa only aggravated his homesickness. Later, Pierce said that
he was able to stand the discipline and to graduate because the
hardships were not so tough as they had been represented. Older
than the average plebe and with more military experience than
most of the neophytes, he wrote his parents that he suffered less
from older cadets than did other members of his class, "but it is
hard for me to see them run the others so hard."

The first week Pierce and other plebes drilled in squads and
took preliminary physical and mental examinations. The academic board, composed of the superintendent, commandant, and

the professors of the Point, sat at small desks arranged in a crescent in Academic Hall. All of the "brass" of the highranking officers impressed Pierce tremendously. He passed the examinations without difficulty, and was luckier than Camp and the appointees from South Carolina and Alabama who had accompanied him to West Point. Ironically, on the boat trip up, the appointees had talked and laughed saying that some of them would be going back on the same boat in a few days. "Unfortunately for some of us our joke turned out to be a sad reality for out of four of us on the boat only one passed the ordeal," he wrote home, adding, not without a touch of pride, "and that was your unworthy son; the other poor fellows sure enough had to return in the same boat before the week was out." Plebe Young felt that the Northerners got along better than Southerners since they generally were better prepared and educated than Southern men.

For the first two months Pierce and the other plebes were trained in military matters at Camp Putnam. Nothing excited him more at Camp Putnam than the "thundering explosions of heavy artillery" or the smell of gun powder. He described in detail to his parents the "fiery charge" of the battery and stated that he did not see how anyone escaped injury. Although there were many discomforts, the Georgia cadet adjusted and began to enjoy the military training. By the middle of July, even though he was still undergoing the rigorous schedule at Camp Putnam he confessed to his parents that West Point was a fine place and that he liked it, but added, "it is hard to those who have never before tried it." He warned his folks not to expect too much from him, "for it takes more brain than I've got and a d--n sight more than I'll do."

Whenever Pierce wrote home about his difficulties, his mother and sister were sympathetic; but his brother Robert did not pamper him at all. Instead he encouraged, cajoled, advised, admonished, and challenged his younger brother. Robert concluded one letter by saying, "Fame cannot be attained in a day. You must bend your mind and soul to the schemes of glory and renown and worship faithfully and devotedly at their altar before you can make a name. You are the only member of your family who has ever had it in his power to raise up a name and reputation for our prosperity—and to you I confidently look for that result." Efforts to get sympathy from the South Carolina relatives were also unsuccessful. In reply to his hard luck letters, they expressed confidence in his ability but warned him that he must not relax his "efforts in the path of usefulness and eminence," and must prepare himself for later action by a rigorous application in his youth; "and no maxim is more true than that 'man attains nothing great *sine magno labore.*' "

Although every moment of the plebe's time was devoted to training, the interest in politics which Pierce had shown at Georgia Military Institute continued despite the arduous tasks of encampment. He tried to keep up with the gubernatorial and congressional races of his home state. In a letter to his father he wrote that he did not like the nomination of Joseph E. Brown for governor of Georgia for it spoke badly for the party.

One of Pierce's worries the first few months at West Point was that he had not received his G.M.I. diploma; he was concerned as to what the administration at the Institute would do. He requested his father on July 15 to send him all the news about the Marietta commencement and to let him know if the administration made any alteration in his diploma; if so "I authorize you to send it back to them and tell them that I do not want it and will not accept it." Six days later Louisa wrote him that his diploma had been delivered in a metal case specially built for the purpose by his friend Captain Camp. His sister explained that on the diploma was a marginal note by Colonel Brumby stating that Pierce had left before completing his studies but that it had been conferred "in consequence of the very short period which he had to remain before graduation, and of his general good conduct. . . ." Louisa added that she did not like the note but that Dr. Young and Bob did not object to it. Pierce found that twelve former classmates had signed his diploma.

By the time the plebes moved from the two-months encampment on August 30 Pierce had begun to like the Academy and expressed his growing satisfaction in his letters to the various members of his family. The family had become deeply concerned over Caroline, for when her son left she became sick and seemingly could not recuperate. Though worried and anxious for his mother's health Pierce did not let her know of his concern. In his letters he purposely omitted any news that he thought would cause her to fret; instead he described the barracks, his room and equipment, and his roommate Watts from Kentucky. In one of his letters Pierce explained that classes began with about eighty men. Since his name was low on the alphabet he would begin at the very foot of his class, "the lowest section in the Academy." He predicted that he would rise to a higher section, for forty plebes would be found deficient in January and sent home; *"but fear not for your son*; I'll not be found in the January failures . . . for I would be ashamed to appear at home under circumstances in which you would not like to see me; no act of my life shall ever lower the name which I inherited purely, high and honorable— if it moves it must ascend."

Cadet Young soon realized that if he stayed at West Point he would have to study; he wrote his family not to speak of his "standing high for the Lord knows it's enough for one to graduate without studying his few brains out. I know I will not stand high for I do not stand as well as I did at first." Human as he was Pierce blamed some of his poor grades on one of his instructors, whom he described as "an old scoundrel whose disposition is made sour by fighting Indians and he don't like me because I got mad and faith if he wasn't an army officer I would have broke his head with my book before this time; but (military discipline) I would have been put in the dark prison and fed on bread and water for a month, which would have hardly paid me for my revenge."

Although the regulations of the Academy forbade any cadet to receive money or boxes of food from his parents, or from any other person, without permission from the Secretary of War or the recommendation of the superintendent, the cadets used George Stevens at Buttermilk Falls as the intermediary to receive money or packages from home. Pierce soon advised his parents how to circumvent the regulation. He assured them that the authorities would not open letters. "The authorities do nothing unmanly or ungentlemanly. As a matter of course this law is broken every day in the year, and they have no manner of means of finding it out and they do it merely to scare off parents and guardians." However, when Louisa sent a Christmas box addressed to Cadet P. M. B. Young, in care of George Stevens, his assurance was virtually destroyed. The package was held by the quartermaster's office, and Pierce stated that he would be punished by several extra tours of guard duty on Saturday evening. When the predictions did not materialize Cadet Young became bolder in his visits to Benny Haven's, a small eating place some two and a half miles from West Point, where contraband liquor and delicacies could be bought. His love of good food and drinks made the risk worthwhile. As he explained to his mother, "West Point cadets are held so tight that when they do get on a spree, its a regular *binder*."

Unable to spend the Christmas holidays at Walnut Plantation,

Pierce enjoyed his first Christmas season at the Point. Released
from duties on Christmas Day, the cadets enjoyed the turkey dinner. That night Pierce and his friends "ran off down to Butter
milk [Falls] and Old Bennys! We got oysters and lots of good
things for supper. . . . I suppose there has been over twenty gallons
of whiskey drunk by the cadets since Thursday night, a good deal
more. Now you'll wonder if I pitched in and got drunk on whiskey too. Not I, I remembered the pledge, but I had a fine eggnog
—we made lots of it in our water buckets. You may depend that
everything in the shape of a drink got soaked here. The pledge
you know allows eggnog," he added defensively.

Pierce learned about the life of a plebe. He described how he
and some of his friends slipped away to Benny Haven's after taps
at ten. They persuaded some of the other plebes to sleep in their
beds to "cover up." "We got back at 2 o'cl at night and finding
there had been no inspection during our absence we went to sleep
contented; next morning, thought it would be pleasant to sleep
all day as we sat up nearly all night, so as the surgeon's call sounded we went down looking very sour—all had bad colds, of course.
The doctor excused us and prescribed antimony; you know that
isn't good for one's stomach. The old steward of the hospital is a
good friend of mine, so he very thoughtfully turned his back on
me after handing me the dose and so I made the slop bucket swallow the puke which was intended for me. The other fellows let
their pills drop into their overcoat sleeves as they went to swallow
them and put on awful faces, but one poor fellow couldn't escape;
he had to gulp down an awful big tumbler full of salts, tried to
put as good a face on it as possible after smacking his lips; said
'salts wasn't such a bad thing after all and a fellow ought to take
a good dose occasionally.' "

Within six months after his entrance to West Point, Pierce
Manning Butler Young, the pride of G.M.I., had become a rather
subdued plebe. His work was acceptable but not outstanding; his
conduct was far from deficient—he had received only four demerits each month in the barracks. Regulation 72 of the Academy
provided that only cadets who received more than 100 demerits
for the six months prior to the examination in June and January
would be declared deficient in conduct and recommended to the
War Department for discharge.

Pierce was learning to be an officer. For the first months, while
he was homesick and undergoing the treatments of a plebe, he
threatened to resign. He felt that he had made a grave mistake

in leaving home and intimated that when he became of age he would tender his resignation to the superintendent. But after his twenty-first birthday, Pierce never spoke again of resigning until the fateful senior year of 1861 when Georgia seceded from the Union.

In the January semi-annual examinations Pierce passed. He was in the third class, composed of sixty-three members; in mathematics he ranked forty-five, while in French and drawing he ranked thirty-eight and eleven respectively. In a letter to his father on January 2, 1858, Pierce wrote that he was progressing very well in his studies and hoped "to rise a few files at the June examination." Nevertheless he expressed some anxiety about French. "It is no harder to get along here than I ever thought it was. West Point comes up to my previous anticipations." On February 6, 1858, he was transferred to one section higher in class and took the oath of allegiance. The services, held in the chapel, were impressive to him. He was to remember the administration of the oath again three years later when he was torn over the question of what he should do when Georgia seceded.

Although Pierce had matured since his arrival at West Point, the ties to his mother were still very strong and from her he received too much sympathy for his weaknesses and too much money for his personal use. In spite of a rise in 1857 which gave each cadet a total of $30 a month, Pierce frequently asked and received from home money badly needed there. He was acquiring the personal characteristics that typified his father and that were to haunt him most of his life—lack of financial ability and lack of business acumen. He had learned, however, that one should face problems and not avoid them.

Knowing the anxiety of his mother for his health and welfare, Cadet Young wrote often to lessen her worries. He explained how comfortable and warm they were; they were not exposed too much to the cold weather although there was plenty of snow during the winter; guard duty, which was required of every cadet, was held in the halls of the division of the barracks. In fact by January Pierce was writing home that he was enjoying the winter up north and was convinced from experience that one ought to sleep in a very cold room to remain healthy. "I have suffered less with colds than any winter I can remember." He wrote his mother that it was rare for a cadet to die: "It seems with death as most other things outside of West Point, that is that cadets have not time to die, for we have to keep pushing and let outside business alone."

Pierce liked sports, especially horseback riding and swimming; ice skating appealed to him also. His training on the Etowah River was valuable to him. He wrote his father that he planned to learn to skate on the Hudson as soon as it froze over but expected that the ice and his head would come in contact often. Dr. Young knew that he would, too, daring as he was.

Throughout the winter, Pierce continued to be interested in politics. He frequently commented in his letters about national and state affairs. When the United States Senate passed the Kansas Bill, he rejoiced. "There is a step beyond which the black republican dares not pass. They are all cowardly scoundrels from the fathers down to the sons. The southern man is cock of the walk at West Point. I have never yet heard a man say out boldly that he was an abolitionist since I've been here. I would no more think of contaminating myself by associating with a black republican than I would with the blackest hearted puppy in the Georgia penitentiary. The corps may be decidedly democratic—there is many a black republican representative who has a democratic cadet at the Point; in heart, I really believe that there are lots of rank abolitionists among us—we even can often find out that their fathers are black republicans, but they will tell you they are democrats. Well, I wonder what will become of our Union; . . . I am afraid it will not last long. I think patriotism is fast oozing from the breasts of northern men. I believe it is a rare commodity here North. The longer I remain in the free soil states the stronger I grow in my own principles; I believe I am now looked upon by some as a *nester*. I hope I shall never get softer; I don't believe anytime southerners will associate with anyone who entertains principles so adverse, so deleterous [*sic*] in their effect and so directly opposed to the interest and welfare of my active country."

Love for the South and for the principles of extending slavery in the territories was basic to Pierce's home training and education. From this time on he became vociferous in defense of slavery, and became known at the Point for his rabid Southern views. When Louisa wrote teasing him about marrying a Yankee girl, Pierce rejected such an idea. He did admit that he had met some fascinating Yankees but he could never tie himself to "a Yankee gal or get sued for breach of promise. In the first place, I am not national enough to marry north of the line and in the 2nd I think I'll not make the promise; some of the Yankee girls are very pretty, charming, etc., but my prejudices cannot be easily overcome."

During 1858 the promised visit of Robert materialized. Although he enjoyed his brother's visit, Pierce soon found that all was not well financially with him and his family and that he was considering joining the army or, failing that, moving his family to Texas to try his luck. June of 1858 was a wonderful month for Pierce. He passed the examinations, and wrote his mother that he was well satisfied with his work and expected to be made first corporal in his company. Six of his classmates were found deficient and the total number of his class was reduced to sixty-three. He passed from the lowly state of plebe to the higher status of cadet. He enjoyed seeing and commanding the 1858 plebes. With his classmates Pierce "gave the poor devils quite a time." He explained, "I have charge of the plebes and I tell you I give them thunder."

By the end of the first year at the Point, Pierce had become rather sure of himself and did not mind giving advice to the members of his family—whether it was on how to make money or how to get a husband for Louisa, who at twenty-three was an old maid to him. He loved his family and home, and felt free to advise. But the end of the year found him worried about whether the training at West Point would be for four or for five years. His wish was for four years and he informed his father in September that Congress had the matter under consideration. The sooner he finished his training the quicker he would be able to get back home. Therefore he was pleased to hear that Congress had decided to make the training course four years instead of five. His joy was expressed to his mother—"That changing the course was a great thing for us. . . . I only have two years and 8 months to stay here. I dare say the time will pass quickly by."

The pride of Walnut Plantation had matured into a handsome young man with very definite opinions about politics, economics, and young ladies.

IV

◊◊◊
◊

A Rebel at Heart

OMINOUS events in national affairs overshadowed the incidents and happenings at West Point and Walnut Plantation in October 1858, for John Brown, the fiery fanatical abolitionist leader, made his famous raid on Harper's Ferry on Sunday night, October 16. He and five of his followers were captured the following Friday morning by Colonel Robert E. Lee, a West Point graduate. Brown was soon indicted and placed on trial for murder and treason, and on October 31 the jury brought in a verdict of guilty. John Brown was sentenced to be hanged in December. Pierce was very much aroused about the incident.

On November 29 he wrote his father, "I suppose you are stired up to a high pitch in our section of the country, and the excitement no doubt increases as Brown's execution draws near." He hoped that the people would remain cool and firm. "I believe I am as you have taught me, a union loving man and a patriot. I am devoted to my whole country; but to that portion of my country who array themselves under a black republican banner, I am a sectional enemy. I am not an enemy upon the field of argument; but I am a blood thirsty enemy to them and theirs on the field of bloody battle. . . . I do hope that the time is not far distant when it shall be determined whether or not this government is to fall into the hands of traitors. It may be and I believe it will open on next Friday's noon; I believe that the determination will begin on that which shall determine whether the constitution of the American republic shall continue as it has always been the robust legacy ever handed down from one generation to its posterity or whether it shall prove a curse and a disgrace to an enlightened people."

26

The news of John Brown's trial and sentence caused consider-able excitement at West Point and was closely followed by the cadets. Many of the Southern cadets denounced in violent and passionate terms the abolitionists and everyone in the North who shared the abolitionists' antipathy to slavery. One day during the trial Pierce, on guard with Cadet John H. Calef of Massachusetts, got into an argument with Calef over the trial. Exasperated and chagrined, Pierce swore that he wished he had a sword as large as from West Point to Newberg, and had the Yankees all in a row so that he could cut off the heads of "every damned one of them." Fortunately Cadet Calef did not answer in kind to the outburst and no incident took place.[1] One of the first sectional collisions at West Point was between Wade Hampton Gibbs of South Caro-lina and Emory Upton of New York. Personal matters were in-volved as well as politics. Pierce was in the crowd at the fight to see that Southern honor was upheld, and stood on the stairway while the cadets fought in a room on the first floor of the First Division.

Such incidents were forecasts of events to take place three years later when war divided the country into two enemy camps, and classmates and even roommates were pitted against one another. West Point was forgotten in the sectional cause to which each dedicated himself—many to die for that cause.

But John Brown's Raid was fully exploited by most of the Southern cadets. Pierce wrote home in November describing the prank which he and a classmate played when they hanged John Brown's body in effigy from one of the windows at the barracks. Although efforts were made by the administration to find the culprits, the secret was never revealed by Pierce or his companion. His parents laughed about the prank, for secretly they approved of it.

Slowly but surely sectionalism spread like an epidemic among the cadets at West Point. The Southern hotheads and the im-petuous Northern cadets frequently clashed verbally, and some-times, more often than the authorities knew, the clashes ended with bodily harm until honor had been defended. The witnesses to such incidents never reported them.

Despite sectional differences there developed close friendships which knew no section and later withstood the war. One close friend of Pierce's was George A. Custer, of Ohio, whom Pierce and other cadets dubbed "Fanny" because "his bright locks gave him a girlish appearance, . . . coupled with the remarkable fact

of his strictly temperate habits." Among other close friends were
Wesley Merritt and James H. Wilson, who with "Fanny" Custer
never allowed an occasion for a joke or prank to pass, especially
with some awkward plebe for the butt. Frequently the quartet
played pranks on one another, and especially on Pierce, but he
was seldom caught. Pierce was attracted to "Fanny" Custer because of the latter's good nature and also because of his ability
to ride. Custer was known as one of the best riders at the Point,
and Pierce liked horseback riding. Although Custer drank but
little, he seldom missed the secret pilgrimages to Benny Haven's
cabin with Pierce and a few others—mainly for the daring in
getting out of quarters at night.

Pierce was given some relief from sectionalism by a vacation
home after two years at the Point. He was ready for relief too,
for in April of 1859 the course of study had again been organized
for five years. Pierce, very much disturbed, wrote his father, bitterly denouncing the Secretary of War for the five-year order;
he thought it was done for political reasons. Later he wrote his
parents that he would not resign from the military academy even
though the training has been increased.

While vacationing at Walnut Plantation, the young cadet was
dined and entertained as though he were a top-ranking army
official. His mother undertook the fond duty of seeing that he
had every delicacy he had ever liked. He was pleased at every
opportunity to relate his experiences at the Point and was proud
to display his uniforms. He enjoyed the various trips made with
Louisa to Resaca to visit Brother George and his family. He
attended the funeral at Kingston of the wife of his cousin Dr.
Thomas F. Jones. Pierce long remembered the unconsolable grief
of Cousin Tom at the death of his young wife, Kate, who had
died in childbirth. Later he was to recall this tragic husband
and father, for within two years' time the widower married Louisa
and became not only Pierce's brother-in-law but in time his
closest friend. The Georgia cadet found a major problem dis-
turbing his mother. Robert and his family, consisting of his wife
Josephine and daughter Ida, had moved to Waco, Texas, and
Mrs. Young was worried because very little had been heard
from them.

When Pierce returned to West Point he found that the one
major topic of conversation besides ladies and furloughs was
politics, especially the threat of Republicanism and the different
kinds of "abolition Democrats." As he became an even stronger

state's rights Democrat, he became more voluble about the abolitionists and Republicans.

In telling his mother about the Christmas holidays of 1859,
Pierce explained that "a crowd of us made lots of hot punch,
of course we had to smuggle in the materials and I am afraid
it will prove a dear day to some of my classmates,—two were
caught drunk and the poor fellows are now in arrest, but we
have all signed a pledge of honor not to touch a drop of any intoxicating liquor while we are in connection with the Academy,
provided they are not dismissed." Pierce confessed, "We do not
yet know if even that will save them. The pledge is a good thing
for the class." Later he wrote that all of the class signed the
pledge, "the Sect. accepted it and we are now on a pledge and
our fellows' all rights atoned, so no more wine for several years
to come."

The big event of this Christmas season, though, was a surprise
visit from Louisa, Uncle Tom Jones, Aunt Georgia Jones (Uncle
Erwin's wife), and young Cousin Waddy Thompson of South
Carolina. They "all dropped down on me like a thousand of
brick." They had to come across the Hudson on the ice by sled
and remained at the Point only an hour and Pierce saw them for
only half an hour. "They telegraphed me from Washington City
to meet them in N. Y. City; just think of the idea, as if I could
go to meet them in the city, if the whole British fleet had bombarded the place, I couldn't have gone and Sis knew it."

The year 1860 was ushered in with one of the severest freezes
of the past several years. The Hudson River was frozen over and
snow was deep. Nature seemed to have had some premonition
that the year would bring no good. The ill winds of sectionalism
were becoming hurricane in force, and West Point was slowly
swept into its vortex. Pierce wrote his mother, "our country is
in somewhat of a distracted condition. . . . The time is not so
far distant when southern citizens must stand up with a bolder
front than they now do, to crush the despoiling hand of a northern oppressor, when the storm which would seem now but to
be the gentle breeze which mildly fans our soil will lash the waves
of fanaticism into thundering bellows which perhaps shall wreck
our vessel and our national happiness." A year later he was to
realize how prophetic his statement had been.

Pierce still thought lovingly of home and in a letter to his
mother on March 1, 1860, wrote that a home was the happiest
spot on earth—"a place where happiness is not made up of vain

and guilty thoughts and desires; no morbid transient or surface
bliss reigns there, but all is *real pure and holy*. There is no
worldly garnish or guilty splendor required to make that home
a paradise; but around the simple spot one calls home there reigns
a halo of serene sweetness the loss of which cannot be atoned
for by any other spot on earth, but one should leave sometimes
in order to appreciate his home."

Early in March 1860 Pierce heard from Robert, who advised
him to give his whole heart and soul to his duties; "something
that your future career must depend on is the manner in which
you improve your *present advantages*. You can *never* have the
same opportunities of storing your mind with that solid practical knowledge, which must adorn the soldier and statesman as
the present affords you. *Aim* at the honors; if you *should* fail to
get them, your 'stand' will be *higher* than if your aim was only
to graduate. Pardon me for advising! But I can't help it. Do your
duty! Angels can do no more."

Louisa wrote her brother that she was planning to marry Tom
Jones. Pierce disapproved so strongly that he refused to answer
the letter. A month after the wedding he wrote his mother, "I
wish I could forget that *infernal* marriage." Louisa realized that
her youngest brother's refusal to write to her indicated his dis-
approval of her marriage, but she continued to write to him;
and to her mother she wrote, "I am distressed at Pierce's silence,
but am not conscious of having done anything to merit his displeasure. I suppose I did marry against his wishes, but *I do not
think* that my family is disproved by my union [*sic*], or that I
am in any degree worse than formally." She added, "Nothing
that Pierce does or says shall effect my love for him tho' he may
pain my heart." Pierce seemed to be the only member of the
family with such strong objections to Louisa's marriage. Aunt
Mary Thompson, Mrs. Young's youngest sister, wrote Mrs. Young,
"We all grudge her to Tom mightily, but she would have married sometime or other, and we would have disliked it just as
much then." Aunt Mary concluded by quoting from the matriarch of the family, Grandma Elizabeth Jones—"Ma is much better satisfied since seeing them." She added that Grandma Jones
thought the young married couple would do well.

Meanwhile the ill feeling of the Young family toward the
abolitionists extended to all Yankees. Probably Dr. George Young,
the oldest brother, expressed the sentiment of the family when
he wrote that Pierce's opinion of the infernal Yankees and aboli-

tionists was correct. "Dispose of them all, for they are such negro loving chaps that they are all the time at some devilment with them at the South, either trying to steal negroes or get them to burn their homes, and to kill their masters and mistresses and to murder women and children, and do every other bad and wicked thing."

In February Pierce became very much excited about politics. He was fearful that Stephen A. Douglas would be the nominee of the Democratic convention at Charleston, South Carolina. Reading an account of the convention in the *New York Herald,* he denounced to his father the Charlestonians for charging such exorbitant prices for the use of the convention hall and for food. "If it was serving the republicans in this manner it would be all right, but it shows a bad spirit to the national democracy." Then he added: "I hope and trust that Mr. Douglas will not get the nomination; to vote for his squatter doctrine will be to concede to what I look upon as a taint of black republicanism. If men say that he is the only man to save the country from the impending crisis I say in response let the country go to the devil. We have been conceding and giving ground for twenty years, and even longer until concession has ceased to be a virtue, and now it has come to a pretty pass that southern chivalry must light upon a man whose milk and water principles may perhaps get the majority of votes; there are a great many candidates in the field, I believe I would as soon see Gen. [Joseph] Lane the Pres. as anyone who seems now to have a chance."

Dr. Young immediately answered and denied that the *Herald* report of exorbitant prices was altogether true, but he too thought Charlestonians were charging too much. As for the various candidates, he thought that General Lane's prospects were as fair as those of any other aspirants for the presidential nomination and he would be fully satisfied with the General. "Hunter of Virginia and Dickinson of New York are both favorably spoken of in this state; nevertheless, I still believe that Douglas will be the nominee"; and Dr. Young added, "If he is I shall vote for him, but with much reluctance."

Pierce's uncle John M. Jones of Greenville, South Carolina, wrote on March 23, 1860, "All good men . . . would mourn to see the costly and glorious fabric of our union pulled down to the dust forever; yet it will not by the same estimate balance the seals of oppression and ultimate degradation of one half by the other.

"I hope South Carolina will not go out by herself. The only hope I suppose is that the south by united and timely resistance may save the whole country. . . ."

Although the Georgia cadet and his classmates went to summer camp on June 19, where they followed a hard military schedule, he tried to keep up with political events. He read the papers avidly, and while in camp wrote that he was surprised and sorry to see an opinion in the papers that Georgia would not go for Breckinridge. "Alas, I hope the South will awake from her apathy in time to turn aside the thundering storm which is gathering over her. Our people will yet see that they must pull together or all is lost."

By the first of September Pierce and the other cadets had returned to the barracks. Then things began to hum and cadets became more embroiled in politics. On September 15 Pierce wrote his father about a straw ballot in the corps for president and vice president. "There are only 214 votes polled. The results were as follows:

Breckinridge and Lane 99
Douglas and Johnson   47
Bell and Everett 44
Lincoln and Hamlin 24

and we are positively certain that the majority of the small number who did not vote are Breckinridge and Lane. This is a pretty good showing considering that nearly two-thirds of the cadets are from the North," he added boastfully.

Another cadet in the division, writing years later described the straw ballot incident differently, saying that "some evil spirit stole his way into West Point and thence into the room of a couple of bitterly partisan southerners. When the tally was over, only about thirty could be found who had voted for Lincoln, and according to the tellers, every one of these was from west of the Hudson River, the bulk of them north of the Ohio. . . . What happened is not certain, but whatever may have happened according to the tellers there was not a single recorded vote from New England for Lincoln."[2]

Sectional feeling at West Point was forgotten for a few days in October 1860, when the Prince of Wales visited the Academy. Pierce in a letter to his mother pretended to object to royalty, but it was apparent that actually he enjoyed the pomp and ceremony incident to the Prince's visit. He described in detail the arrival of the royal visitor and the parade that the cadets put on for him. He expressed disgust over the "fuss" the Yankees made over the "white headed little fellow," but wrote with pride about how General Winfield Scott met the young prince.

Interest in the prince was soon forgotten in the growing attention to sectional strife. "I hear there is excitement South. Let's all be ready for the coming trouble. I wish my southern brothers here were ready to throw our swords in the balance and offer our services to a southern confederacy *if she will duly act true to herself* and prohibit Lincoln from taking the chair. And there is many a man in the army who in case of disolution will wheel his platoons into the columns of the South. I shall patiently await the action of Georgia," he concluded his letter.

The excitement and ferment of secession were intensified in November with the election of Abraham Lincoln as president by a minority popular vote. Pierce expressed his thoughts in a theme which he entitled "The Union." He wrote that if the Union was not dissolved, the Southern people would be ruined forever; but if Southerners would resist, they would become the most prosperous people on earth. He condemned those who cried submission. "The real leaders are only those who are capable of judging an insult. There is not a true patriot that will cry submission! And the highminded patriot must live, too, in the abominable union which has been trampled upon by the most degraded Yankee. And when the Yankees hear the submissionists talking about this glorious Union they go off among their brethren and triumph over it, and they say we will get them to submit and we will then set the slaves free. And they will make a law to mix the races. Then submissionists will live in slavery, while the patriots will try and if not successful will die in the glorious excuse of defending their rights."

There was one cool-headed person in the family—Aunt Mary Jones Thompson—who after the election wrote to Mrs. Young that she supposed they would all be out of the Union before long. "But I am sadly afraid we will never be as happy a people and cannot help looking forward to the future with forebodings."

Robert in Texas wrote that it was the best armed state in the Union. He stated that Texas was ready for revolution and would probably take the lead in secession. He said that he planned to join the Texas Rangers and "had rather fight the Yankees than the Indians."

On December 7, 1860, Governor Joseph E. Brown issued a special message to the Georgia legislature on federal relations, retaliatory state legislation, and the right of secession. Dr. Young sent Pierce a copy of the message, and he was tremendously impressed by it, especially the part in which the governor stated that the constitutional rights of the people of Georgia, and of the slaveholding states, had been "violated by some of the non-slaveholding states to an extent which would justify them, in the judgment of all civilized nations in adopting any measures against such offending states which, in their judgment, may be necessary for the restoration and future protection of all their rights."

By December 1860 Pierce had begun to question whether he should stay at West Point or resign. Writing in an Atlanta newspaper in 1893, he stated that for several years the question of slavery and the rights of slave states in the territories had formed the principal topic of discussion in the halls of Congress, and "each year they grew warmer and more exciting, til the presidential election in 1860, which resulted in the election of Mr. Lincoln, and the dethronement of the democratic party from control of the government. After the election the excitement grew hourly more intense. All eyes were turned upon Washington City—it was the center of interest. All sections of the Union were being wrought up to most intense excitement, but the body of men most interested in these events was the army of the United States, and the corps of cadets preparing for the army at the time, for they knew that if war must come they would be the first to be called upon the stage to open the great drama that was to decide the fate of the Union. The men of the army were to be the actors to open the play. In case of war, they had to do and to die; so they were making up their minds trying to determine honestly what was the proper course of each of them to pursue when the final moment should come. The cadets at the military academy were deeply moved; each day brought some startling piece of news."

Early in December Pierce wrote Senator Alfred Iverson asking what he should do. On December 4 Senator Iverson replied that he thought the young cadets should remain at the academy at West Point until their states seceded from the Union. Then, he added, "After such a step . . . , no Georgian could in my opinion remain in the service of the Federal government without dishonor. You should then immediately resign, go home and tender your services to the authorities of your own state or to such government as the seceding states may form."

On the very day of Senator Iverson's reply Pierce wrote his father that the country was perhaps nearer to destruction than it had ever been since the foundation of the republic. "These traitorous republicans are just beginning to realize the dangers which they flattered themselves would never occur. They now shrink from the appalling effects of their own treasonable designs. They now would save the Union and are crying peace and conciliation but alas too late to save this once glorious fabric of republican government. Such a crisis has never been occured [*sic*] in our country; workshops and factories are being closed and thousands of men are being sent adrift upon the world with nothing to do and nothing to eat—just two hours ago I heard of the closing of Cold Spring foundry, one of the largest and most extensive foundries in the country and such is the case with hundreds of similar institutions throughout the whole North; two weeks ago not one of these scoundrelly yankees thought that there was a possibility of disunion although the South threatened it. They thought it was all talk as usual, but now there is not one but has terror depicted in indelible characters upon his countenance. There is a complete revolution of opinion and they are now saying that dissolution is inevitable." Pierce thought a few Republican Congressmen were sympathetic with the South but felt that a majority were opposed to any concession. "They despise the South; they despise our institutions and now victoriously shake their clinched fist at us and dare us to leave the Union. Will Georgia remain with such a Union? Will she submit herself to be bound and lashed to a delusion that will inevitably lead to her own damnation? God forbid. I am ready to fight and if need be to die for her, but submit with her—never! I feel entire confidence in our leading men of Georgia and that if she is not righted in the Union, she will right herself out of it. I am in rather a critical position but I shall patiently wait until the time for action arises and then depart for my home, and you must let me know from time to time your opinion of these things and I shall be guided by your council." Fearful that his father would think he was devoting too much time to extra-curricular activities, Pierce added that examinations were approaching and he was well prepared. "I am doing as well or better than I have ever done before, so you may rest assured that I will attend to all my duties until it becomes necessary for us to leave the institution even if it should not be till I graduate. Some of us have occasionally donned the cockade, but the Yankees are mighty still and conservative." Pierce spoke for most of the Southern cadets.

Pierce's relatives were not agreed on what course he should take at West Point. His immediate family cautioned him to wait; the relatives in South Carolina, who favored secession and war, advised him to resign and come home and prepare to fight. In every letter Pierce wrote he spoke vehemently of the Yankees and the rights of the Southern states. When brother George wrote home about the birth of his second son, he added that he had received a letter from Pierce, who had written "on nothing else in the world but politics from the first line to the last; *he is in for the war."*

Meanwhile Pierce wrote his brother-in-law, Tom Jones, that he had supposed Georgia would have striven to be the banner state—"a course to freedom and the best of the South." He continued, saying that the free states were all under "the control of the black republican party—they elected their speaker in congress last year, having now elected their president and vice-president, they have long since committed the overt act, by violating the constitution and laws of congress on the subject of the recovery of fugitive slaves by refusing to admit a state [Kansas] into the Union with a constitution tolerating slavery—they have declared we shall have no more slave territory—and they will abolish slavery. In their violation of the constitution on the subject of the recovery of fugitive slaves, they have broken the constitutional compact, and hence we are under no obligations to adhere to the compact. Are these the people we are to compromise with? Is there any hope (if we fail to act now) that they will surrender all of this catalogue of wrongs, and can the South be satisfied with anything short of complete restoration of all her constitutional rights, with such constitutional guarantees as shall enable her to maintain her right, by equal power in the general government, both legislative and executive? Without these rights we cannot safely consent to live in a government with the North, and who is simple enough to believe, that if the South now stays her action for the hope of compromise, that these rights will be surrendered to her?

"Believing as I do that the states of this Union are sovereign and independent, and that they have the right to assume the power delegated in the formation of the Federal Union; and seeing that this right is now denied by a considerable portion of the people of the states; I regard it as all important, that the southern states should now, not only assert the doctrine but put it into execution, in order to test the rights of the states under our government; for it is evident the tendency of the government is to consolidation and despotism, and the sooner the tendency is rejected, the better it will be for the states of the South, whose rights are now in eminent danger and can only be secured by the right to withdraw from the Union, and formation of a southern confederacy. Are the states sovereign, and independent parties to the constitution compact? They entered into the compact each for itself—each is entitled to two senators, and by withdrawing their senators, the government will be at an end—without a senate no laws can be made, and the functions of the government destroyed. There is no power to compel the states to elect senators or representatives, and hence the power of forming the government is with the states—the people of the United States, as such, have no powers of government independent of the separate power of each state, and show conclusively that the government is not a consolidated one, and possesses no power to compel a state to submit to its laws or remain in the Union after she has seceded. I mean of course constitutional power. South Carolina has again and again asserted the right of secession, and that to preserve her rights she would exercise the powers. She, as also several of the states, has declared that the refusal to protect the rights of the South in the Territory, that the refusal to carry into effect the fugitive slave laws, and the election of Mr. Lincoln upon the principles laid down in the Black Republican platform, would be sufficient cause for Her to exercise the rights to send, and for that purpose she has called her convention."

Pierce condemned President Buchanan for stating that he had to endorse the collection of revenues and for repairing and strengthening the forts at Charleston Harbor. He thought the President's idea of sending messengers to South Carolina begging the state to stay her action was ridiculous. He explained to his father: "I don't believe she will do so; if she does she will be the dupe of timid and timeserving politicians; her prestige will be gone and with the balance of the South will sink into insignificance and disgrace. She won't do it, but will brave the storm and lead her sisters of the South, who are almost ready to follow in her footsteps, to honorable death or glorious victory. If difficulties betide the South it will be her own fault. To use the

expression of Georgia's noble [Augustin] Clayton, 'He who dallies
is a dastard, and He who doubts is damned.' "

He continued, "What I mean by equality in the governments—
is equal legislative powers in the senate, and a dual executive
(as proposed by Mr. Calhoun many years ago), viz. a southern
and northern president or executive and that no act of congress
should have the force of law, unless sanctioned by both execu-
tives. This kind of government is the only one in which the
South could have her just rights in connection with the North.
In a general government with the North (as heretofore) her
interests are so different from those of the South, and her members so much greater, that it would be a miracle if her legislators
should not become not only oppressive but intolerable; in other
words we should be the subjects of a despotism unequaled in
the world."

More determined than ever to do something, Pierce wrote to
Colonel W. J. Hardee of the First Regiment of Georgia at
Savannah offering his services as well as those of another Georgia
cadet, Joseph G. Blount. Replying for Colonel Hardee, who had
been called to Montgomery, Alabama, Lieutenant Edward Willis
told Pierce that his services were "needed in Georgia and if
your intention is to come, it is your duty to come at once," although all of the appointments had been made in the regiment.
"Of course if you and Blount should remain at West Point (a
thing which I could hardly believe) take a cut for old and former
friendship sake. But to my advice—if you are coming to Georgia
and want to enter the army write at once to Leroy R. Walker,
Confederate Secretary of War, at Montgomery, Alabama, state
your age, all your education, birthplace, residence, etc., the arms
of service you prefer—artillery, cavalry, or infantry." Then he
continued, "All old Brown's appointments will be knocked hell
west to make army officers and West Point cadets high up; not
one of them will be dropped." Willis liked his reserve officers
only "pretty well; one or two of course are d—n fools, who are
disgustingly supercilious, but they will sink to their correct level
before long and find the first duty to an officer is to keep his
d—n mouth shut lest he should convince those capable of knowing that he was an ass."

One reason for Pierce's anxiety about what he should do was
the action of several of his classmates who were resigning and
returning home. On November 30, Cadet Henry S. Farley of
South Carolina offered his resignation—to take effect on the

nineteenth of December. South Carolina seceded from the Union on December 20; immediately all of the cadets from that state resigned except one—John Y. Wofford.

The bitter misunderstanding on sectionalism that had been increasing for more than a decade had by January 1861 grown to such proportions that no power seemed able to stop the cyclonic fury which it had reached. On December 26, 1861, Major Robert Anderson transferred his small federal forces from Fort Moultrie to Fort Sumter in Charleston Harbor, and he refused to return when the South Carolina authorities ordered him to do so. The next day, the collector of the port and all the custom house officials resigned from the national government in Washington and proceeded to raise the Palmetto flag over the custom house. Under orders from the governor, the South Carolina state troops on December 30 seized the United States arsenal and the large quantities of arms and ammunition found there. It was a time when reason seemed to have become silent, or spoke so feebly that few paid it any attention.

Even the cadets at West Point became embroiled. In the series of newspaper articles that Pierce wrote for the *Atlanta Constitution* more than thirty years later he described the average cadet of that time as a pretty independent thinker, who studiously perused the papers; "In their leisure moments they discussed freely all the current topics of the day. . . . The cadets at the Military Academy were deeply moved; each day brought some startling piece of news. The 'Star of the West' a government steamer fitted out in New York, attempted to land and reenforce Sumter in Charleston Harbor. She was fired into and forced to retire; she had on board several hundred men and a large quantity of stores and provisions for Major Anderson's command in Fort Sumter. The firing into this vessel by the South Carolina batteries was the first hostile act of the war."

Several years after the war George Custer related a dinner conversation which he had with Pierce at West Point during the time when the possibility of war was a constant topic of conversation. All the cadets talked about the impending war in a free and friendly manner; those from the North discussed earnestly the power and motive of the national government; the impulsive Southern cadets argued about invaded rights and future independence. "Finally, in a half jocular, half earnest manner, Young turned to me and delivered himself as follows: 'Custer, my boy, we're going to have war. It's no use talking; I see it coming. All the Crittenden compromises that can be patched up won't avert it. Now let me prophesy what will happen to you and me. You will go home, and your abolition Governor will probably make you colonel of a cavalry regiment. I will go down to Georgia and ask Governor Brown to give me a cavalry regiment. And who knows but we may move against each other during the war. You will probably get the advantage of us in the first few engagements, as your side will be rich and powerful, while we will be poor and weak. Your regiment will be armed with the best of weapons, the sharpest of sabres; mine will have only shot-guns and scythe blades; but for all that we'll get the best of the fight in the end, because we will fight for a principle, a cause, while you will fight only to perpetuate the abuse of power.' "[3] Custer stated that the prophecy "was destined to be fulfilled in a remarkable degree."

Events were moving fast. Rumors were rampant. Pierce was carried along with the growing emotional excitement and frenzy, and frequently took the leadership at the Academy in urging that some action be taken. His sense of urgency and his enthusiasm were further heightened by the news from his brothers. George, in Resaca, Gordon County, Georgia, wrote that a company of volunteers had been organized and he had been elected captain. The orders were that the company would stay in Georgia to defend the state, but George wanted a captain's commission in a regiment where his medical training would be used. Early in January, brother Robert spent one night with Pierce while in New York on business and told him of being commissioned a captain in the Texas Volunteers. The news from George and Robert made the youngest brother even more anxious to take action himself.

"You know I am the strongest fire eater in the country, and the very moment Georgia has need of it, I am *honor bound* to be there," he wrote his mother on January 10. "I believe it would not be honorable for me to remain here after the state passes the ordinance of secession. Nearly all of the Georgia delegation have their resignation ready to hand in as soon as the state goes out and some of them would go now, but they are awaiting my discretion as I am the senior member from Georgia." Pierce continued thoughtfully, "Now I am not in favor of blustering around seceding and then having a reconciliation and come back into the Union. I am opposed to such a move from personal as well as patriotic motives; it would ruin my prospects for now I consider that I am sacrificing everything. I have in throwing up my pay, renounced my commission and with it a bright and certain future. I would not do it for twenty thousand dollars in hard cash under any other than existing circumstances. Now this will be my loss, provided there is a reconciliation which God in His mercy forbid. Now I shall want to enter into service as soon as I get home, but as my family is one which rather awaits the coming events, than pushing them forward, I suppose that I will have to wait till I can see myself that plebeian governor and recommend myself to him before I can get a respectable rank and then probably they shall have all been filled. I have devoted 9 years to my profession and am ably qualified in all its branches and can get certificates of the same. I would like to have a position secured for me from the governor if possible; if not I will try my hand when I get there and if I fail I will take nothing low in rank for I would rather fight as a private than a subaltern to an officer less proficient than myself, but I will be moderate enough in my demand."

Pierce included in his letter a note to his father seeking advice as to what he should do, and he wanted Dr. Young to write a short letter to General Lane in Washington enclosing his consent for Pierce's resignation and asking the General to hand it in "when he thinks that I ought to resign; and you may depend there is more confidence to be placed in him than any man in the country and the General is a warm friend of mine and will do it with the greatest pleasure and advise me to resign when he thinks it is right; I expect he will judge so as soon as the state goes out." Pierce confessed that he had already written General Lane himself and that he would be on the lookout for his father's letter. Fearing that the family had not heard the news, Pierce concluded his letter: "Reinforcements have been sent to Sumter; I hope the little republic will sink the ship before she lands although I have several good friends as officers on board."

Dr. Young did not answer, but he got Louisa to write cautiously on January 17, "Father is at a loss to know how to advise you as regards your resignation; he fears the state will not need your service and the difficulties will all be amicably adjusted by the time you would reach home, and then you would lose your place at the Point at a very great sacrifice. However, he says he will write to Gen. Lane as you requested and submit your resignation to his discretion." Then Louisa added on her own account, "That appears to me to be the best thing he can do. Father thinks

there would be no impropriety in your remaining at West Point
even if our state should go out of the Union, provided the state
does not need your service. I should think the prompting of
your own feelings would better decide the point."

The family at Walnut Plantation was worried for fear that
Pierce had already resigned and was on his way home, because
no one had heard from him in over a week. Louisa wrote to find
out where he was and reported the news that the state convention
was in session at Milledgeville. She presumed that Georgia would
be "the last state of all the Southern States" to secede but it
would "go out by a desperate effort." She went on to say, "We
scarcely deem ourselves safe here as there is quite a company of
Lincolnites in the county. On public days they come down from
the iron works hollering for Lincoln and for negro equality and
still they go unmolested. . . . Dr. Jones is pledged to South Carolina and is only waiting orders to go; should his services be
called for . . . , I may accompany him but think I will stay with
Mother. Tom thinks I would be safer in S. C. than here but I'm
not afraid to remain here with my six-shooting gun and your
sword which is one of the most prominent mementoes of my
room." She concluded her letter by asking Pierce if he had read
Toombs's fearless speech in Congress, and by telling of the rumor
that Joe Brown, the governor, had taken possession of the federal
forts in Georgia on January 3. The rumor indeed was a fact, for
Fort Pulaski was seized by Governor Brown's orders on January 3, 1861.

The Georgia convention met in Milledgeville on January 16,
1861, and after a terrific debate adopted a secession ordinance
on January 19. After this events moved too quickly for a cadet
drawn between two loyalties—his love for his home state and his
oath to the national government. Pierce tried to be practical,
even though he spoke and wrote rash statements, but such times
were not conducive to rational thinking. A few days after the
adoption of the secession ordinance, the Georgia convention appointed delegates to meet with representatives from other Southern states at Montgomery, Alabama, on February 4. Meanwhile
on January 23 all of the Georgia senators and representatives
resigned from Congress, and returned home.

Though mindful that Pierce had ever been an obedient son,
Dr. Young realized the urgency of the times and knew that a
young man's impetuosity would hold only so long. He wrote to
General Lane asking advice, including Pierce's resignation to be

used whenever the General thought expedient. On January 27, General Lane answered, expressing serious doubt in any adjustment between North and South, for "the North will not agree to such terms as the seceding states can accept. Besides this in less than three weeks a southern confederacy consisting of Georgia, Alabama, Florida, South Carolina, Mississippi, Louisiana, and Texas will be organized; a president will be appointed and a *de facto* government will be put in operation and in a few weeks will be recognized by all the powers of Europe. And after mature reflection, I have this moment enclosed to him at West Point your letter of permission to resign."

Impetuous Robert Young wrote his mother from Texas that he was astonished to hear that his father was undetermined as to what course Pierce should pursue. "Father should remember Pierce is but a boy and needs council [*sic*] in his movements. Senator Albert Iverson wrote to the Ga. Cadets 'When Georgia secedes from the Federal Union I am of opinion no Georgia cadet can remain longer in honor at West Point, until that time my advice to you is to pursue your studies and attend your duties.' I wrote Pierce . . . to not wait one moment if he was still there but to leave instantly, even if he had to go off bareheaded, barefooted, in his shirt tail and beg his way to some southern state. It is certainly a dishonorable, disgraceful, and degrading position for him to hold longer, and his own sense of right and pride of character should have taught him this earlier."

Now that Pierce had his father's consent to resign he was not so sure that was the thing to do. He suddenly realized how much he was surrendering when he resigned. He wrote his mother a long letter in several installments, saying in part, "Sometimes the idea of remaining under Lincoln's government presents itself to my imagination in a very repugnant manner—then I think cooly of the matter and feel and know that the people will not appreciate the sacrifice that I should make in resigning; and this is not all, some of them will think I was found deficient because you know almost every man that has represented the 7th Dist. at this place has been sent off before remaining a year; in fact, you know comparatively speaking that a very few have graduated here from our state. The people think a man cannot get away from here without being sent off; you know we thought so before I came. Well, now it is a hard thing to throw up a diploma from the *greatest* Institution in the world when that diploma is in my very grasp and you know that diploma would give me preemi-

nence over other men in *any* profession. Whatever now I say it is
a hard matter to renounce all this when I know that my position
is not appreciated and when I have no position or employment
ahead. If there is war trust to me then, for then I will be needed
and can serve myself and my countrymen at the same time. And
no matter how low I should begin, success would be certain, for
the loggerhead and feather bed soldiers would willingly skip out
and let the deserving take the lead. War is a matter of life and
death and a battlefield is not the puny place which it is reported
and the whistling of balls and the groans of the dying and the
wails of the wounded are not the sweet and seraphic music that
novel writers would make us believe. . . .

"But I am getting off my subject, you see I am very touchy and
justly so upon giving up my position. It is now my opinion you
need have no fear of *Civil War,* for South Carolina cannot attack
Sumter without orders from the southern government. Why she
did not attack it when the President refused to give it up and
when she had it in her power God only knows, for I cannot possibly imagine. That fort ought to have been taken a month ago;
it would have been much better than to have waited, but, My
Dear Mother, it would have been a hearty enterprise and many a
one of these gallant fellows would have hit the dust and never
seen the inside of Sumter. It can be taken and they have the men
there to take it, and why have they not taken it? Well I would
like to know. And again I would like to know why the Miss.
troops left Fort Pickens. I suppose because they could not get Old
Chase to let them pitch in. Now I do not like all these things and
they make me afraid to give up all before I see my way clear before me. Nearly everyone says wait. Of course you have read the
speeches that Lincoln has made on his way to the Capitol; they
are flimsy, childish, pointless and uncomprehensible. He knows
that if he attempts to take back the southern forts by force of
arms that it will be the first set act of war, and that the border
states (who will not otherwise go out) will stand to their guns
and defiantly bid a last and bloody adieu to the American Union.
Lincoln is well aware that he stands above and hears the murmurings of a terrible volcano which at the slightest menace from his
little finger will burst forth with all its terror to spread death,
desolation, and destruction throughout this whole fair and happy
land. He has at his right hand a man who is one of the greatest
statesmen the world has ever produced, though a corrupt one.
That man as you may see from clauses in his speeches would like

to send his name down to posterity as the savior of his country. I speak of Senator William Seward. You see he is coming round and there are a host of others who only await for some leading republican to break through the platform and they will follow like sheep.

"Now I do not anticipate a settlement of this trouble during the administration of Lincoln, neither do I anticipate coercion or war (they are the same), but at the same time I can very well see how the government *might* act during Lincoln's term as not to take back the facts, not to offer any hostilities and at the same time not act in such a manner as would cause the doctrine of disunion to spread and also to prevent the border states from going out. If this should be the case, and if after Lincoln's term is over the northern states and the southern states which may still be in the Union (for some will not go if Lincoln governs as I have supposed) should elect a democrat for the next President, then I can see it is very possible those states would come back. Though I should not like it, I very much fear the conservative principle that is yet distinguishable in the revolting states may one day bring them back. God forbid it should be under a republican."

Pierce ended his letter on February 18, "My action will depend upon the advice of Father and the advice of these gentlemen to whom I have written. . . . The last letter I wrote home was for leaving, but the more I am convinced the more I am determined that I cannot do without bread to eat and clothes to wear, and I hope you will see me as your neighbor with a pretty little gal and a big plantation. Not that I have picked her out, for My Dear Mother, before I do that it will be with your full knowledge and approbation, so fear not. But, she must have a mighty big plantation and lots of little darkies."

Still unable to decide whether to resign or not, even though he had his father's consent, Pierce wrote to the leaders of Georgia—Robert Toombs, Alexander H. Stephens, Howell Cobb, and Governor Joseph E. Brown—and to Jefferson Davis of the Confederacy, seeking advice as to his course of action. Typical of the letters he wrote was the one to Governor Brown in which he told of his qualifications, education, training, experience, and his references. He commented, "As Georgia is out of the Union I do not consider that I should remain here consistently with honor and duty after the 4th of March. I shall therefore leave here very soon. . . . Sir, you will do me a great favor if you will give me a commission on my arrival in Milledgeville. I have been engaged

in acquiring the profession of arms about nine years and I hope
I am prepared to serve my state in the capacity of a soldier."

To Jefferson Davis, Pierce wrote on February 6 a similar letter,
stating that he believed it would not be consistent with honor and
duty "for me to remain in the Academy after the 4th of March.
Is this met with your opinion?" He explained that he would enter
the 1st Class in June, and it had always been his most cherished
hope to graduate at the Academy. He would not resign his position for any consideration if he thought he could hold it with
honor, "but I am afraid it would not be right and moreover I
consider it my duty to tender my services to my section immediately. I am advised that a regular army of the Southern Confederacy will be immediately formed. It is my desire to get a commission." Then he proceeded to give his qualifications, with the
hope that Davis could "to some extent judge in a rough manner"
of his ability. "I am informed that you will probably be at the
head of the government or at least of the War Department."

Not waiting for a reply to his letter, Pierce sent a telegram on
February 22 to President Jefferson Davis offering his services and
requesting a commission. Meanwhile his brother George bitterly
opposed Pierce's resignation from West Point, for he did not
think that his services would be needed for two or three years. In
a letter to Mrs. Young, George wrote, "He is now being paid to
get a more thorough education than he has and becoming better
able to serve his state and country. . . . he will . . . command a
better position with a diploma from West Point than he can now
without one. He should stay at the Point till he graduates so he
can do so with all honor. . . ." George explained that Georgia in
its convention ordinance had exempted cadets so that they could
remain at West Point and get a first class military education to
serve the South. He concluded his letter: "I have not written him
from the fact that it was too great a responsibility for me to
(perhaps) blast his hopes and prospects of future usefulness if not
greatness."

Pierce heard from a former West Point classmate, Edward Wil-
lis, who had already resigned and joined the Georgia militia. He
explained that Pierce and Blount had both been appointed sec-
ond lieutenant, and added, "Both you and I are in Hardee's
Regiment. I was in Walker's (Old Billy), but was transferred.
Our pay is one hundred and eight (108) dollars per month.
Savannah is the headquarters of Hardee (1st) Regiment and
Augusta the headquarters of Walker (2nd)." Willis further re-

ported that recruiting depots were being established all over the state and preparation was being made for the worst. He explained that after the two regiments had been organized, they would be presented to the President of the Confederate States so that they would be in the regular army of the Southern Confederacy. Willis stated resolutely that he had resigned his cadetship of course, and would never serve again a government which belied its statement and violated a compact which it was sworn to preserve inviolate. He continued, "My dear friend, the only question for you now to decide is will you stay or come; don't be offended at this because I know you are as true to Georgia as the magnet to the steel. Still I am also aware of the fact that you think a reconstruction [*sic*] may be effected and then you would be received; this I think is natural and right but my advice is come and not only come but do it at once. You are wanted. . . ." Willis also asked Pierce to get the cadets from Virginia to come South to join up with them.

Pierce was disappointed when he was offered only a second lieutenant's commission in the militia of Georgia. He expressed to his father, on February 28, his surprise at the low rank of the commission, "considering all the circumstances. They have appointed some of my old Marietta classmates 10 or 15 years ahead of me in rank, that is it would take me that long from 2nd Lieut. to reach the positions they occupy when these men have been doing nothing ever since they graduated, while I not only commanded them at Marietta, but have been diligently devoting myself to the profession ever since. Now this is humiliating." Then Pierce continued, "Father, I see from the list they have put down sixteen-year-old boys ahead of me. This may arise from the fact that my friends were too late in bringing forward my name. Being absent I did everything in my power, but I suppose that man Brown thought I was a beardless boy. I knew that these people could never appreciate the sacrifice that I am making. I wrote back to Lt. Willis and told him I would not accept, but as I have not been officially informed of my appointment, I suppose it will be kept open till I get home. I may by the force of circumstances be compelled to accept it. My friends here are indignant at the manner in which I have been treated and urge me not to accept, but as I have offered my services and as Georgia is considered in danger it would not look well for me to give it up immediately, but if they should not keep it open till I come, I shall not care a whit; curse them, I expected better from my state. Have not yet received the draft. . . . The idea of giving me a second lieutenant when in a year I would have been offered the same position in the most aristocratic and highly educated army in the world is indeed hard; especially when they put men above me whom I taught to drill 5 years ago." Pierce concluded his letter—"I'll get off soon; you'll see me in March sometime; don't know when." He promised his father that he would be friendly with Louisa's husband when he came home.

On March 4, 1861, Abraham Lincoln, the backwoods lawyer of Illinois, was inaugurated President of the United States. His inaugural address was received with mixed emotions by Pierce's family. Aunt Mary Thompson, the practical member, wrote Louisa on March 8, that in her humble opinion they had "a proclamation of war in Mr. Lincoln's inaugural address. . . . I think it is an able address written perhaps by Seward who is a great statesman. If they carry out those sentiments, I suppose we will have bloody work to do. . . . It will be decided shortly." The family at Walnut Plantation were worried over what would happen, for they feared that the address meant immediate war, and they had three sons and a son-in-law who would be called into service at once. Not only was their safety involved but also the care and protection of three families.

Cadets at the Academy were restless but officers outwardly carried on as usual. Daily routines went on uninterrupted, and examinations were held at the beginning of the year as rigorously as ever. It was unfortunate that P. G. T. Beauregard, of Louisiana, a graduate of West Point, was appointed superintendent of the Academy on January 23, 1861. After serving for only five days he was dismissed, after telling a cadet he would go with his state if it seceded. Beauregard explained his dismissal as resulting from a disagreement between the Secretary of War and the U. S. Senator from Louisiana. Many cadets thought Beauregard had hesitated to resign outright for fear of what the Southern cadets would do.

On May 7, Pierce and the other Georgia cadets had a meeting. After a brief but serious discussion they all handed in their resignations. George Custer described the resignation of the Southern cadets as a bitter experience that disrupted the intimate relations existing between the hotblooded Southerners and his more phlegmatic schoolmates from the North. "No school girl could have been more demonstrative in their affectionate regard for each other than were some of the cadets about to separate for the last time, and under circumstances which made it painful to contemplate a future coming together. Those leaving for the South were impatient, enthusiastic, and hopeful; visions filled their minds of a grand and glorious confederacy, glittering with pomp and pageantry which usually characterize imperial power, and supported and surrounded by a mighty army; the officers of which would constitute a special aristocracy."[4]

Writing in the *Atlanta Constitution* in 1893, Pierce stated, "About the middle of January [1861] the seven states that had already seceded appointed delegates to a convention at Montgomery, Alabama. They met in convention and formed a provisional government. I felt then that the separation was permanent and war was certain. I was in the graduating class; in less than three months I would have my diploma, and I was very anxious to have it. Georgia seceded in January. The convention in Montgomery had formed a government. I thought I surely must go.

"While deliberating on the course to pursue, I naturally turned for advice to my superior officers, the professors, and the military instructors. They all advised me not to resign. The beloved old superintendent Bowman urged me to remain and graduate, said to me, 'Taking your own view of the case, would you not begin your career, even if you should go South, on much more advantageous grounds, if you should present yourself with your diploma?' This was a strong argument, but I felt it was bad faith to remain and receive pay when I knew that I must join another so soon as I graduate, so I took the final step, and the day that I broke the ties of comradeship and severed my connection with the service was one of the saddest of my life." Pierce went by Headquarters and signed his cadet check book with a great flourish —"My address is P. M. B. Young, Savannah, Georgia."

Pierce received $18.94 as a balance due from the amount of his credit. Then he bade sad farewells and left for New York. From the one day he spent in New York he took time to write a letter to Leroy Walker, Secretary of War for the new Confederate States of America, in which he said, "Sir, I have just resigned my commission as a *cadet* in the U. S. Service and I am desirous to obtain a commission in the army of the Confederacy."

V

◊◊◊
◊

A Dashing Cavalier of the Confederacy

AFTER leaving West Point Pierce spent one day in New York and then left for Washington. There he met many army officers whom he had known at the Academy. He saw that troops were concentrated in Washington; new commands were being formed and everything connected with military affairs about the Capitol was creating the greatest interest. While in Washington, Pierce attended "one reception at the President's—almost all of them were in uniform; everyone talked of war; the clank of sabres and the rattle of spears were heard upon every pavement. Then I realized the fact that war was inevitable."

The only Southern senator the ex-cadet could find was Louis Wigfall of Texas, who gave Pierce some dispatches for President Davis and urged him to hurry on to Montgomery. He met his friend Senator Ira Harris of New York, the father of his classmate Cadet William Harris, and told the senator of his resignation. The senator advised him to return to West Point immediately to finish his course and said he would see the Secretary of War and have the young man's resignation recalled. Pierce assured Senator Harris that it was impossible, for he had already accepted a commission in the militia of Georgia.

In Washington Pierce tried to get as many prominent people as possible to assist him in getting a commission in the army of the Southern Confederacy. Although he had accepted a second lieutenant's commission in the First Regiment of Georgia, Pierce wanted a commission from the Confederacy because he hoped to get a higher rank and he believed that a Confederate commission would give him a greater opportunity to serve. Therefore he

50

asked his friends to write the leading Confederate officials and use their influence to get him a commission.

While in Washington Pierce received letters of reference from two of his officers at West Point, Captain George W. Desser of Company D of United States Cadet Corps and Captain Charles S. Shields of Second Cavalry. Captain Desser wrote that P. M. B. Young's character had "those marked and characteristic signs of the true military man which ever should guide the judgment in selecting persons for responsible posts, viz. firmness, fidelity, and fearlessness in the discharge of duty." He emphasized that Pierce's military qualifications and talents were of the highest order; in addition he had "other leading qualities of the officer and gentleman which ever made it a pleasure to be associated with him 'on duty'; it is without hesitancy that I can commend him for a position of trust and responsibility."

He deeply appreciated the letter of Captain Shields, his cavalry officer, written to Jefferson Davis, whom Shields had known when Davis was superintendent at West Point. Captain Shields informed Davis that Young had completed the theoretical course in cavalry, was an accomplished horseman, and a gentleman, and would "whenever the opportunity occurs, give additional lustre to the chivalry of the South."

Pierce left Washington in forty-eight hours and went as rapidly as he could to Montgomery, Alabama. There he called upon Mr. Davis, who received him with kindness and informed him that in a few days he would receive a commission in a brigade then being organized. In the meantime Pierce was granted fifteen days' leave of absence to visit his home in Georgia.

Meanwhile Pierce's father had written Secretary of War Leroy Walker to request his assistance. Dr. Young's very good friend Dave S. Printup of Rome, Georgia, also wrote Howell Cobb asking him to help. Printup explained that he had been appointed the visitor to West Point in 1859; "At that time Young had been at West Point two years and Col. Delafield superintendent and Colonel J. Hardee commandant both informed him that Young was one of the most efficient officers if not the very best *officer* in his class." Printup knew him personally and had been acquainted with his family, "his father Dr. Young of Cass County, for several years being [from] among the most excellent families of the state."

One of the first things Pierce did upon reaching Walnut Plantation was to send his resignation to Adjutant General Henry C.

Wayne of Georgia, saying, "Having just arrived from Montgomery, I find the commission tendered to me by the Governor of Georgia; and in consequence of my appointment in the army of the Confederate States; I have to inform you of my now acceptance of the commission in the army of the Confederacy."

While Pierce was at home, he received a joint letter from several of his closest friends at West Point. They wrote of the latest events since his resignation, and told how much they missed the Cass County cadet. Some praised Pierce for his resignation and expressed regret that they were not Southerners. One said he wished "Old Abe would inaugurate war" so he could resign. Others also expressed a wish for war and the opportunity to resign. George A. Custer wrote, "We all miss you very much and many are the regrets I have heard expressed at your going. When you write do not fail to remember me, and I know that because we happened to be born and raised on different sides of the Mason's and Dixon's line you will still consider me as your true friend." Though such letters brought fond remembrances of West Point, there was no time for sentiment.

On April 20 Second Lieutenant Pierce M. B. Young was ordered to report "without delay to Pensacola, Florida, and report for duty to Brigadier General Braxton Bragg Commanding."[1] He was to be aide-de-camp to General Watts I. Walker. Bidding his family farewell, Pierce spent the night with a friend at West Point, Georgia, en route to Montgomery. He tried in Montgomery to get his orders changed to an assignment in the adjutant general's office, but was told of his need as an artilleryman at Fort Barrancas at Pensacola. No changes were made. Before leaving the city, Pierce called upon Mrs. Jefferson Davis and her sister, Miss Margaret Howell. He wrote his mother that he had a pleasant time. "Miss Howell, Jeff's sister-in-law, is a very pleasant and pretty girl. I knew them at West Point. Mrs. D— treated me very kindly and pressed me to come frequently."

In 1893 Pierce described in the *Atlanta Constitution* his arrival at his post: "General Bragg occupied the United States Marine hospital as headquarters. The Confederate States government was expecting an attack at the navy yard from the fleet and the garrison in Fort Pickens, and active preparations were going on to defend the place. Forts were being built along the coast in front of Pickens, and mortar batteries were being placed to command the fort in case of attack. General Bragg was a very strict disciplinarian. The force under his command was the best material, and could easily have held their ground against ten thousand men. We expected an attack by land and water, but it never came. The army, however, was in splendid condition and was becoming more efficient every day."

Back at Walnut Plantation the Young family was upset not only over Pierce's departure for Pensacola but also because the doctor son, George, was, according to his wife's letter, "like a war horse, snorting for battle" and threatening to start immediately for Charleston, Virginia. His wife wanted him to get the advice of his parents; with a wife and four babies to care for, she wanted the advice of the older people in the family. She wrote Mrs. Young that George had not received the appointment for which he had applied. The Secretary of War wrote George that he thought it very probable that surgeons would be appointed from those who had resigned from the United States Army. George later was appointed on July 19, 1861, assistant surgeon in the 14th Regiment (Brumby Regiment) of Georgia, Volunteer Infantry.

As for Pierce, he was never more serious. He began his work earnestly and assiduously, as any second lieutenant at his first post. One of his chief worries was that the war would begin and end without his having an opportunity to participate. His letters home from Fort Barrancas complained of the hot weather, poor food, inconveniences, and lack of work. He felt that his training and talents were being wasted, and he tried unsuccessfully to get his father and George to raise a regiment for him to command. The only pleasant features of his tour of duty were the visit of inspection by President and Mrs. Jefferson Davis in May and the daily rides on his horse.

On July 21, the long smouldering embers of sectionalism, hatred, and misunderstanding broke into flame along the small stream, Bull Run, in Virginia, between the Northern forces of General Irvin McDowell and the Confederate forces of General P. G. T. Beauregard. News of the success of the Confederate forces spread rapidly throughout the South. On July 23, the news was received at Fort Barrancas; cannons were fired and rebel yells shook the walls of Fort Pickens, which was being held by the northern forces in Pensacola Bay.

Immediately upon receiving the news, Pierce requested and was granted from General Bragg a special leave of fifteen days.[2] He went home and then immediately left for Richmond. "Everyone was anxious to get to Virginia; it being apparent that the

ole mother state must be the battleground. I desired to get into
the army of Virginia, it being at that time the most active in
the field. . . . Richmond was full of soldiers; the greatest activity
prevailed in every department; troops were arriving from all of
the southern states; corps, divisions, brigades, and batteries were
being organized for the autumn campaign. Richmond and its
environs formed one grand camp. The adjacent fields were covered with canvas. The hospitals were full of the wounded from
the battles of Manassas and Bull Run. There seemed to have
been a grand gush of patriotism throughout the South, and troops
were being tendered to the government by the tens of thousands
from all the states of the confederacy. Arms were scarce, muni-
tions of all kinds were in demand, troops were being rushed to
the field.

"While the army of the union was reorganizing and preparing
for another advance McClellan took command of the Army of
the Potomac in the field, and the vigor of his discipline was
immediately felt by every soldier in his command. This army
was soon in splendid condition. Early in the autumn he began
to abandon the lines around Washington and transferred his
operations to the peninsula."[3]

While at the Spottswood Hotel in Richmond Pierce met
Colonel T. R. R. Cobb, who asked him to be his adjutant.
Pierce accepted the offer. From the first he admired Colonel
Cobb, and twenty-eight years after the War ended said that
Cobb "was one of the most perfect characters" he ever met.[4]
A month after accepting Cobb's offer Pierce received a letter
from Colonel Henry Benning informing him that he had been
elected a colonel of Benning's regiment and giving orders for
him to report to camp near Lynchburg. Of course he could not
accept.

The commissions for lieutenant, colonel, and major had not
been filled in Cobb's Legion when Pierce accepted the place as
adjutant to Cobb. Writing later he said, "This was my first
step toward promotion and for which I shall never cease to be
grateful to this noble gentleman and able soldier. Between
Colonel Cobb and myself there had sprung up a deep friendship and when I prepared to leave him and join my regiment,
he objected in terms that induced me to remain, bringing me
at the same time the commission of major of his battalion of
cavalry." Aware that there were older men in the Legion, Pierce
explained, "I accepted on the condition that the captains of

the cavalry companies would request me in person to accept the position. These gentlemen were all much older than myself and several of them distinguished men. They were Ben Yancey, Wm. Lawton, Thos. F. Stovall and Wm. G. Delony. After a long consultation with Colonel Cobb they came to my quarters and made the request. I accepted and in one week marched for General Magruder's Command on the peninsula at Yorktown."[5]

Pierce felt that the rank of major entitled him to a servant. He wrote his mother before leaving for Yorktown: "I am in want of a servant. Am using Cobb's horses; if you send a boy on [have him] to report to Brown, as directed to Richmond. It will be alright. . . . There is no chance of my command having any fighting to do in Yorktown. I hope therefore to be removed from there soon."

Pierce was placed in command of the four companies of cavalry while Colonel Cobb went by train with the infantry to Yorktown. While on the march, Pierce wrote his mother that he had four hundred horses and twenty wagons; "So you see with my men, horses, and wagons I have a pretty rough time. I have to be pretty rough with these old captains of mine and strict with the men. I have to ride along with the advance guards and order all the barrooms closed. I march from fifteen to twenty miles a day. My trains detain me much." Then with pride he continued, "You know I am in command of the whole command and nobody to dictate to me." He told his mother how kind the people along the way were to him and to his men. The young major was proud of his command and wrote home that he and his men "were universally admired on the road. I had a most delightful march from Richmond"; but he added, "I have no horse and no servant as yet but my captains have acted most kindly to me always, sending their negroes to wait upon the major and pitch the major's tent. If Father has sent me a boy, he will get transportation from Richmond here, which is about 6 hours ride on the railroad and steamboat. Wm. Brown, Ast. Sect. of State will fix it all."

As soon as Pierce arrived at Yorktown, he realized there was much work to be done to get the men drilled, disciplined, and prepared for active service in the field. In describing his experience he wrote, "I think one of the cavalry companies had fifteen wagon loads of baggage. There were sixty men in this company and they also had forty-five colored servants. This was a sample of the cavalry companies in the Legion. Their idea of war

was certainly amusing. When they had to send home most of
the servants and turn in for storage all of their baggage, there
was a howl of discontent that arose in that camp that threatened
to become mutiny. The negro servants were as angry and disappointed as their masters, for they expected to have a big time
in the war, and really, the negro servants did enjoy the war.
They cooked, groomed horses, served their masters, sang and
danced, as they had no fighting to do. I never heard of one
who deserted his master."[6]

At Yorktown Pierce and his cavalry took a position on the
Warwick River. He wrote his sister on September 22: "We
arrived here safe on Friday morning after 4 days march and one
day's sojourn at Williamsburg—an old town about 13 miles
from here. I found General Edward J. Magruder at that place.
He treated me with every mark of consideration and I took
dinner with him and staff. When I arrived here with my command I found the infantry portion of the Legion on a very
beautiful camp ground surveying the route for miles." In another
letter he wrote Louisa, "I'll bet there are more negroes in my
small command than in any regiment on the field. While the
column was marching, it was amusing; it looked as if almost half
of each company was composed of negroes in rear of companies."

Pierce showed his anxiety for the welfare of the men under
his command. He was always on the lookout for better food for
them, and wished for cold weather so that they could eat fish and
oysters without any harm. When a storm hit the camp on
September 21, and blew down many tents, his included, he
expressed anxiety that his men might become ill. The young
major realized that only healthy cavalrymen were an asset, and
tried to keep his men well and ready to fight.

On October 2, Henry, the Negro boy Dr. Young sent to be
Pierce's servant, arrived at Yorktown. He brought money from
Mrs. Young to her son. Master and servant were happy to see
each other. Henry was proud of his young master, and asked
to be remembered to everyone at Walnut Plantation whenever
Pierce wrote home.

The infantry of Cobb's Legion was put in the brigade of
General Howell Cobb, brother of the Colonel. "General McClellan was marching up the peninsula," wrote Pierce, "and began
forming his line along the Warwick River. Johnston was moving
down from Fairfax and forming in front of McClellan. Skirmishes
occurred daily between the outposts of the armies. In one of

these, the Gallant Captain James Barrow was wounded, leaving General Howell Cobb without an adjutant general. I was transferred from my command temporarily to General Cobb's Staff as adjutant general."[7]

Despite the excitement and chores of camp life Pierce usually wrote home twice a week. His affection for his family deepened. He worried about whether Tom Jones was in service, and fretted about his mother's anxiety over her two sons and a son-in-law in service, and about her grief over the death of George. Just before Pierce left Richmond, he heard of George's serious illness; he wrote immediately to his mother to allay her worries, saying that he had heard that George was in a country house and was "waited on well. He is going to resign and come home as soon as he gets well." Four days later he wrote Louisa of his uneasiness about their brother's illness. "I am so anxious about George. They tell me over 500 of Brumby's regiment were on the sick report at the same time." George died on September 21, but it was not until October 1 that Pierce received Louisa's letter with the sad news. He was heartbroken and wrote his mother: "Sister's letter came to me some days since bringing me the sad, startling and almost unbearable tidings of my dear brother's death. I somehow have been afraid to hear from home ever since I heard he was sick and as soon as I looked at the seal I knew as well as if I had read it the contents of that letter." In his grief over his brother's death Pierce wrote his mother, "It was God who gave his life, God took it from him and we pray and believe that God now has him in his keeping." The young officer had not become accustomed and hardened to death, for he had not yet fought his first battle. He concluded his letter: "How sad must be the appearance of home. This is the heaviest blow that has ever befallen upon me and it falls heavily. We must fall one by one from earth, that enemy to man [death] separates us only for a short time. We must be content, and bless God that there is hope of a happy reunion in the world to come. We are separated from eternity, that world of everlasting bliss and harmony, but by a veil, by a filmy mist—a mere nothing—a cord whose notness [sic] snaps at the least shock. Oh, Mother we are closer to our dear dead than we would imagine."

It was not until many weeks later that Pierce was to learn the details of George's death. He had died from typhoid fever, which had swept through the entire 14th Regiment of Georgia.

Yet to weep for the dead is never the duty of a soldier; it becomes a responsibility of those at home where time passes more
slowly and permits loved ones to mourn. Pierce was too busily
engaged in training and caring for his men to spend time in
mourning for his brother. But he continued to console his
mother; and when the Richmond papers on October 25 described
an account of a fierce battle around Yorktown, Pierce immediately wrote her that there was not a word of truth in the account
of the newspapers. Again he said that he did not expect any
fighting at Yorktown and confessed, "If it comes I fear that my
cavalry will have no chance, for there is no good ground for the
operation of mounted troops here." To try to take his mother's
mind from her sorrow, Pierce pictured in detail his tent with
a wooden floor, and described the building of log houses by
the regiment for winter quarters. He wrote that he had just
received "a beautiful little stove, . . . from Richmond and in
fact the major of cavalry they say is better fixed than any man
in camp." He told how Henry, the servant, "goes out often and
brings in a mess of squirrels. We are about 7 miles southwest
of Yorktown." Also he described several of the beautiful young
ladies he had met in Richmond.

His subordinate officers respected and liked the major of
their regiment. The men liked his daring and respected and
obeyed his commands. One of the young lieutenants while on
leave at Petersburg, Virginia, talked about the handsome Major
Young so much that a young lady wrote anonymously to him
saying that she was anxious to find out something about him.
Although flattered, Pierce thought she was too forward, and did
not reply to the letter.

Events moved so slowly at Yorktown that Pierce began to
regret that he had not accepted the commission as colonel offered
by Colonel Henry Benning, whose regiment in October 1861
was near Manassas.

Early in November, Lieutenant Colonel Richard B. Barnett,
who had been a captain of the Sixth United States Infantry and
a veteran Indian fighter, was promoted in Cobb's Legion to a
brigadier general, and the senior major, Ed F. Bagley, was
killed by his own men who mistook him for the enemy. Then,
Pierce was by common consent promoted to Lieutenant Colonel
of the Legion. Proud of the promotion, he was determined to
merit it by hard work in training and disciplining his men for
battle.

On November 7, while training with his cavalrymen, Pierce had a severe chill. Although he tried to carry on, his fever rose so fast that he was almost delirious before being carried to his tent. In spite of all that could be done for him by Dr. White, the regimental surgeon, Pierce's fever continued to rise each day and he remained delirious most of the time and kept calling for his mother. Dr. Young was sent a telegram describing Pierce's condition, and he immediately set out for Savannah and Yorktown to see his son. He had considerable difficulty in getting to Yorktown, as he had no passport and had to run the blockade. He finally arrived at night on November 13. He wrote his wife that he found Pierce much better—"He had been quite sick, but never very dangerous; he is at a private house, comfortably situated, a good large bed, comfortable room and enough of everything to eat; his landlord [is] a good and kind physician."

Two days later he wrote that Pierce was "still mending, has had no fever since my arrival, sleeps well and has a good appetite; chicken cannot be had at any price, but Henry kills him plenty of squirrels. We get two pints of milk for him daily, also some eggs at 50 cts per dozen." Immediately Dr. Young put in for a furlough for his son so he could take him home to Walnut Plantation—"Whether Pierce can procure a furlough to home" had not been ascertained, "but we will do all in our power. No fighting is expected here during this winter, but," he added with parental pride, "he is regarded the best officer in the Regiment; therefore the Colonel is not willing to give him up."

Through the efforts of the regimental surgeon, Pierce was given a thirty-day leave to go home to recuperate. Dr. Young wrote to his wife on November 16, explaining that they would not leave before the middle of the following week in order to give Pierce time to recuperate. He concluded, "We will have to go by Richmond; there we may be detained one or two days. I shall reach home as soon as I possibly can." But Pierce was not able to travel to Walnut Plantation with his father, and he did not arrive until the middle of December. Henry traveled with his master and took care of him. At home, Pierce found it hard to realize that a war was being fought, except to see "Ginnie," George's widow, and her three children living there. With the aid of the servants, Mrs. Young and Louisa nursed him as they would a small boy. Special foods were provided, and Pierce began to improve immediately. While at Walnut Plantation, he learned that his brother Robert had joined the Texas Sixth Infantry, located at

Fort Herbert near Galveston, Texas, and that his family—
Josephine, his wife, and daughter, Ida—had been left as a safety
precaution near Fort Sullivan on the Brazos River in Robertson
County, Texas. Pierce also learned that Robert was expecting to
receive at any time his orders to march for Missouri or Kentucky.

After he recuperated Pierce traveled throughout north Georgia
trying to raise volunteers and to buy horses for the cavalry. He was
not successful at all in the first effort, and he did not find many
people willing to sell their horses. On March 7, he received a
brief note from Colonel T. R. R. Cobb, with the following news:
"A telegram informs me the Legion is ordered to Suffolk and
leaves today. I hurry on tomorrow. . . . I learn that there are
5,000 minnie rifles in the hands of Brown's six months troops.
See the Governor and try to secure them for us as soon as their
service expires."

Pierce immediately left for Milledgeville to see Governor
Brown, but he was not able to get the rifles, because the governor
wanted them kept in Georgia to protect the state. Only the
previous December Brown had a terrific fight with the legislature
over the transfer to the Confederacy of the Georgia troops called
out for service on the coast. If the troops were not transferred,
the legislature wanted them disbanded in order to eliminate the
expense of maintaining them. Governor Brown thought such a
plan was fatal with the enemy on our soil in force. Consequently
Pierce had no luck in securing guns for his outfit.

Leaving Walnut Plantation on March 20 to join his outfit,
Pierce wrote his mother five days later from Weldon, North
Carolina. He was there awaiting the arrival of his legion, which
would pass through on the way to Goldsboro where it had been
ordered. "We have been thinking that Burnside would attack
that place, Goldsboro, but I see this morning that he has fallen
back, and it was but a feint upon Goldsboro to detract our attention from other points. It is supposed this morning that he will
go towards Suffolk. Troops have been crowding to Goldsboro
for some days." Major Benjamin C. Yancey relieved Pierce, who
thought there had been some wire pulling, for Pierce believed
that the battalions wanted him for colonel. He, however, was
placed in charge of transportation.

By April 6, Pierce was back with his legion near Richmond.
From the Spottswood Hotel, on April 7, he wrote his mother
that the plans were to march the next day "for the neighborhood of Fredericksburg. You know the infantry of the Legion

is yet on the Peninsula or rather with Johnston's army retreating. I have been ordered up to take charge of our cavalry. Johnston's army is still falling back from the Peninsula; I suppose they will make a stand about fourteen miles from Richmond. Our programme is now to take the offensive. I think within three months all the troops will be withdrawn from the Georgia, South Carolina and gulf states and concentrated in two columns to march north." Then he advised his father for the first time, "You had better be looking out for a mountain home to be safe."

In a letter to his mother on April 16, composed while he was at a camp near Lee's Mill on the Peninsula six miles east of Yorktown, Pierce said that after leaving Walnut Plantation he met the Legion at Goldsboro where they were joined with General Howell Cobb's Brigade. After a week with the group he received orders to return to the Peninsula. They looked for a fight; he wrote "Our force here is now about 30,000 reinforcements pouring into us by the thousands. Gen. McClellan commands the enemy here which is reported to be a hundred thousand strong (which we don't believe and do not care a whit if it even is so)." He explained to his mother that they had light skirmishing "all along the line every day but that little damage had been done on either side. I shot at a Yank the other day, but he was so distant that I fear that I did not hit the dog. The Yankees have passed Dr. Powers house where I was sick. The Dr. and my trunk I suppose are with them."

Pierce longed for a real battle, and he thought his men were ready for action. "We are behind breastworks and throwing stronger ones daily; if they will hazard a fight we can lick them. Our troops are in *fine spirits* and the rascals are so eager for the fight that it is hard to restrain them. I was just noticing some of the sick this morning and thought some of them had better be sent to the rear. Would you think it? They would not hear to it. *There is not a man in the Legion who could be forced to take a furlough at this time.* Noble fellows, I begin to believe all the patriotism is in the army and very little out of it."

Although he was at the battle front, Pierce continued to keep up with the political news of his state and the Confederacy. In a letter home on April 11, he wanted to know what his mother and father thought of the enactment of the conscription act and how it was being received. He tried to relieve his mother of any worry about his safety. He assured her that lieutenant colonels remained in safe positions and were in no danger; then, too, "We will whip the Yanks all hollow here if they fight, which I doubt exceedingly." He asked his father to buy him a good horse, and informed his parents that he had sent a Lieutenant Williams in Atlanta some money to be used in buying a new saddle and "Billy Rowland's mare."

Writing from camp near Lee's Mill, on April 21, Colonel Young said, "We have been skirmishing for several days." He told his parents that General Joseph Johnston had been placed in command of the Peninsula and "if the army that we have here cannot whip this fight we had just better quit." The horrors of the skirmishes and minor battles on the Peninsula were brought to Walnut Plantation by Pierce's letters. "The infernal dogs would not ask permission to bury their dead and they became so offensive to our men in the trenches that we had to send over a flag of truce and make the proposition ourselves which was accepted by them; only thirty-four bodies could be found. It is supposed that we killed many more and that they were taken off under cover of night. It is strongly suspected that the storming party was bribed; in fact a prisoner who we took said it was so; another thing was that no officer was among the killed or wounded. . . . The prisoner said that the stormers were not aware that we had rifle pits in that position, but when that sheet of lightning burst upon the unsuspecting dogs, those who were not sent to the devil were sent a kiting to the other side. They are throwing up strong entrenchments. They depend greatly upon their artillery, but we too have plenty of that here now."

Whenever possible, Pierce went on leave to Richmond. He began to feel the increasing cost of living. He wrote the latter part of April that the price of horses and saddles was rising very fast and blamed much of the rising cost of living upon the civilians of the South who he believed were lacking in patriotism.

On April 30, writing to his father, again from near Lee's Mill, Pierce told him: "No general action has taken place as yet though General McClellan is making vast preparation; it is reported that he has 150 thousand men—we have about 80 thousand and ought by all means to gain the victory as we have the advantage of position. I am afraid that the enemy will not give us battle here, but move to some point south where we have no troops. We are skirmishing heavily constantly and I consider that the siege of Yorktown has partially begun. The woods around us are strewn with shells. The slow but constant boom of the enemies' cannon is now thundering in our ears, but he does little or no damage. He has not dared to assail us in close contact since the desperate struggle of the 16th ult. in which the flower of his front line was left to rot upon our soil." Pierce added, "The appalling news of the fall of New Orleans has burst upon [us]. May God grant that it be not. If they have New Orleans they have the Mississippi River—then Memphis must fall. They have pierced the femoral artery of our little republic; but do we despair? Never! God forbid. We are strong and hopeful. Our hearts beat proudly yet and if our citizens at home will not disgrace us their soldiers in the field will yet bear them to victory. You know not the meaning of war. May God grant that the people of Savannah will not follow the example of Nashville and request that their city be not burnt; burn it, I would not have a piece as large as a straw. I would make it a cinder before it should be polluted and governed by our disgraceful and damnable enemy and if the people are too cowardly and penurious to burn it, I would burn them and let them perish in the ruins, for they deserve not to be free."

On May 8 Pierce was ordered to retire to the line of the Chickahominy River near Richmond. The entire army was under General Joe Johnston, who had retired to the river bank before General McClellan's army.

Pierce wrote his father on May 14 from Camp Caroline near Fredericksburg, "I arrived here on last Saturday after a pleasant march of three days from Richmond. It is about 60 miles from Richmond. I am about four miles from Fredericksburg which you know is in the hands of the enemy. This is the most beautiful country I have ever seen; it abounds in beautiful fields of wheat and clover, which refresh the eye for miles down its verdant valleys. My men are healthy and horses thriving. I now get plenty of milk and butter, but pay high for it. I left the army of the Peninsula last Friday a week ago. . . . I am now in sole command of the cavalry. I am in sight of the enemy every day. We don't know when the Legion will be together again. I will soon be in command of nine companies of cavalry." He reiterated that they did not expect a battle for several days; however, the army of the Peninsula had fallen back to within about ten or fifteen miles of Richmond.

While on sick leave at Walnut Plantation Pierce had bought some horses which he expected to bring phenomenal prices in Richmond because they were scarce and in demand; he asked Dr. Young to buy more whenever the opportunity arose. Back in

Virginia Pierce wished for his horses, and wrote for his father
to send them, along with his servant Charlie, who had replaced
Henry. Whether homesick or fearful of what might happen,
Pierce's letter to his father included an apology and a promise.
"I hope, my dear Father, that you may never have to save my
life again, for I am as certain that I would have died as I am
writing this minute, had you not been with me, and I hope ere
this that you have forgiven me for my apparent ingratitude during my convalescence, for I know I was unreasonable, and head-
strong and disobedient to the best Father in the world, but not
ungrateful and I know that you attributed it to the proper cause
and that was the ill temper attending pain and bodily suffering.
If my life is spared through the war, it will be my aim through
life to be the pride of my dear parents."

The living quarters at Camp Caroline were not any better
than on the Peninsula. Each night Pierce used two planks as a
bed and did not remove his coat, pants, boots, and spurs the entire
stay. He did not write his family of the hardships because he knew
his mother would be disturbed. Again Pierce warned Dr. Young
that the war might come to them and for him "to hunt a nook
and have it ready" when the Yankees came. He knew that if the
Federal army tried to take Atlanta it would pass through Cass
County and probably near Walnut Plantation.

In May the young Georgian was pleased to learn that Dr. Tom
Jones, his brother-in-law, had gone to war, but was sorry that he
went as "a member of a guerilla band for he will labor under
many disadvantages." Pierce added, "I would have accepted
another cavalry company into the Legion cavalry. All my companies have all the advantages of irregular cavalry and none of
the disadvantages, for I frequently send them out on a several
days scout."

Pierce enjoyed Camp Caroline during May 1862, and described
the country around the camp as "indeed a land of milk and
honey," the most beautiful country he had ever seen. But all was
not harmony; he wrote on May 19, "I saw a touching incident
yesterday. I went out night before last on a scout of about twenty
miles, had only eight dragoons. I got in half a mile of the Yankee
lines about ten ocl—away up on the Rappahannock yesterday and
halted near the house of a gallant rebel who is in ranks serving
his country. We rushed in with cocked pistols, but found only his
beautiful wife, who looked as if she was about eighteen and most
beautiful she is, but not a bit frightened. She invited us in and

showed to us the wreck that had been caused in her house by the worthless enemy who had just been there. They went in her splendid parlors and took everything even the lamp chimneys and stole all of her daguerreotypes. She ordered them out and with so much pluck that they left after taking about all that she had and threatening to hang her husband if they ever caught him. She was just packing up to leave and she was escorted off under the protection of my gallant troopers; in a few minutes after she left her husband came in with the Va. Cavalry scout, and he treated us as I have never before been treated. He opened his cellar and I suppose an hundred men filled themselves and can-teens with milk and honey. There must have been forty gallons of the finest milk you ever saw. He took us out and showed us a long row of bee gums and told us to pitch in and they did pitch in. You ought to have seen them knock off the heads of the gums and pour out the honey. The gentleman invited me to move down and make his house a barracks and use his cows, negroes, clover fields, corn, fodder, and everything as it all belonged like himself to the Southern Confederacy. Well I got some of the good things and left."

The best news Pierce had to write his family was that his servant Charlie and the horses had arrived at Richmond, which was only three hours' ride away by railroad. He especially enjoyed the large box of provisions—cooked and uncooked—which his mother had been kind enough to send. He regretted that his father was not able to buy any more horses for him.

The family did not hear from Pierce again for several weeks. During that time the Battle of Seven Pines for Richmond was fought. The Northern Army under General McClellan had tried to capture the capital of the Confederacy, which at that time was being protected by General Joseph E. Johnston, who had withdrawn from the Peninsula in order better to protect Rich-mond. Pierce wrote his sister on June 5, "You know the army retreated from Fredericksburg in a hurry. I had to cover the retreat, but did not get into a fight as I expected, so now we are all before Richmond for the big fight." Then he told of the Battle of Seven Pines and added, "I have heard our loss in killed and wounded estimated at two thousand. I think it not so great as that. I being with cavalry was not in the fight. Infantry was used on that occasion. We whipped them off their ground, but we have since fallen back for a better position to our original position. General Johnston was wounded. General Lee now commands.

There is not a doubt that we will conquer this fight. Our success
is certain."

After the Battle of Seven Pines there was a month of inactivity.
The Federal army remained within its strong position at Harrison's Landing, and the Confederate army was withdrawn nearer
to Richmond. General Stuart placed his two brigades of cavalry
alternately on picket duty on the Charles City front, and in camp
at the intersection at Hanover Courthouse. Pierce was stationed
at the latter place. There continued to be frequent skirmishes
between the two armies. On August 5, at Malvern Hill, Pierce
with his Georgia legion had a skirmish. His first official report
to General Wade Hampton stated that a courier sent by Lieutenant Jubal Early reported to him at 12:15 A.M. on August 5,
with word that the enemy was advancing with a large force of
cavalry upon the left flank of the North Carolina cavalry pickets.
Immediately Pierce directed his adjutant to write a note to
General Hampton informing him of the state of affairs, and
ordered the courier to return and direct Lieutenant Early to
send him a scouting party. The scouting party did not discover
anything. Throughout the night couriers were reporting that
the enemy troops were advancing. They attacked at 5:30 A.M.
Pierce reported in detail the retreat and gave high praise to the
officers.

A study of the official report shows Pierce's keen insight into
military movements, his alertness to conditions around him, and
his care for reporting in detail. In addition it demonstrates
Pierce's fairmindedness in appraising his men and officers and in
giving credit where credit was due. For his account and for his
alertness at the skirmish, Pierce was commended by General
Hampton in his report.[8] On August 11, General Robert E. Lee
wrote to General J. E. B. Stuart as follows: "The report of
Lieutenant-Colonel Young of the operations of his command
at Haxall's Landing and Malvern Hill is received. I desire that
you will express to Lieutenant-Colonel Young my sense of the
courage and efficiency which marked the conduct of himself, his
officers, and men, and of the success which attended his efforts
against a superior force of the enemy. Colonel Young has performed the duty assigned to him in a manner creditable to
himself and his command."[9] To Pierce, such a commendation
was the highest reward he could receive.

Because fighting increased daily, he had little time to boast
about the commendations, for there was again a major battle at

Manassas on August 30. Although Pierce was on the field around Richmond and not in the main battle, he wrote his mother that he rode over the field five days afterwards. "The ground for a mile was literally blue with dead of the enemy. It was a fascinating though sad sight. It is my opinion that not less than two thousand Yankees now lie unburied on the field and it has been five days. The fighting was desperate and the victory glorious. Thousands of prisoners were taken and paroled on the spot and sent over to their lines as we were unable to feed them. McClellan was on the field. The prisoners say their men were deceived; they were told that Jackson was surrounded and they had only to cut him to pieces. They fought desperately but their closed ranks melted away before the death by fire of our brave troops like dew before the morning sun. It is said that the enemy are fast retreating over the Potomac. We expect to cross today and now, ho, for Maryland. We have them decidedly on the hop."

It was not until September 20 that Pierce was able to write his mother again, for he was with General Lee in his invasion of Maryland. He wrote from Charlestown, Virginia, "I have not had an opportunity of writing to you since we crossed into Maryland. We had a fine time going through the towns in Maryland; some of the ladies would wave their handkerchiefs and sash flags at us, saying, 'Hurrah for Jef. Davis!', and others for the federals." Then he wrote his mother that he had been wounded. "You will be surprised to hear that I am lying in a beautiful house in this town waited upon by the kindest people in the world and all together very pleasantly wounded and very slightly. On last Saturday whilst marching from Middletown, Md., towards Harper's Ferry the enemy was pressing us and Gen. Hampton saw a regiment of a cavalry which he feared would attempt to cut off our column. He ordered me to charge them with my regiment and I did it and they say I did it well. I tell you the clash of sabres and the shout of my gallant troopers was deafening. My horse was shot dead under me and I was shot through the calf of the leg, but no bone broken. I am now doing finely. The pretty girls treated me splendid," he teased his mother, "after I was wounded in Maryland. I crossed at Harper's Ferry the other day and came into Va. in a carriage. I saw the thirteen thousand Yankees who surrendered to Jackson. There was a terrible battle fought at Sharpsburg, Md., on Thursday. We gained another splendid victory. Our troops are all in Maryland. I suppose it will be three weeks before I can ride. If I was in Richmond I would come home, and I may yet manage to do it; do not be uneasy. I am doing finely. I peeled a Yankee's head in real trooper style. I think we killed and captured 20 or 30. I lost 20 in killed and wounded. I routed them *completely*. We have been doing wonders in the last two months. Our army is invincible. . . . You ought to see the pretty girls bringing us flowers and fruits. Do you think some rich girl in Georgia would give compassion on a fellow on crutches?" he asked jokingly of his mother.

Captain F. Edgeworth Eve, of Richmond County, Georgia, writing in the *Augusta Chronicle* of July 8, 1896, described the battle at Burketsville on September 13, 1862, when Cobb's Legion, Georgia Infantry, first asserted its individuality under the leadership of Pierce: "I can never forget the picture—we had to charge down a steep, rocky land between stone fences—from whose shelter their dismounted men were firing, over a narrow plateau where we deployed into company front at the run. The Dougherty Hussars of Albany charged, then the Richmond Hussars, his favorite always. And as we passed Colonel Young who was lying surrounded by dead and wounded, men and horses, in front of a little church, his dead horse pinning him to the ground; as we came by at the full run his voice rang out clear and distinct above our yells: 'Give 'em hell, boys; give 'em hell!' Waving his plumed hat over that handsome face, illumined by the fierce excitement of the charge, P. M. B. Young's and Cobb's Legion reputation was established."

The feeling of the soldiers toward Pierce at this time was shown by one who wrote several years later: "The other officers were older and we respected them. It was not the same feeling we had for Pierce Young. As Colonel Baker of the 1st North Carolina Cavalry told him at Middletown, Maryland, September 12, 1862, where after a hard day's fighting, incensed at some slighting remark that Baker had made of a charge of the Cobb's Legion: He challenged him to mortal combat then and there, 'on horseback or on foot, with sabre or pistol, or any way he would fight.' 'Why Pierce, you are nothing but a boy; you forget yourself. I came here to fight Yankees, not as good a soldier as you.' Unmindful of the emphatic berating of his junior officer, conscious of his own courage, demonstrated in many a fierce encounter, instead of arresting him for disrespect, he laughed at the boyishness displayed even before his own regiment, who with the older men of Young's regiment always so regarded the affront. Far from being perfect, we forgave his faults, even as a father would those of a spoiled child—for a spoiled child in many of his actions was Pierce Young. . . . Being born a soldier and with his military training, it was easy for him to infuse into that command, then consisting of six companies of infantry, four of cavalry, and the afterwards famous Troup artillery of others, the *esprit de corps* they were so noted for."[10]

Pierce's daring, fearlessness, and leadership won for him the esteem of the common soldiers as well as of the officers. They learned to respect his ability to fight and to admire his courage and devotion to the Southern cause.

By November Pierce's leg wound had healed and he was back in the saddle again, and a pleasant surprise was the receiving of his promotion to colonel. He immediately wrote his parents that he thought the promotion was given to him because of his leadership in the recent skirmishes. The young colonel immediately had the three stars of his rank placed on his uniforms and went to Richmond. His friends teased Pierce by calling him the "beau brummel" of the cavalry, for he was considered handsome in his colonel's outfit. He had a flair for making the most of his dramatic good looks. At one of the balls in Richmond he was the youngest officer present. His new uniform gleamed with gold lace, his high boots glistened, and his silver spurs and jewel-handled sabre clanked as he strode into and through the length of the hall. A Southern beauty whose tongue was as keen as Pierce's sabre called out to him so that everyone could hear, "Colonel, why didn't you ride in?" Undaunted, the dashing colonel ignored the sarcasm.

In December Pierce received a leave and visited Walnut Plantation. His father and mother were overwhelmed with joy to see him. From the first Pierce was restless and after a few days traveled throughout north Georgia trying a buy a horse to replace the one that had been killed under him. Returning home unsuccessful, he persuaded his mother, sister, and her two children to go with him on a visit to Greenville, South Carolina, to visit Aunt Mary and then to White Oak, North Carolina, to visit Grandmother Jones. Mrs. Young was anxious to show off her youngest son, and he wanted to get the approval of his grandmother. After a few days with the family in Greenville and White Oak, however, Pierce's restlessness returned and he went on to Richmond.

After Pierce left, Mrs. Young received the message that her son Robert had been wounded and captured and placed in Prison 2, Camp Chase, Ohio. Although Robert had an attack of fever soon after he was imprisoned, he wrote that the aid of clothes and money from Uncle Tom of Newport, Kentucky, was helping him to recuperate. As soon as Pierce received word of Robert's capture, he tried to get a leave to return to Walnut Plantation, but his request was turned down. He wrote his mother that he was still in command but that Butler would take over about the first of March and then would know what was to be done with him "I do not yet see where they are going to assign me."

On December 13, the young colonel suffered a personal loss, for Major General Thomas R. R. Cobb, the head of the Georgia Legion and the man who had offered him his first big opportunity in the cavalry, was killed at the Battle of Fredericksburg. In writing home Pierce told of his love for General Cobb, who had meant so much to him, and said he felt as though he had lost a member of his family.

By the end of winter Pierce had become somewhat reconciled to his grief over the loss of his friends. He sought the various entertainments, such as charades, parties, and dinners, offered by the Southern ladies of Fredericksburg and Richmond. His friends began to speak of him as a ladies' man. In his letters he frequently wrote of the wonderful time he was having with the young ladies of Virginia.

Pierce was made happy on April 4, 1863, with the news that Robert had been exchanged as a prisoner of war. He was able to get a few days' leave to meet his brother in Richmond, but was shocked at the emaciated, trembling man who met him—a living skeleton with clothes draped on him. As long as he lived Pierce never forgot the haunted look in Robert's eyes. He immediately got him some food and kept him in bed to rest for a few days before sending him to Walnut Plantation. Pierce was heartbroken over his brother's physical condition—it was the first time he had ever seen him lifeless and spiritless. He was determined that the Yankees would pay dearly for their treatment of Robert.

It was hard to recognize Robert in the gaunt emaciated looking soldier who made his way to the front door of Walnut Plantation in April 1863. He was so weak that his mother and sister immediately put him to bed; there he stayed as listless and lifeless as one exhausted and in a deep coma. In despair Louisa wrote her husband that she feared for his life, for "he suffers dreadfully at times with pain in the region of his heart. He is entirely unfit for service, and I think it will be suicide for him to return to it." Louisa's heart was broken to see her once proud brother crushed, haggard, and spiritless. She added a note to her husband's letter that Robert's constitution was entirely shattered and he could not bear the least noise, "and if a fly lights on his head it shocks him all over. Those abominable Yankees are the cause of his ill health!" Only time and careful nursing could cure Robert.

On Saturday, March 16, 1863, Pierce met his friend John Pelham, a West Point classmate, at the old hotel at Culpeper Courthouse to celebrate Pelham's recent promotion to lieutenant colonel. They celebrated by going across the street that evening and calling on the young ladies at the house of Judge Shackleford, just opposite the hotel. In fact John Pelham at the time was paying his addresses to Miss Bessie Shackleford. Both young men enjoyed the company of the young ladies and retired rather late to their hotel rooms. "Pelham was in fine spirits," Pierce wrote in an account in the *Atlanta Constitution* in 1893. "I am sure that night his dreams were tinged with roseate hues. But when morning broke we were awakened by the thunder of artillery."

The Yankee cavalry under Major-General William W. Averell had left Fredericksburg and marched up the Rappahannock, and at daybreak on Sunday, March 17, crossed at Kelly's Ford and advanced along the Culpeper Road toward Brandy Station. Then aides reported to Fitzhugh Lee at brigade headquarters for help. As soon as news was received, General Stuart and "the gallant John Pelham who loved a fight borrowed horses and went to see the fight." Pierce's *Constitution* article described how "Pelham rushed off to the scene of action. He rushed forward into the thickest of the fight cheering on our men and animating them by his example. When one of our regiments advancing to charge was received with such a terrible fire by the enemy as to cause it to wave, Pelham galloped up to them shouting, 'Forward, boys! Forward to victory and glory!' And at the same moment a fragment of a shell, which exploded close over his head penetrated the back part of the skull. . . ." He was carried at once to Culpeper, where the young ladies of Mr. Shackleford's family tended him with sisterly care; but he never again recovered his senses and died the same evening.

The death of this close friend upset Pierce as though Pelham had been his own brother. He wrote, "He was brave as Caesar and gentle as a girl. He shared my couch the night before his death. . . . He died the next night in the same house where we had spent the evening so delightfully the night before. . . . I never knew a better friend, a braver soldier. His name is immortal."[11]

Throughout the first part of the year 1863 Pierce was in command around Richmond. The real fight in Virginia, except for skirmishes, did not take place until May 1 to 4, when the Union forces were defeated at Chancellorsville; there were battles at Fredericksburg and Salem Church on the same days. At Chancellorsville, when Stonewall Jackson was mortally wounded by his own men, the South lost one of its most fearless officers. On the fourth the Confederates raised the siege of Suffolk and rejoiced over their success.

On June 9, Pierce engaged in the cavalry battle at Brandy Station. It was here that he attempted to live up to the promise made to Robert. Pierce described the battle in detail in his official report and commented on how he and his men supported the First North Carolina until ordered by General Hampton "to throw forward a body of skirmishers." Later learning that General J. E. B. Stuart's headquarters were in danger of being captured, Pierce and his men charged the enemy in close columns of squadrons and swept the hill clear of the enemy. Before the battle ended the young colonel gave support to Major R. F. Beckham's artillery, and later opened communication with Stevensburg. Pierce reported three officers and forty-one men killed, wounded, and missing. He reported that all of his officers and men "acted in a gallant and praiseworthy manner. All acted so well that it seems unfair to mention the names of any particular individuals; but I cannot fail to mention the intrepid personal gallantry of my lieutenant-colonel, W. G. Delony. Among others whose distinguished conduct came under my personal observation, was my adjutant, Lieut. W. L. Church; Capt. J. E. Ritch, commanding sharpshooters (who, I regret to say, while dismounted, was captured by a cavalry charge) and Lieutenant [J. L.] Clanton, of Company K. Captain [B. S.] King also deserves praise for the manner in which he commanded his sharpshooters. I desire also to mention the most distinguished gallantry of Privates McCroan and Landrum, who, on foot, refused to surrender when surrounded by the enemy, but cut their way through safely."[12]

Pierce's report was substantiated in the official reports of Colonel John L. Black, First South Carolina Cavalry.[13] Brigadier General Wade Hampton and Major General J. E. B. Stuart praised Pierce along with the other officers "for a large part of the success" and commended them for handling "their commands with skill and judgment, while their conduct was marked by conspicuous gallantry."[14]

In the battle on June 9, 1863, there were two tragic losses. Colonel M. C. Butler's right leg was cut off above the ankle by an enemy shell which after striking the ground ricocheted and killed his horse. Another loss to Pierce was the death of Lieutenant-Colonel Frank Hampton, a brother of Wade Hampton. He was mortally wounded while engaging one of the enemy with his sabre and died that night.

After the Battle of Brandy Station Pierce described the fighting: "The whole company crossed the Rappahannock and again started for Md. and Pa. On the 18th of June my regt. was called upon at day break to open a pass in the mountains through which the cav. corps could pass. We charged and were again victorious —the day after which we crossed the Potomac near Deanville. The army having crossed above . . . we were at Rockville near Washington, D. C. My regt. was in three miles of Georgetown and in sight of the church spires. We marched on day and night taking prisoners and transportation until we reached Hanover (29th June), Pa.; here we were met by a strong force of cav. under General Kit Patrick; my regt. was again successful and camped by Gen. Hampton. Late in afternoon of the 2nd of July whilst marching up to take our position on the left of the line of Gettysburg, Hampton's brigade was attacked in rear vigorously by a large column of cav.—my regt. being on that day the rear guard was first attacked. We immediately turned and fought desperately till night—most of the time hand to hand with sabre. Here I lost in one charge during ten minutes six commissioned officers killed out of my own regt. This was a great mortality for the length of time engaged. My Lt. Col. [Delony] was badly cut with a sabre while leading the charge. Another horse was killed under me at this place. We were victorious in this fight at Hunterstone; on the next morning early we took our position in the line and owing to the great loss in my regt. the day before I was assigned to the support of a battery of artillery and on this day we were lightly engaged but the regt. acted as reserve to the columns. On that night our army began its retreat from the bloody field unpursued by the crippled enemy. We marched covering the retreat of the army until arrived at Hagerstown, Maryland, we formed line of battle and marched one day and two nights. On the last night my regiment took up the line of A. P. Hill's corps which

crossed the Potomac at 12 o'clock. We of the cavalry remaining
till day light. To my regiment was assigned the honor of covering
the rear of the army over the Potomac. On the 12th of July
we took position at Hedgersville. Here we fought every day for
thirteen successive [days] in which engagements I lost many brave
officers and men. We retreated from Martinsburg through Win-
chester thence up the Staunton Pike and over the mountains
to Culpeper Court House taking up our old line on the Rappahannock. Here we remained until the 1st of August when the
enemy's cavalry advanced in large force and from strange circumstances the only force brought to oppose five brigades of cavalry
was Hampton's small brigade which from the heavy inroads of
death, wound and disease of the late campaign had been reduced
to about eight or nine hundred men in the saddle. We com-
menced fighting at noon on the same memorable bloody field of
Brandy Station on August 1, 1863."[15]

Fifty horses were killed and thirty-seven out of the 150 soldiers
were lost. When Colonel L. S. Baker, the commander of Hampton's brigade, was wounded in the early part of the battle, Pierce
took the command of it as well as of Cobb's Legion. While leading his men Pierce was shot in the chest and fell from his horse.
He was moved by his men from the battlefield and carried to
Richmond. Knowing that his parents would be anxious, Pierce
had the following telegram sent to Walnut Plantation: "Wound
did not enter cavity. Pistol ball passed through flesh and came out.
Doing well. Enjoying a novel." Two days later he telegraphed
that the wound was in his chest but that his lungs were not
injured.

General Robert E. Lee in his official report of August 2, 1863,
described the cavalry skirmish and reported the loss was small,
"but among our wounded, I regret to say, are those brave officers
Colonel [L. S.] Baker . . . Colonel Young of Cobb's Legion, and
Colonel Black, of the First South Carolina Cavalry."[16]

Pierce's wound, though not serious, necessitated his staying in
the hospital for about ten days. As his sister wrote her husband on
August 7, "I doubt not but that he will receive every attention."
Although Pierce enjoyed the company of the young ladies who
visited the hospital, he soon became restless and longed to visit
Walnut Plantation, especially while Robert was there. Receiving
a sick leave, he left after giving detailed orders to his adjutant. He
traveled by train to Cartersville, where his father and old Jim
met him with the surrey and drove him home. His mother and

sister wept with joy, and Robert, who was still frail and weak, patted him on the back. The Negro servants tried to outdo one another for the young colonel, who enjoyed all the attention.

Pierce was kept regularly informed of activities at his head-quarters by his adjutant, W. S. Church. He was grateful to hear expressions of concern for his health from his men, and pleased with the news from them. The best news the adjutant wrote was the promotion of Wade Hampton to major general. Church added to this news, "It is generally thought that in case such is a fact, you will command this brigade. Everyone thinks such ought to be and none of the brigade but what desire it."

The young colonel enjoyed his rest at home. He learned to know Robert better; he saw in his brother a man striving for recognition and success, and was glad to see that he was recuperating from his ordeal in prison. Pierce also talked and advised with his parents and sister about evacuating Walnut Plantation if the Federals should march into Georgia, for by the middle of July the Confederate army under General Bragg had withdrawn from middle Tennessee and fallen back to Chatta-nooga, which was approximately seventy-five miles from Walnut Plantation. For months refugees from middle Tennessee and Chattanooga had been passing through Cartersville on their way to Marietta and Atlanta. Pierce made tentative plans for his family to evacuate to Penfield, Georgia, and for George's widow and her three children to go to her sister's farm near Thomasville. He instructed the older and more trusted slaves to assist the family; one or two servants were to be left at Walnut Plantation; the household goods and all available food were to be placed in wagons and in the carriage and taken with the folks to Penfield. Dr. and Mrs. Young thought their son was too pessimistic and did not believe that the plans were necessary, but agreed to follow his instructions.

Early in September Pierce returned to his regiment to find that there had been a reorganization of the cavalry corps of the Army of Northern Virginia. Major General J. E. B. Stuart was in com-mand. Pierce was disgruntled and disappointed that M. C. Butler had been given command of the brigade and had received the promotion to major general, for he expected to be placed in command. Pierce remained commander of Cobb's Legion, and continued to be the fearless leader to his men.

VI

◊ ◊ ◊
◊

Testing a Rebel's Courage

ALTHOUGH Pierce never actually met face to face in battle any of his former comrades at West Point, he and they often opposed each other in battle. Several times Pierce recognized with his glasses General George Custer. "He was in full uniform and always wore long sleeves." In his 1893 autobiographical sketches in the *Atlanta Constitution* he described an incident that occurred during one of the first cavalry fights just after the Gettysburg campaign. "It happened at Buckland Mills, ten or fifteen miles north of Warrenton. We had been marching nearly all night in the direction of Warrenton. My brigade was marching in rear next to the enemy. It was a little after dawn and the enemy had attacked us in the rear. I drove him off and was just moving off, when one of Stuart's aides dashed up and said General Stuart sent him to say that a regiment had been sent to relieve me, and that I must come to him in person immediately at the Hunton house, which was near the mill. When I entered the house General Stuart was at breakfast and two beautiful girls were attending him. They were the two Misses Hunton. He presented me and they invited me to breakfast. Stuart finished and left me, telling me not to be long, as we were forming on the other side of the creek and the enemy might catch me. When I was about through a shell exploded over the house, and my courier called out: 'They are coming, sir, we must hurry or be cut off from the bridge.'

"I left the young ladies and the breakfast with many regrets, saying I would return, mounted my horse and rushed for the bridge just in time to get over safely. We returned slowly toward Warrenton, sending Fitz Lee's division down the creek. We set a trap for our friends, the enemy, and they walked into it. As soon as we left the mill, Custer's command came up. Custer himself rode up and politely asked the young ladies to have breakfast prepared. They told him breakfast was on the table, a confederate officer had just left it. He inquired all about who had been there. The ladies told him that General Stuart and myself had just left, but that I had not finished my meal and it was now on the table; Custer said: 'Very well, ladies, Young and I are friends. I will take his breakfast.' So he took it and enjoyed it. He chatted on gaily, telling the young ladies of our former intimacy, and when he had finished he said: 'Now, young ladies, be so good as to have something prepared for dinner for myself and staff, as I am likely to be about here till after dinner.'

"General Stuart's ruse worked well. We attacked in front and flank at a charge, and as the boys say, 'Wiped him up.' As Custer passed he stopped a moment at the gate saying: 'Ladies, give Young my compliments and tell him I took his breakfast, he can take my dinner and please give him this picture of myself and tell him to send me his,' and he galloped away for he was crowded." After the war Pierce and Custer renewed their friendship and laughed a great deal over the above incident.

For his brave leadership at the Battle of Fleetwood, or Brandy Station, Pierce was promoted in October to the rank of brigadier general. However, he did not have time to think much about the promotion, for on October 14 the Confederates fought the Federals around Bristoe Station. By adroit maneuvering combined with hard fighting, Pierce and the rest of the cavalry compelled the enemy's cavalry to recross the Rappahannock River, thereby saving the commissary and quartermaster trains of the Army of Northern Virginia. General Stuart in his official report stated that Pierce's brigade captured eighty-seven of the enemy, and "the conduct of the officers and men of the command generally is best exhibited by the fact that after two days' incessant fighting, they still charged with an ardor and gallantry which resulted in the total rout of the heavy forces of the enemy opposed to them with the advantage of position and supported by infantry."[1] He also described the ruse Pierce had used in dismounting three fourths of his brigade and "deployed them along the wooded range known as Slaughter's Hill. . . . A brisk fire of artillery and sharpshooters was kept up until dark, when Colonel Young ordered campfires to be kindled along his entire front and, his band of music playing, bivouacked on his line

of battle."[2] During the battle Pierce was struck on the head
by the fragment of an exploding shell but was not seriously
wounded.

In praise of Pierce's skill and leadership, General Stuart
reported that he and Colonel Rosser had driven back an entire
division of cavalry together with an entire corps of infantry
from Southern supplies. "The determined reception which they
met with when they reached the position occupied by General
Young, evidently impressed them. . . . And the defeat of an
expedition which might have proved so embarrassing entitles
the officers who effected it to the award of distinguished skill and
generalship."[3]

The fighting continued, with Pierce and his brigade taking
an active part, and capturing 250 prisoners, "together with eight
wagons and ambulances, Brigadier-General Custer's headquarters baggage and official papers, with many arms, horses, and
equipment . . . and the whole division dispersed in a manner
graphically described by one of their writers as 'the deplorable
spectacle of 7,000 cavalry dashing riderless, hatless, and panic-
stricken' through the ranks of their infantry."[4] Pierce and
Rosser had much fun the next day examining "Fanny" Custer's
equipment, and both laughed much about the complete rout of
the Federal cavalry.

The day after the battle, Pierce's wish to transfer was approved.
General Robert E. Lee by a special order had Pierce to report
to Major General J. E. B. Stuart, "for assignment to the command of Butler's brigade."[5]

The jealousy created by promotions among officers was revealed in Pierce's letter to his father: " 'Tis true [James B.]
Gordon was promoted first but my commission was dated the
same day and as I ranked him as a colonel I now rank him as
brigadier-general. I did not lose a brigadiership by stopping
to flirt with the girls after all, but got the general commission
and the kisses to boot. Old Gordon is very much disappointed
for he thought as he was appointed first he would certainly
rank me."

Pierce's command over the Butler Brigade was only temporary until General Butler recovered from his wound. He
was sure that Stuart wanted him to remain, but if Butler did
return and wished to retain his brigade, Pierce planned to go
south. He was anxious about conditions around Walnut Plantation, especially about Robert who seemed to recuperate too

slowly. He was concerned over the possibilities of a Federal invasion, and reminded his parents to follow the plan agreed upon while he was at home. He was worried about his father's poor health and about the Negro slaves and what they would do when the Yankees arrived near Cartersville. He wrote his sister on December 25, "I know plenty of people who have lost negroes, had their houses burnt, and not a rail left on the place."

When the family wrote Pierce complaining of their discomforts caused by the war, he scolded them: "To speak of suffering from the war, you all have suffered practically nothing compared to others that I know. . . . I am now on the last little piece of timber that a poor farmer has yet he murmurs not; before I leave I will have to burn the last stick. Bear up for God's sake. It is the cowardly and the weakhearted who sink under difficulties and troubles, but it is the noble and brave who rise triumphant above it all. No Christian will have trouble."

Pierce wrote Louisa that he had been attending "starvation parties" given by the young ladies of Fredericksburg, Virginia. He described these parties as ones where the very simplest of refreshments, if any, were served. But on December 24, because it was Christmas Eve, the starvation party was an exception—the young ladies gave a most delightful little supper. "We are living very well, plenty of oysters and birds; of course, it takes about all one can raise to live as we do, but you know," he confessed, "I am to eat if its to be had."

Early in December General Hampton submitted to General Lee a detailed suggestion that a brigade be formed for General Young. Then Butler, Young, and Gordon would "each have a full brigade ready for the spring campaign" provided the horses were sent away where forage was abundant and where an opportunity of procuring fresh horses could be made. General Hampton's suggestion was made because he was prompted by an earnest desire to place his command "in the best condition before the opening of the spring campaign."[6]

As if an omen of the next year for the Confederacy, the weather in December 1863 was terrifically cold and inclement. Pierce suffered from toothache, which the weather agitated, and he reported that each time he stepped outdoors his mustache froze. He remained near Fredericksburg with his command. On January 3 there was a cavalry engagement at Jonesville, Virginia, and from January 29 to February 1 there were cavalry skirmishes at Medley, West Virginia. Pierce apologized to his mother for not writing, "You would have heard from me more often during the last two weeks had not the enemy been moving. The enemy forced a passage over the Rappahannock several days ago and at the same time they advanced up the Peninsula, so we were in a considerable stew and hardly knew which way to march first to meet them. They have all gone back now and we are ever more snugly fixed in our old camp" at Hamilton's Crossing near Fredericksburg.

In a letter of February 11 he advised his mother to move, "for our army might have to fall back [from Chattanooga], but leave someone to take care of the house for it will be ruined even by our own troops if no one is there to protect it." Still carrying the enthusiasm with which he entered service, Pierce concluded, "I think things are looking brighter now than they have for a long time. You must always look on the bright side. There is not reason now for looking at the dark side." His high morale was typical of the Confederate Army at this time.

Tragedy struck again at Walnut Plantation in March 1864. Louisa's husband was captured and sent to Johnson's Island, Ohio. Louisa took the news of her husband's imprisonment bravely. She felt she had to be brave for her two children and her parents. She wrote Pierce that she longed for Tom's exchange, for she remembered how Robert had been treated while in prison. Pierce was grieved for his sister, but he was too busy with his command to brood over things at Walnut Plantation.

Pierce was kind to his men but realized that he had to be firm in order to control the older ones. He would not permit any insubordination; so when Major A. R. Venable accused Captain F. E. Eve, Company K of Cobb's Legion Cavalry, of being intoxicated on duty, Pierce brought charges against the latter and sent them to General Stuart for approval. General Stuart commended General Young for his action but felt that the evidence against Captain Eve was "not considered as sufficiently comprehensive" and recommended that no further action be taken if Captain Eve would pledge to Pierce "to abstain from all *intoxicating drink,* wine included, *so long as he remains a soldier in the service of the Confederate States.*"[7] Pierce agreed to the recommendation of General Stuart.

Reports of Pierce's ability to handle men spread. On April 15, Colonel Andrew Young, Commander of Eleventh Georgia Cavalry Regiment, wrote to Captain W. L. Clark, Assistant Adjutant General, of the "deep disaffection in his regiment and

the loss of soldiers going A W O L." Colonel Young advised
the sending of help to bring the deserters back. Then he added:
"I think it would have a good effect for General Young to
visit my Regiment as early as possible to speak to my men."

On April 30, Pierce was placed temporarily in command of
the North Carolina Brigade. Before he left for his new command he delivered a brief speech to his men. "My command has
been enlarged and my field of operation changed. If I have
acquired reputation as a commander, to your strong arm and
stout hearts, I am alone indebted. On a hundred battles you have
illustrated the chivalry of Southern hearts and amid the carnage
and shock of arms, borne in triumph and honor the proud flag
of your country. With you the post of danger has ever been the
post of honor—your decimated ranks, your glorious battle flag
battered by the storm and pierced by the unsung bullet of the
enemy on almost every battle field, your unsullied reputation
are all living testimonies of your gallantry and heroism. With
pride let it be remembered your flag has never trailed in the
dust, nor been ignominiously surrendered to the enemy—sustain
your already enviable reputation—buckle on your sabres with
renewed hope and energy for the coming contest—your homes are
invaded, your property destroyed, your cities, towns and private
residences are burned to the ground. Your mothers, wives, sisters
and daughters have been insulted and driven from their homes,
families, and houses. No man of honor and courage can submit
to such degradation. Let us renew the vows upon the altar of
our country to avenge the wrongs and as sure as the sun rises
and sets, we will drive back the invaders from our soil, and
accomplish our independence."

While Pierce was in North Carolina, he was main speaker at a
Confederate patriotic rally on May 4, 1863. In a rousing address
he appealed to the loyalty of the soldiers to support the cause
for Southern freedom. Never had he spoken better; his firm,
sonorous voice rolled out to thrill the soldiers, who yelled furi-
ously when he stepped down from the wagon which served as
a platform. That night a military hop was given in his honor
at the city hall in Columbia, S. C. Major Allen Green acted
as "herald." Dressed in full dress uniform, the handsome black-
haired Georgian was the pride of the young ladies. He was the
dashing beau of the evening and flirted with all of them. One
of the special visitors was Miss Mary Brooks, daughter of Preston
Brooks of South Carolina. She fell in love with Pierce after the

first dance. Pierce appeared to have fallen in love too. Before
returning to his command he proposed to the beautiful South
Carolina belle. Though she was engaged to another young man,
Mary accepted the dashing young general, and they promised
to write to each other. On May 14 Mary wrote expressing her
love. "How can I prove to you that my heart is indeed your
own? If you think me or my love not worth having—cast it
off. . . . Am I not right when I think that you are opposed
to being bound? You wish to remain single and free for some
time longer. . . . Until I met you I thought I would never like
to marry anyone who had loved or been engaged before. But
I am changed. I know I am unworthy of your love, but if you
wish it, it is yours. Did I not prove to you dearest that I
loved you?"

In a letter written three days later Mary described to Pierce
her breakup with her fiance, Colonel James P. Adams: ". . . on
Saturday night, I received a letter (or rather a note) from Col.
Adams, informing me that he had arrived and would call the
next day. I therefore did not go to church in the morning, but
waited for him. . . . He at last came and remained only twenty
minutes. You see we did everything up in quick style. Well,
we are to each other, nothing more than strangers now, only
mere acquaintances. I don't regret it. I am delighted it is broken
off. I loved him once very dearly, but that is past forever. . . .
He minds it dreadfully but tries to disguise it and be very
proud." She sent Pierce a tiny ambrotype which she thought was
much better than the photograph she had given him on May 4.
She concluded: "Write to me often, my dearest. There are
a thousand rumors as to the cause of my engagement being
broken off. Nearly all center upon you. I have written to mother
of our engagement." Then she reiterated several times her love
to Pierce. "I am so happy, my darling, in having your love."

By May 15 Pierce was back in Virginia busily engaged in
training his cavalrymen. Upon his return he learned of the tragic
death of General J. E. B. Stuart on May 12, after receiving a
mortal wound the previous day at Yellow Tavern, Virginia, and
of Brigadier General James B. Gordon, who was also killed at
the same place. The loss to the Confederacy of these two men
was irreparable, and to Pierce each was a great personal loss.
He had served under Stuart's command for more than a year,
and had worked with Gordon and learned to love him as a

brother. The young officer did not attempt to hide his emotions when he heard the news.

Pierce was so busy with his cavalrymen that he forgot the promises that he had made at Columbia to Mary Brooks, but she did not. She wrote on May 30 that she had not heard from him in two weeks, scolding him and accusing him of seeing other young ladies and forgetting her. She repeated her love for Pierce and continued, "Tell me *anything* my dearest, by which I can prove to you that my heart is yours *entirely*. But *first* tell me if you are changed; do not deceive me Gen. Young. Do not make me believe that you love me unless you *really* do. Write me candidly, and if you are no longer what you were when you were in Columbia please tell me. . . ."

Mary told him she was returning to her home in Edgefield, and requested that he write her in care of her mother. She added, "If you do not reply to this letter, I *may* make one more trial after I return home. No, I think I *will not*. For Gen. Young I will be forced to believe that you do not love me, and that some of your Virginia sweethearts have stolen your heart from me. Gen. Young, please tell me the truth, do you love me as much as you made me believe or were you flirting with me?" She described her visit to the park to sit where they sat while he was in Columbia, and told how it brought sad and painful memories. "If you love me, my dearest, as I *trust* you *do,* my one desire through life, shall be to make you happy."

General Young, however, was too busy to write, for he was engaged in the cavalry skirmishes at Hanovertown and Salem Church. On May 30, the Federals attacked at Ashland, and after a sharp fight drove Pierce and his cavalry through Hanover Courthouse.[8] Pierce was again seriously wounded, in the chest this time, and was removed from the field. His adjutant general, Major Church, and assistant adjutant general, Captain Robert Aldrich, thought him mortally wounded. Major Church, believing that General Young was going to die, asked Captain Aldrich to pray for him, but the captain replied that he did not know how, and in turn, requested the major to pray; but the latter acknowledged that he too did not know how to pray. Major Church then asked Sandy Dooker of Barnwell, Georgia, the orderly of the staff, to pray for the General. Sandy gave the same excuse as his superior officers, but when the Major turned his request into a command Sandy had to obey orders.

The orderly took off his cap and knelt by the stretcher on which
the wounded General lay. "He began to pray and to talk to
the Lord in quite a favorable manner about as follows: 'You know
Lord, the General is badly wounded, and not liable to recover;
have mercy on him, for you know he has been a wicked man.'

"Just then the General interrupted, and said: 'Sandy, what is
the use to remind the Lord of that? Why don't you say something good in my favor?'

"Sandy being interrupted, was disconcerted and ceased praying, remarking that he couldn't pray much nohow, and if he
couldn't do it his own way, he wouldn't do it at all.

"The General said that such prayers reminding the Lord of his
shortcomings, were not calculated to do a man in his fix much
good, and did not urge Sandy to proceed any further."[9]

While Pierce was recovering from his wound he received a
letter from one of his young lady friends at Fredericksburg saying that the Yankees had occupied the town three weeks previously. "You can form no idea of what we had to go through;
at one time we had thirty thousand wounded in town, and not
less than seventy-five thousand passed through. My only amuse-
ment was watching them bury their dead. I got quite fond of
looking at them. They just carried them off in wagon loads—
wouldn't start until the wagon was full. They evacuated last
Saturday—horrible wretches! I pray they may never return."
She described the miserable conditions of the town and continued: "I am going to Lynchburg as soon as I can get away,
but the only thing in the shape of a vehicle here is a wheel
barrow—everything in the shape of a horse was stolen. You never
meet or see a creature on the street, and to think there is no
prospect of having the cars. . . . All the servants in town went
off and most of the lower class of white people." One of the
most interesting bits of news she had for Pierce was an account
of the wedding of George Custer on the previous February 9,
at the Presbyterian Church at Monroe, Michigan. The young
lady reported that Custer had cut his hair and wore a plain
uniform. She said that she had heard of Pierce's being wounded
and that it was first reported by a little boy who had got it from
some Southern scouts. "Even the Yankee papers carried it and
spoke of the gallant Young," she told him.

Although Pierce's wound was serious and he was confined
to bed, he worried more about his family than about himself;
he learned that from May 19 to 22, the Confederates had made

an unsuccessful stand at Cassville, twelve miles from Walnut Plantation. By May 30, the Federals under General Sherman had captured Cartersville and were driving toward Atlanta. Pierce fretted about whether the original plans of moving the family to Penfield had been carried out. What had happened to the house, animals, slaves, and farm? Where was Robert? A thousand unanswered questions tormented the young man and hindered his recovery. He could not hear a word from any of the family, for all means of communication had been cut off.

The dashing young officer received some degree of comfort from various young lady friends. Mary Brooks was deeply concerned over his wound and wrote that she was miserable at not hearing from him for more than three weeks. She asked him to write or to get someone to write how he was getting along. She wanted to know when she could see him and begged him not to deceive her in love. In spite of his serious wound Pierce did write Mary a short note, to which she replied almost immediately, insisting that he not try to write again until he was better. She repeated several times how much she admired him for his bravery and how much she loved him.

On June 27, Pierce was taken to the house of a Dr. Gibson; there he was able to walk around the room, although his right arm was temporarily paralyzed. The extreme sultry weather did not help him to recuperate very fast. By July, hearing that Sherman and his troops had destroyed Walnut Plantation, Pierce felt that he could not stay in Richmond any longer. In spite of his weakened condition he set out immediately for Greenville, South Carolina, to find out what had happened to his parents, Louisa and her two children, and Walnut Plantation. He also planned to go to Penfield and stay there until he grew stronger.

Some of Pierce's comrades teased him about his arm's being temporarily paralyzed so that he could not hug the young ladies or squeeze their hands. On the way south Pierce did not go by to see Mary Brooks. At Greenville his Aunt Mary told him of the tragic flight of his family to Penfield, and a cousin wrote him that everyone felt sad that his mother's beautiful flowers, "nurtured by her own hands—all of Dr. Young's nice arrangements—had been destroyed by the polluted and vile hands of our degraded enemies, but worst of all they were compelled to leave and seek a home 'amid strangers afar.' For a long time we knew not *where* they were, and felt uneasy about them." After a day's rest with his relatives in Greenville he hurried on, anxious about his parents and about the fate of the plantation. On July 3 he arrived at Penfield. The family could hardly believe that the thin, tall, gaunt soldier was Pierce. The hardships of new surroundings were momentarily forgotten while his parents and sister tried to reassure him. But Pierce was worried about the limited facilities of the refugees; especially was he concerned about his father, who was sick but would not go to bed. The one bright spot was that all the slaves had been loyal and had stayed with the family. Not one had fled or tried to escape.

As soon as she could, Louisa told Pierce about the family's flight—how the last carriage loaded with clothing and household goods left Walnut Plantation while the thunder of the battle of Cassville could be heard. She described the heart-breaking scene of leaving the house under the care of the servant Henry, and told how brave and calm her mother had been. She told him of the almost impossible travel through Atlanta and Decatur, and of the road crowded with other refugees, and of the breakdown of one of the wagons at Covington and the long delay before the wheel was fixed. She spoke of the nights spent along the road en route to Penfield, as well as of the precautions necessary to protect themselves from marauders who crowded the roads. Louisa further related how kind the people along the way had been in giving them water and allowing them to stop and rest. Then she confessed how she was almost crazy from worry in not hearing a word from Tom since his capture. Pierce was proud of his sister and praised her for the care she had taken of their parents.

Seeing his parents as refugees, living on bare necessities, Pierce swore that when he returned to combat he would make the enemy pay. He tried to comfort his family by reaffirming his belief that the South would not be defeated. He took what money he had and tried to buy food and make the family more comfortable. While at home he learned that Robert was back in service and in a camp three miles south of Atlanta. He was disappointed that he could not see his brother—Robert could not receive a pass from his command, and Pierce was unable to travel. General Young never saw Robert again, although he received a letter from him, saying that General Bragg was in camp, "for what purpose I do not pretend to know. Hope he will let General Johnston alone; we are all confident we can whip Sherman whenever he will give us a chance. The army is in fine spirits, and anxiously expecting a fight. Atlanta is being depopulated by the citizens."

Planning to go by Columbia to see Mary Brooks on his return to Richmond, Pierce was joined by Louisa and her two daughters, who decided to go with him as far as Laurens, South Carolina, to visit her husband's family. They left by train on August 4, although Pierce was still weak. After Louisa and her children left the train at Laurens, General Young went on to Greenville where he stayed for several days before going to Columbia to meet Mary. Finding that she had returned to her home at Edgefield, Pierce visited her there for two days. He treated Mary with such devoted attention that she was giddy and in turn she was so admiring and adoring that he saw she was expecting him to marry her. So the general left after the second day, insisting that his leave was up and that he had to report to duty—not, however, until he had promised to write every week and to return sometime later for a visit. Then Pierce and his servant Charlie went to Danville, Virginia, where they stayed a week with a friend. He wrote his mother and Louisa about his entertainment in Edgefield and in Danville, saying that he was having a grand time "eating ice cream and drinking mint juleps." He explained that marriage was not for him and the marriage of each of his lady friends to someone else was "one off his hands."

His mother worried about Pierce's flirting with the young ladies, for she felt as did Louisa, who wrote her mother in her first letter from South Carolina, "He will yet get himself into difficulty about the girls." Both women knew that the handsome young man was a target for many a young lady anxious to get married. Pierce, in a letter of August 10, described his romance with Mary Brooks to his sister—"Well Mary and I stand just about where we did before I told her that I was too poor to marry, and did not know when I would be better off, so we stand. God knows what will become of all my gals. . . . They are getting more numerous every day. I suppose I will have to compromise, kiss all and marry none, for I can't marry them all. . . . I am told it is all over South Carolina that I am going to marry Mary Brooks. Confound the people, tell them it is not so if they push it upon you."

Driven from her beautiful home, and having to care for the slaves and her sick husband, Caroline Young was almost heartbroken. The loss of her oldest son, the lack of news from Robert,

and the absence of Louisa caused Mrs. Young to feel that she
had given to the Confederacy more than she could bear to lose.
Yet she never grumbled—not a letter did she write complaining
of her losses and wellnigh insuperable hardships. In fact Caroline Young felt that in contrast to the conditions which her
sister Mary and her mother were suffering, she was blessed. The
failure of the fruit crop in South Carolina in the summer of 1864
made the already scant food precious. Furthermore, the deserters
in the mountains made raids upon the White Oak District,
stealing animals and molesting women. Aunt Mary, in a letter
to her sister, Mrs. Young, on July 27, wrote that they slept very
little. The deserters "broke in the smoke house and stole butter,
turkeys, etc., and I think if [W. W.] Holden, the Union candidate, is elected governor honest people cannot live here. But
the whole Confederacy is in such a whirlpool that it is enough
to run one crazy to reflect upon it."

Louisa in her first letter from South Carolina to her mother
described the difficult times: "Provisions here are very scarce,
meat especially and I do not feel that it is right for me and
my crowd to consume so much. I have been trying to find out
where I can purchase some meat or chickens but so far have
been unsuccessful."

On August 11, Pierce left the little village of Danville for
Richmond, hoping that he could go on duty, though his arm
was still stiff. Before leaving he wrote his sister how proud he
was to hear that Joseph Wheeler was doing so well in capturing
the raiders in Laurens. Upon his arrival at Richmond he wrote
his mother not to worry about him, for though he was with the
brigade he was not yet on duty—"Just going along seeing how
I can stand it." Pierce continued to worry about Robert, who
was with the Confederates in the defense of Atlanta, for he had
not heard anything from him since leaving Penfield. Communication had almost broken down, and it was weeks after he got
back to Richmond before he had a letter from his mother. Such
delay made Pierce anxious about his family, for he knew only
too well of the numerous raids the Yankees were making throughout middle Georgia.

On August 30 Pierce wrote a hurried note to his mother
from near Petersburg describing the success on the 28th when
Hill's Corps and the cavalry together captured 2,500 prisoners.
"We had a pretty brisk little fight; we surprised the enemy
and charged his breastworks. For twenty minutes the fire was

as severe as any I ever heard. We are now resting; I think
the hard fighting is all over here." Pierce was engaged in the
siege of Petersburg and participated in three battles: Jerusalem
Plank Road, Globe Tavern, and Ream's Station, on the Weldon
Railroad. The Seventh Georgia, which was at this time attached
to Young's brigade, arrived in June and when it reached Richmond had 1,000 men. On September 2, it had only 400 men, of
whom twenty-five were mounted. The main problem in the early
days of September was low morale which resulted in many
deserters.[10] Desertion continued to be a problem to the Confederacy throughout the rest of the war. Throughout September
the battle raged around Petersburg. The casualties increased
daily and with each battle Pierce lost one close friend or more.

General Hampton, Pierce, and his close friend General Rosser
made a raid against the Federals on September 16 and captured
2,468 beeves, which were a godsend to the hungry Confederates.
Years later Pierce and Rosser were to laugh about their famous
"cattle" raid. Many years later the *New York Times* described
the role of Pierce in the raid on the Federal corral. "This capture was one of the most brilliant and successful raids of the
War, in which General Young had played a gallant and conspicuous part. . . . The conception and plans were Hampton's.
It was arranged that a picket body of 500 cavalry, under Hampton, should sweep General Grant's rear, capture the corral and
drive the cattle into the Confederate lines, while General Young
should come to the support of the corral guard. The scouts
had gathered every detail of information needed. They knew
the exact location of the cattle, the number and quality of
the troops on guard, the relative position of the great army of
Grant and how long it would require for him to dispatch assistance to the guard when attacked. Hampton relied upon Young
to keep back the entire army, if necessary, until he could get
the cattle out of reach. As cattle have to be driven slowly, and
over fairly good country, it was necessary for Hampton to drive
them quite close to the enemy's line, making the risk very much
greater.

"Everything worked smoothly until the cattle had been captured. The Negro guards were soon disposed of and the corral
of 2,500 head of cattle was shortly being driven toward the
Confederate camp. To reach the rear of the lines Hampton
and Young and all of their troops had been in the saddle day
and night and had ridden fifty miles almost without halt. Despite

the fatigue of horses and men a forced march had to be made
by Hampton, while Young and his weary cavalry had to face
the entire federal lines and draw fire until the raiders were out
of harm's way. General Young accomplished this in a most brilliant style.

"He stretched out his 2,500 troopers into so long a line that
it seemed as if nothing less than an army division could occupy
the space. By rushing from one point to another a considerable
body of his men and concentrating fire on the federal advance
he succeeded in keeping up the deception. The federals expected momentarily to engage the Confederates in force, and so
advanced cautiously, feeling their way. The dashing cavalry
officer was playing Napoleonic tactics in miniature. Before the
army of Grant realized that it was putting forth its great strength
against a handful of daring horsemen, Hampton was safe, and
the special lines of the grand army of the Confederates closed
up and galloped away, having completed the most reckless foray
of the War. 'The federal cattle,' added Young, 'formed the basis
of our supplies for the rest of the campaign.' "[11]

A week after the foray General Wade Hampton, in a note to
General Bragg as commander, requested a promotion for Butler
and stated wishfully, "I hope that in the reorganization of the
cavalry both Rosser and Young may be able to obtain larger
commands than they now hold."[12]

On September 28 and 30 the Federals attacked but were re-
pulsed. Much of the success was because Wade Hampton's cavalry
with Rosser, Young, and Fitz Lee in command, and Archer's
brigade gave an excellent account of themselves.

In Georgia events were gloomy. Atlanta surrendered to Sherman on September 2. Robert Young's regiment which had at one
time 1,050 men, was reduced to ninety-six. Mrs. Young wrote
Louisa, "God only knows what will become of us. . . . I fear
our army is not sufficient to contend with the enemy; then our
state will be overrunned. We [at Penfield] are now open to
raids. . . . What slaughter; still it goes on. I fear we will lose all
our men or the greater part of them."

Louisa, in Laurens District, South Carolina, feared for the
safety and welfare of her parents. She worried much because she
could not hear anything from Robert, and advised her parents
to forget their garden, chickens, and sugar cane and to leave
everything to the Yankees when they began attacking the countryside. Her major worry was not hearing from her parents. "I some-

times feel as though I could not longer bear this horrible suspense. I would to God I had never left Georgia. True I am safe here, but what is my own safety worth when all my family are in danger and I cannot hear from them." The one salvation for Louisa was the weekly letter she received from her imprisoned husband, who told of his love for her in each letter. It was his devotion that helped Louisa to carry on under the difficult and adverse circumstances. Being in prison did not embitter him; he seldom wrote Louisa of his hardships; rather he cautioned her, "We must bear the ills we have and hope and pray for brighter days."

Back in Penfield under Mrs. Young's careful supervision, the family and servants fared well. In the early fall they had an abundance of watermelons that were kept cold in the spring house. In addition they had potatoes and peas, the chickens did well, and the sugar cane was the best they had ever had. Mrs. Young kept the Negro women busy weaving clothes for themselves and for her daughter and grandchildren. She did not allow herself to grieve over her sons, but prayed that God would protect and return them safely to her. Mrs. Young encouraged Louisa to be hopeful that her husband would soon be exchanged and returned safely to his family. Her amazing strength and confidence fortified her family; she was able to meet their demands, and the demands of the servants and of the farm. As the tension of social and economic conditions increased, her strength seemed to increase in proportion.

In the winter of 1864, the best news that Pierce received was in the letters from his mother and sister. He worried over Robert's long silence and feared something serious had happened to him. He was still receiving letters from Mary Brooks, but as early as September 1864 he was too busily engaged in military duties to write to her often. Then, too, he had begun to tire of her forwardness, which he thought was not a proper attribute of a lady. But Mary continued to write often, pleading for letters from him and telling how disappointed she was not to hear from him. Not hearing from Pierce by the last of the fall, in a ten-page letter she told him that she would not write again until she had received a letter from him. She concluded: "I never *thought* to have stooped to ask any man's love. . . . I *never knew what it was to love before.*" Unmoved, Pierce still refused to answer.

In the fall Pierce received a letter from J. E. Ritch, a fellow prisoner on Johnson Island, Ohio, with Tom Jones. The letter

puzzled and distressed Pierce. Ritch explained that he and Tom
did not want to spend another winter in prison and sincerely
trusted that Pierce would use his influence to get them exchanged.
He proposed to Pierce that two Federal captains from among
those captured be "paroled" on condition that he and Jones be
exchanged or the Federal men would lose their parole. He explained that Tom Jones was sick and could not stand another
winter in prison, for the "unceiled quarters" were very airy and
afforded poor protection from the wintry blast that swept across
the lake. He said the food was poor and a majority of the prisoners were suffering from undernourishment and malnutrition.
Pierce tried unsuccessfully to assist Tom.

Another anxiety to Pierce was occasioned by the insistence
of the Carolina relatives that his mother and father move to
White Oak. When Mrs. Young wrote him of such a proposal,
Pierce replied immediately for them to stay in middle Georgia
and if they had to move to go near Albany or Americus, Georgia.
He knew that the relatives did not want them, and that Louisa
was unhappy because the relatives did not want her and her
daughters eating their scarce food. "It does not matter much
where you go, but I believe I would take a house to myself no
matter where. . . . I would not live with our relatives. They have
always been our poorest friends. I would not for any consideration be under obligation to any of them. I would rather pay a
year's rent for all of you than to see you under obligations to
any one of them. Can't Father get a place to himself? I think
you will not be troubled for the winter where you are by the
Yankees."

Knowing that his sister's health was impaired by improper diet,
Pierce wrote her: "I would not remain with the Greenville kin.
I can't think they like us or ever did." He worried about her and
about his inability to get Tom exchanged from prison. Still
fretting about the lack of any news from Robert, he was partially reassured when his mother wrote on October 14 that
Robert was on the other side of the Chattahoochee River with
General Hood in Granberry's brigade, Clebourne Division, 10th
Regiment Jones Infantry, Army of Texas, attacking General Sherman's army from the rear and trying to cut off the Federal supply. The younger brother was glad to learn, too, that Robert had
been recommended for a commission as a brigadier general in
the first vacancy.

General Young wrote his mother on October 14 that he had

been very busy, for they had some hard fighting at Strassburg, Virginia, on October 12 and lost some good officers. Then he described how Uncle John Jones, his assistant adjutant general, was captured. "It was all on account of his negligence. I suppose he was in ten feet of me when he was taken, but I had to ride hard and well, I can tell you, to get out or they would have captured me." The shots missed his head by inches and only his horsemanship and agility saved him from being captured. One soldier reported that when the Federals called upon Pierce to surrender, he yelled, "Surrender, hell!" and proceeded to escape in a burst of gun fire. Major M. H. Beaumont, Commander of the First New Jersey Cavalry, in his report to Joel Parker, Governor of New Jersey, confirmed the incident: "Sergt. Charles Watts, of Company C, seeing a group of men dressed apparently like our men, rode up to one who proved to be General Young and asked him, 'How in thunder are we going to get out of this?' The general seemed to be as much puzzled as Watts, as he had taken the charge of Lieutenant Hughes for the advance of a mounted force, and had delayed his own attack upon our flank long enough for us to regain our works and be in readiness to repulse him. Private Miles Downey, seeing that they were the enemy, seized upon Captain Jones, assistant adjutant-general to General Young, and brought him in a prisoner."[13]

Pierce wrote his mother that he heard that Uncle John had been quite well since his capture. "And the Yankee officers were much pleased with him as they said he was the most perfect gentleman they had ever met; and most of all he had nearly everything he possessed on his person—his fine watch and my chain, my field glasses and my silver cup; he had about two thousand dollars on him." Pierce consoled his mother by telling her that he would try to get a special exchange for his uncle as soon as possible.

Despite the heavy fighting and high mortality rate, Pierce was still enthusiastic about the success of the Confederacy. He wrote in October, "I think we have heavily used up this army of Grant's, and from all I can hear I think you will all be at our old home again soon." But, he added, "We can hear nothing just now from Georgia except that Hood is in rear and Sherman is moving from Atlanta. God grant it may be so."

Five days later Pierce repeated his optimism in another letter— "Everything now looks bright. I think brighter *than ever*. I certainly expect to hear of your being at our old home in a few

months. I am trying to bring my command to Georgia for the
winter. Don't know I'll succeed." Then, ever thoughtful of those
who served him, Pierce told that Charlie, his servant, was well
and sent love to his folks, saying of him, "He is a good boy
and helps me a great deal."

In a letter written a week later Pierce told Louisa about his
envy of the promotion of certain officers in the cavalry corps.
Especially was he jealous of the promotion of Matthew Cal-
braith Butler to major general, for he thought Hampton was
pushing him too much. "I think it is evident that Gen. Lee does
not want to promote him as Hampton has been pushing his
claims for two months and there is no promotion yet, but I think
he will be promoted soon as he is the ranking officer in our
division, and that is the only reason he will be promoted. Gen.
Hampton has done and is doing all in his power to promote
Butler. You know it is all a political click [sic]. The division
is composed of Butler's, Rosser's, and Young's brigades, and
Butler was made brigadier before Rosser or myself so he ranks
us and Rosser ranks me. Well, Rosser and I at first declared that
we would not serve under Butler as we had both seen a great
deal more service, but Butler and his friends talked to me and
Hampton told me that Gen. Lee would not promote Butler
unless Rosser and I were willing to serve under him, and so I
got magnanimous and called upon Gen. Lee and told him I
would be willing to serve under Butler or anyone else he would
put over my division, but Rosser would not do this. So at last
accounts Butler was expected to be promoted, but it has not been
done, and he is very uneasy about it. . . . "He and I get on well;
he pretends to think the world and all of me." Then he cautioned
Louisa, "You must never allow yourself to talk about this subject as you might say too much—just hold on it will all come
right soon. Gen. Lee wants to promote me and the President
wants to promote me, and neither of them wants to promote
Butler. But Hampton wants to promote Butler and he commands the corps, and, being a real soldier, some consideration
must be paid to his recommendation."

Learning that General Sherman was planning to march through
Georgia to the sea after resting a while in Atlanta, Pierce forgot
his prejudice toward the relatives and encouraged his mother and
father to go to South Carolina to escape the raids of Sherman's
troops. However, he wanted them to be independent, and suggested that his father find enough tillable land and put the

Negroes to farming. Pierce still opposed his parents' moving to White Oak, North Carolina, to live with Grandma Jones or any other relative.

When Sherman left Atlanta on November 16, to begin his march to the sea, Mrs. Young, as soon as she heard of the Federals' leaving Atlanta, packed as much of the household goods as possible and went by way of Augusta to Greenville, South Carolina; after a rest of two days there she went on to White Oak to visit her aged mother and her daughter and grandchildren. Dr. Young went as far as Greenville, where he left his wife, and then returned to Penfield, intending to place the remainder of the household goods in wagons and head for Spartanburg, South Carolina. But without Mrs. Young's help and direction he was not able to leave Georgia until the first week in December.

On November 24, General Hampton issued Special Order Number 71, which ordered Pierce to proceed to Augusta in charge of a detachment of men to procure horses. He was also ordered to collect and rendezvous at Augusta all men from the command then absent in Georgia and South Carolina. He was authorized to use his men so long as it was important for the defense of Augusta or such other point in Georgia as was deemed necessary by the officer commanding in that locality; when the emergency had passed he was to allow the men to go, under suitable officers, to their homes to procure horses and return to their commands in Virginia in as short a time as practicable. After he had completed these orders Pierce was commanded to report in person at Hampton's headquarters.[14]

General Braxton Bragg sent a message on November 28 to Colonel John B. Sale, Military Secretary, Richmond, Virginia, confirming that Pierce and his men had arrived in Augusta and later would be sent to General Wheeler, "Who will . . . be able to mount most of them from his capture." General Bragg reported that devastation marked the enemy's route through Georgia. Two days earlier General Sherman had sent a large cavalry force toward Augusta and General Wheeler immediately followed, leaving a portion of his force to confront Sherman and to attack the Yankees at Waynesboro, Georgia.[15]

On December 2, a deserter, M. Carter, of the Sixth South Carolina Cavalry, reported to Brigadier General D. McM. Gregg, Commander of the Second Division, that about 1,500 dismounted cavalry, under General Young, had been sent South.[16] The next day other deserters confirmed Carter's report but admitted that no troops had left the front of the army of the Potomac except the dismounted cavalry under General Young. So when the Federal cavalry tried to cross Hatcher Run, General George G. Meade reported to General U. S. Grant that they had found Young's brigade of cavalry, "which prevented any farther progress."[17]

Because of Pierce's courage and leadership, and his willingness to serve, the Georgia representatives in the Confederate Congress felt that he should be considered for promotion to major general. They sent a round robin letter to President Jefferson Davis on November 29, recommending Pierce for promotion to the rank of major general. They sketched his colorful military career and described his sacrifice and dedication to the Southern cause—"He has by devotion . . . exhibition of a high order of military talent, and conspicuous gallantry justly won the spurs of a Brigadier. Thrice has he shed his blood upon the battlefield. He is now at the post of duty, and has left it only when disabling wounds compelled him to withdraw temporarily from the field. We are grateful to learn that his name has been mentioned for promotion by his chief commander. Upon inquiry, we learn that in the Army of Virginia there are five cavalry regiments from the state of South Carolina, and that she has two major generals, and two brigadier generals of cavalry. We also learn that Virginia has the same army, fifteen regiments of cavalry, and four major generals, and five brigadiers, whilst Georgia has in the same army six regiments of cavalry, and one single brigadier. We mentioned these facts, not for purpose of showing that any proposed injustice has been done to Georgians, but for the purpose of showing that in view of these facts coupled with the further fact that General Young is the ranking brigadier for cavalry in this army, that he eminently merits promotion and that the inducements are very strong in favor of granting the request which we respectfully prefer to your excellency." The letter was signed by the following Georgians: George N. Lester, William E. Smith, H. A. Bell, Julian Hartridge, Warren Akin, James M. Smith, M. H. Blanford, Clifford Anderson, Herschel V. Johnson, and Benjamin Hill.

On December 24, General P. G. T. Beauregard telegraphed from Charleston to General Samuel Cooper, Assistant Adjutant General, Richmond—"General Hardee recommends Brigadier General P. M. B. Young of cavalry as one of the major generals I applied for yesterday. He is now in the front and would probably answer." This message was submitted to President Davis by John M. Richy and copies were also sent to the Secretary of War, to General Lee, and to General Bragg. On December 30, the A. G. Office sent a memorandum that Pierce be promoted with company rank.

A Richmond paper, *Weekly Dispatch,* had this to say of Pierce's promotion: "It gives us great pleasure to announce the promotion of this gallant officer. This is the sort of men we want here now, fighting men. The general is said to be a bad mathematician—never learned his multiplication tables well— and understands better the rules of subtraction than those of addition. We present our respects to the general. We like that sort of man. He is one who, when he sees a blue belly, sees somebody to kill, and goes at him with the purpose, and only fails to do so when the blue bellies actually prevent him from his good intent by force of arms.

"It is our regret, however, to state that the General is ordered on duty in Southeastern Georgia. He has our best wishes for his speedy return here. We want him."[18]

The *Charleston Courier,* upon hearing of Pierce's promotion, on December 27, 1864, wrote admiringly of him and predicted success for the future of the Confederacy with General Young in command of a division of cavalry in Georgia.

General Lee wrote to President Davis on December 5 that he had sent Pierce "with about 400 cavalrymen without horses and ordered all those previously sent to Georgia and South Carolina to report to him at Augusta. . . ."[19] Pierce had already been sent to join Major General Joe Wheeler near Waynesboro, Georgia, to receive his orders; but he was delayed and it was not until several days that with 250 mounted and 550 dismounted, General Young was moved by rail to Pocataligo, South Carolina, to observe the left bank of the Savannah River.[20]

From December 13 through 17, Pierce and his troops skirmished the Federals in the defense of Savannah. On December 20, General Young won fame for his courage and leadership. General Sherman had almost surrounded the city. There were approximately but 1,300 troops within the fortification which surrounded Savannah, and there were not enough Confederate soldiers to defend the city against the large Federal army. Five days' rations were all the provisions on hand, and it was necessary for the soldiers to retire before they were exhausted. Evacuation of the city took only a matter of hours. Pontoons were

laid down across the river to the South Carolina side, but because of some mistake the evacuation was delayed twenty-four
hours after the time it was first ordered.

The decoy gave the enemy great advantage. They immediately
"crossed over a considerable body of troops," who were in the
line of battle near the road—a dam across the rice field was the
only route the Confederates had by which to make their escape.
The road was straight and very narrow with deep wet ditches
and marshy ground on either side, and the Federal lines had
already been pushed forward to the high ground and near to
the point where the road left the rice fields. If the enemy extended their lines so as to reach that point and placed a single
battery in position to enfilade the road, escape was impossible.

One of the soldiers recalling his experience wrote: "A few of
those who knew the position of affairs, did not sleep that night,
the danger of being cut off was so imminent. By the dawn of
day, a scout mounted his horse and rode across the bridge,
so as to get a view of the Federal position. It was a difficult and
somewhat dangerous undertaking, as there was no cover by
which his approach could be concealed. He, however, at length
reached a house, from the top of which a view of the troops
on that side of the river could be had. They consisted of infantry
and artillery, and to his great joy he discovered that these troops
were busily engaged in cutting down trees and throwing up a
breast work.

"The scout immediately hastened back to the city. On the
way he met Gen. Hardee accompanied by Gen. P. M. B. Young.
He gave these gentlemen in as few words as possible, the situation on the South Carolina side, adding that it was evident they
feared an attack and as long as that apprehension lasted it was
not possible any forward movement would be made. Young said,

'You think they are expecting an attack?'

'Yes,' was replied: 'That is evident.'

'Then,' said he, 'they shall not be disappointed,' and putting
spur to his horse, he dashed over the bridge at full speed.

"There was some cavalry on that side of the river and a few
light pieces of artillery under his command. Disposing of those
so as to make it as formidable a display as possible, Young at
once began the attack. It is true this great demonstration was a
mere skirmish. It could not have been otherwise with his handful
of men, but he conducted that affair so skillfully as to leave the
impression that a very large body of cavalry were hovering near

them, and the Federal troops were content to remain quiet within their lines."[21]

When night came, the road by which the Confederates were to escape still remained open. Under cover of darkness, the troops marched safely out of the city, crossing on the pontoons, and moved along the causeway within speaking distance of the enemy's lines; and by daylight the whole of the Confederate forces were safely beyond the enemy's reach. General Young's daring strategy had proved a success, and thirteen thousand men, mostly Georgians, escaped being taken prisoner.

Pierce was complimented again for his gallantry, and in general orders, dated December 1864 at Savannah, General Hardee reported that had it not been for the gallant fighting of Young's men under the most adverse circumstances, the Yankees would not have been driven from their positions at Argyle Island. If Pierce had failed, General Sherman could have captured both the dirt road and the Charleston and Savannah Railroad, thereby cutting off the last line of retreat of the Confederates. Pierce lost in the retreat between forty and sixty men killed and wounded. None was captured. One of the soldiers, F. E. Eve, after the war stated that it was amazing that more men were not lost, for "the boys swore the mud would bog a saddle blanket off of the rice dams."[22] Similarly many à Southern soldier years later thanked Pierce for his daring exploit in saving him and his friends from captivity at Savannah.

Sherman captured Savannah on December 21 and remained in the city until February 1, 1865, when he began his march north toward Columbia, South Carolina. Pierce and his men moved from Savannah to Augusta. While in Augusta he received a letter from his mother, who was still at White Oak. She was frightened, for there was "never meaner society on earth; the country is filled with thieves and deserters," who stole everything from Grandma Jones. "This is a dark corner. We cannot hear any war news good or bad. God grant we may drive Sherman from our soil. I do pray that every Yankee may be made to surrender to our army. God surely will come to our help in time of need; our country is in an awful condition; provisions are scarce and very high here. We cannot obtain it here with Confederate money. Factory yarn or salt will buy anything. . . . This is no place for us and the sooner we are off the better. They grudge our food—too severe perhaps." In the same letter Louisa reiterated her mother's opinion—"I never was very clannish, and now in this house of adversity I had rather go to another stranger for kindness than any relative I have out of our immediate family."

Both women were deeply concerned for Pierce and Robert; they had not heard from the latter since the last of October and feared what might have happened. Louisa wrote, "We are very anxious about Brother Robert, having seen that two officers by the name of Young had recently been captured from Hood's army." The fear of the women was well founded, for Robert was with General Hood, who had withdrawn into Tennessee in an effort to draw Sherman away from Atlanta. At Franklin, Tennessee, on November 30, 1864, Robert Young was killed; he was buried near Columbia, Tennessee. Pierce was not to hear of his brother's death until the last days of the war, when he was fighting for his own survival. The death of Robert was a tragic blow for Mrs. Young—only the fear of what might happen to her baby son overshadowed her grief for the older. She informed Pierce of the sad news and begged him to be careful.

Pierce grieved for his brother but was able to send his mother only brief notes of encouragement. When he mailed her a picture with his new promotion insignia, she was pleased but noted that he was thinner than when she had last seen him. She prayed for his safety. Louisa was concerned about her husband; she had written to Colonel Robert Ould about an exchange, but the Yankees wanted two officers of similar rank in his place.

Although General Sherman had marched through Georgia, cutting a wide area of destruction, and had occupied Savannah, the chief seaport, Pierce as late as January 1865 was optimistic over the success of the South. He chided his mother and sister about their attitude, writing them, "You must not get despondent or allow those around you to be so. There is a bright day ahead for us. The spirits of the brave fall not before gathering storms, but as trouble thickens rise like beacon lights to the weak and weary. Let us battle on; my future at least shall be independence or a bloody grave. I hope my poor and deluded countrymen will bear up a little longer and lend confidence and strength to our armies, and not make our zeal less by cries of whipped and conquered. We are doing well; let us all take confidence and put our trust in God and fight the harder and all will yet be well."

A serious problem concerning his troops confronted Pierce in January. Too many were leaving and returning home. To remedy the matter he issued an order requiring all men on leave to report without delay to their command, sending one of his soldiers, T. W. Jones, throughout south Georgia to deliver his order.

On February 3 the first rumors of peace were heard by General Young and his family. Aunt Mary Thompson wrote Mrs. Young that it was true that Commissioner Francis P. Blair had been twice to Richmond and three commissioners from the South had gone to Washington "but no one knows what will come of it. We hear that Europe, Asia and Africa are going to recognize us on the 4th of March. . . . I hear that Pierce is near Charleston and says he can whip Sherman with 15,000 more men. Hood's army is coming to help him and Butler's men are in Columbia. Things begin to look more hopeful." She deplored the scarcity of food in Greenville, especially coffee and salt.

While Pierce was in Charleston, he heard of Sherman's destruction of Columbia from a friend, Miss Sallie A. Aldrich, who wrote him inquiring as to the whereabouts of her brother. She described how the entrance of Sherman brought many changes in the old capital, "to say nothing of the terror impressed into the hearts of southern women, which however, bear the test and remained steadfast to the glorious cause. I hope you will soon meet and remind them on the battlefield for the injury done South Carolinians." She described Columbia as a city of ruins.

Pierce received on February 7 a special order from General Hardee assigning him to the command of Iverson's division of cavalry and ordering him to proceed without delay to Georgia and assume command. By the same order Major General Wade Hampton was assigned to the command of Butler's and Young's divisions of cavalry. The special order sending Pierce to Georgia was in answer to his request and was granted in recognition of his work at Savannah. He wanted to get into Georgia in order to help his parents return to their home; having his command in Georgia would afford a greater opportunity to assist them. He had been in Georgia less than two weeks, however, when General Beauregard wrote him of the movement of the enemy in South Carolina and directed him to move as rapidly as possible in the direction of the Santee River, "cross the stream and operate on the left of Butler, announce your arrival and report to General Hampton." General Beauregard further wrote: "Should you think it advisable you are *authorized* to use a part or the whole pontoon train—to arrive in Augusta with the Engineer troops—in crossing your command over the Sumter—and returning the pontoon train under the escort of your smallest brigade to Augusta with orders to the commanding officer to escort all trains and troops coming this way to guard the approach to the city of Augusta."[23] The general ordered Pierce to make whatever arrangements were necessary for his troops, saying "the enemy has passed over a portion of the country through which you are to pass; it must be devoid of supplies, of forage, and of subsistence."

Heavy rains in February and March washed away bridges, so that Pierce was hindered in his efforts to move his men, for they had to go many miles out of the way. Not only was the weather a problem, but there was also the problem of men and animals, since the enemy had seized, stolen, or destroyed almost every available farm product. Pierce endeared himself to his men by sharing with them whatever food he foraged, and eating the same fare that they had. When food was scarce, he did without, as his men did.

As rumors of peace increased, more and more of Pierce's men deserted and went home to their families. Because he and his men were engaged in combat, he felt that deserters should be court-martialed. On March 29 he held court in Chester, South Carolina, to court-martial some deserters who had been captured. Several days later he held another court-martial in Newberry.

It was in March when he tried to buy some cloth and provisions for his family that he found civilians unwilling to accept Confederate money and insisting on payment in gold. He asked a friend, J. P. Thomas of Augusta, to sell his buggy and convert the payment for it into gold. Pierce realized for the first time that when the war ended he would be bankrupt. Added to the worry about impending bankruptcy was a letter from his father saying that he was unwell, and that "We still find it difficult to get provisions here. I have some fears that I shall not be able to support my family here, but will do the best I can."

The only good news during this time was Louisa's letter telling of the exchange of her husband and of his return to his family at Spartanburg. She reported that although Dr. Jones was not well he wanted to return to duty as soon as he was able. General Young rejoiced over the good news, noting that for the first time in over a year Louisa sounded carefree. She wrote of the recent rumor she had heard of Pierce's engagement to Mary Brooks, and teased him about Mary's not denying the rumor. "Now, my dear brother, if this be so just be so kind as to give me a hint to that effect that I may form some idea what to reply when interrogated on the subject." Pierce did not mind his sister's teasing him, for he was glad to see her happy again.

As the Federal troops moved into North Carolina, General Young began to receive requests from owners whose animals and property had been impressed into service that their possessions be returned. Typical of the requests was one from a Mr. Townsend of Columbia saying that his two carriage horses had been impressed and he wanted one to be returned, for his son who was in one of the cavalry companies needed a horse. He wanted General Young to send the horse by a soldier, fearing that lawless men would seize it from anyone else.

Captain W. S. Phillips, of 2 M Lewis Kentucky Brigade, wrote on April 12 to Major General J. M. B. Lovell, Commander of the District of South Carolina, informing him that the Union army was expected at Camden, South Carolina, the following day. When General Lovell transmitted the message to Pierce, he added that Colonel Caldwell had left camp with his command to meet the Union forces. A week later Young heard from a friend, Kate L. Ferguson, that at Rumpinville "the deserters were acting very badly—committing all their depredations at night. They are formed in bands and reported as having hung one man for his gold. I think it would be advisable for you to send a good body of scouts there. They are reported to be coming in this direction, and I fear them even more than the Yankees."

On April 20 Pierce received a copy of an order General Lovell had written to General Potter of the United States Army while he was near Manchester, South Carolina; the order was for Young to send a flag of "truce to the commanding officer of the forces opposed to you and give him a copy of the enclosed dispatch just received from General P. G. T. Beauregard at Greensboro. Inform Maj. Gen. Gilmore that a *truce* for the purpose of a final settlement was agreed upon yesterday between Generals Johnston and Sherman, applicable to all forces under their command. A message to that effect from Gen. Sherman will be sent him as soon as practicable. The contending forces are to occupy their present position. Forty-eight hours notice to be given in the event of resumption of hostilities."

Pierce received on April 22 a letter from his friend J. P. Thomas of Augusta, who reported that "everyone is dealing gold; excitement intense on account of Lee's surrender. The Yankees hold

Macon, Georgia. Everyone feels like the bottom has dropped out
as the government seems to have no head. . . . Confederate money
will soon be of no account."

When he knew that the war was almost over Pierce began to
make arrangements to care for his men. He tried to make plans
which would make it easy to turn his command over to the
enemy. At the same time he was plagued with many requests
from people throughout South Carolina for help in finding sons
and husbands and in recovering their horses which had been impressed by the cavalry.

The Army of Northern Virginia surrendered at Appomattox
Courthouse on April 9. Pierce knew when he heard the sad
news that it would be merely a matter of a few days until the
Army of Tennessee would have to surrender. On April 26, General Johnston formally surrendered at Greensboro, North Carolina, to General Sherman.

Pierce surrendered on April 22 to Brigadier General Edward
E. Potter at a little hamlet known as Fulton Post Office. Four
days earlier he had said goodby to his men. In his farewell
speech, delivered with tears streaming down his face, he followed
General Lee's last message, encouraging the men to return home
without any bitterness or hatred within their hearts against the
United States. He advised them to hasten home and get a crop
started.

General Lovell issued on May 22 the following order: "In
accordance with the terms of the Military Convention, entered
into on the 26th day of April 1865, between General Joseph Johnston, Commander of Confederate States Army and Major General W. T. Sherman, Commander, United States Army in North
Carolina, Major General P. M. B. Young, C. S. A., has given his
solemn obligation, not to take up arms against the Government
of the United States, until properly released from this obligation, and is permitted to visit his home, not to be disturbed by
the United States authorities so long as he observes the obligation, and obeys the laws in force where he may reside."[24]

Discouraged and broken hearted Pierce kept his feelings to
himself. He hurried to Spartanburg to get his father, who on
April 12 had written him about his doubt of being able to
return to Walnut Plantation because of his health. Louisa in
a letter four days later wrote that her father had been "quite
indisposed" and that she hated to see him go to Georgia alone,
but "I trust God will direct him, and restore him safely to us

again in health." With a few Negroes and some household goods
Dr. Young and Pierce hastened to Walnut Plantation. Along
the roads were groups of former Confederate soldiers. The gaunt,
emaciated, ashen grey cadaverous features haunted Pierce for
many years. Many were barefooted and in rags, as they made
their way home from Lee's army. Some were crippled and were
being assisted by friends as they hobbled on makeshift crutches.
Pierce picked up a few soldiers and allowed them to ride behind
him on his horse or on the crowded wagon. He encouraged,
praised, advised, and even wept with these dejected and wretched
comrades of the Confederacy. Whenever he could he shared what
clothing and food and money he had, though he had little money
to offer. By the time Pierce and his father arrived at Walnut
Plantation they were penniless. Their destitute state was momentarily forgotten, however, when they saw that the house had
not been destroyed, although it was in a bad state of repair.

They found that a widow had taken squatters' rights in the
house and had gathered or stolen in the neighborhood a large
number of feather mattresses, so that every room was filled. As
soon as she was forcibly ejected, Pierce and his father found that
the house had been used as a hospital and the northwest upstairs
front room had been used as an operating room by a medical
unit of the Union army. The floor was stained with blood, which
no amount of soap, lye, sand, or water could remove.

The seriousness of the situation—for there was neither ade-
quate food nor seed for planting—made Pierce decide upon a
desperate action, an action which meant humbling himself before his relatives, which he had sworn that he would never do.
In May he tried to borrow money from Uncle Tom, promising
to mortgage part of the plantation as security. He also wrote
to one of his army friends, R. G. Stover of Paris, Kentucky, telling of his plight and saying that he would even marry a Kentucky lady if he could find one who had money and would assist
him and his parents. Stover replied immediately that he wanted
Pierce to visit him and mentioned that he had a lady whose
finances were "unexceptionably" ready for him. But Pierce
could not leave his father. The conditions at home were such
as to overwhelm even a stouthearted soldier. Although Dr. Young
had received his amnesty papers on May 29, he and Pierce were
not able to get enough food to feed the servants. Dr. Young
wrote his wife on June 5, that there were plenty of Federal soldiers
stationed at Cartersville, "for the purpose (they say) of keeping

order in the country." He explained that they were orderly and quiet, and had certainly put down the robbers who were quite numerous before they arrived; "a great many negroes are going to them and going North. None of ours have left, nor do I believe any of them will go." However, all of the neighbors had lost a part and some had lost all of their Negroes.

Then Dr. Young explained that although provisions were scarce, he hoped to be able to feed the servants with at least bread and milk, for he had found a cow on the plantation, and "I shall be able to save some rye, which I found growing in my fields. I have got the crop in pretty good order, and have a fine prospect for a plentiful supply of corn for the next year. . . . Confederate money is not worth anything here. I have not been able to use any of it since I arrived home. . . . We have no mails here; we have the promise of one soon. A full assortment of goods are looked for at Cartersville in a few days; sugar is purchased for 20 cents per pound. The cars are running to Etowah River; the bridge [destroyed by Sherman] will be finished in a very short time; then the cars will run to Atlanta; it is running thence to Augusta now."

Dr. Young had returned almost to the pioneer conditions of twenty-five years before when he had first settled on the banks of the Etowah River. There were some things to be thankful for, such as the preservation of the house and the safe return of Pierce, but the future was too gloomy for much of a ray of hope to penetrate. During the four years of war the Young family had lost two sons to the Confederate cause, and the entire wealth of the family had been wiped out, with only the land and house remaining. But neither Pierce nor any member of his family became embittered. To Pierce came the knowledge that his father, gradually weakened by the trials of the war, had turned to him as the responsible head of the family. Dr. Young was a tired old man—too tired to enter upon the reconstruction of his Southland. Pierce understood and gradually took up the lines of control which his father slowly surrendered, not knowing what reconstruction might bring but willing to face it as he had faced death on the battlefield. General Pierce Young had no apology for his war record, and he entered the era of reconstruction with his head held high, determined to make a new start for his family and for himself.

VII

◊◊◊
◊

A Neophyte in Politics

THE YEARS 1865-1874 in Georgia history have been described as "that anomalous, undefinable period . . . that must stand as the indescribable incongruity of her existence as a commonwealth. It is an epoch that baffles description. Neither war nor peace; marked by the anarchy of war without its dignity and a pretence of peace without its reality; ruled under a scorching travesty of law, alternating with bayonet despotism governed by mob caprice; . . . . It was the cruelest bit of political harlequinade ever practiced by an enlightened civilization."[1]

In this perspective Pierce Manning Butler Young chose to follow Robert E. Lee's advice to Southern leaders to remain and share the fate of their respective states. His entire training had been that of a soldier, not of a farmer or of one trained technically or professionally. The results of the war had ruined his military career, but Pierce never expressed one word of remorse for casting his lot with the Confederacy. He gambled and lost—he had no regrets.

As soon as he assisted his father to get settled back at home and helped gather the meager grain crop, Pierce set out on horseback throughout south Georgia attempting to buy cotton. He found people unwilling to sell unless they were paid in gold or greenbacks. Pierce had little of either and by July 24 had made a profit of only $151 on his speculation. The money was immediately spent for much-needed food and medicine for the family.

Everywhere he traveled General Young saw Georgians facing the winter in almost destitute circumstances, with little food and inadequate clothing. He wrote a friend in the fall of 1865: "It is so mortifying and humiliating to come to the life we have now to live, born and reared to everything people want and now stripped of it all and unprepared to combat our lot. . . . Our privations are very great, no furniture and few comforts we used to have left at all."

Although it was rumored by his friends that the ex-Confederate officer was to be arrested, he was never apprehended by Federal troops. On September 22, Pierce applied to James Speed, Attorney General of the United States, for a special pardon under the third exception in the proclamation of the President on May 29, 1865. He stated in his application that he had served in the Confederate army for four years in various capacities, the last of which was as major general of cavalry, and that he was educated at West Point. In addition he swore that there were no proceedings for treason or conspiracy against him in any of the courts of the United States, and that he owned no abandoned lands and property outside of the United States. Finally, he swore that he was not a slave owner and that he would never again recognize the institution of slavery and use slave labor. His acquaintance with several of the Union officers while at West Point helped him to obtain his special pardon without any delay.

Ruined financially because of the loss of slaves, farm equipment, and animals, he felt during the fall and winter of 1865-66 that the fates took delight in destroying the small crops that had been planted with seeds purchased at a fabulously high price. There was a drought also, in an already desolate area, to add to the misery and wretchedness of those who tried to farm. Money, if it could be borrowed at all, was obtained at a high rate of interest. Crops were mortgaged for several years to come—thereby instituting the crop lien system of the farmers in Georgia.

The Young family was impoverished, but Pierce found that most of his relatives and friends were in an even worse situation. His Uncle John Jones wrote to him in October of 1865 asking for financial assistance, saying that he had lost fifty thousand dollars and did not have enough money to buy sufficient food for his children. The death of the matriarchal Grandma Jones in July 1865 added to the problems, for her estate was heavily involved in debt and no one was able to buy it. Her children's families were almost destitute.

General Young tried unsuccessfully to borrow money from his Uncle Tom, from the banks, from friends, from any source he could think of, in order to buy seed for the plantation. Added to his problem of finances was a labor problem, for by the end of the year most of the former slaves had left the plantation in search of freedom and the fulfillment of promises made to them by the government. By January 1866 only two remained at Walnut Plantation to rent land on shares.

Pierce secured for his father a special pardon similar to the one that he had received. In November 1865 he was able to secure (from Lieutenant Colonel Charles Reams of the 29th Indiana Infantry, who was in charge of the Union soldiers at Cartersville) three Enfield rifles and two United States firearms for sporting purposes. The rifles and firearms had been taken by Colonel Reams from certain freedmen in the neighborhood of Walnut Plantation, who had been killing stock at night. The Federal officer authorized Pierce to procure, if possible, all of the United States arms in possession of the freedmen in his neighborhood. The Youngs used the guns to hunt, and thereby added game to the family larder.

Late in November Pierce moved his mother back home from North Carolina. As soon as he had her settled he began making plans to move Louisa, her husband, and their three children back to Georgia. General Young was worried about Dr. Jones, who, after trying unsuccessfully to get a job, had threatened to resort to quackery to provide food and clothing for his family. By the early part of 1866 Young's plans had materialized and the Jones family was moved to Kingston, Georgia.

Throughout 1865 and 1866, Pierce resorted to various means to relieve the financial strain so as to make his family comfortable. He tried to sell land but found that people did not have any money to buy. In general, land owners had an exalted opinion of the value of land and thought anyone would be foolish to buy until he found out what effect the enfranchisement of the Negroes would have upon farm labor.

Pierce was discouraged because he was unable to get steady employment to relieve the poverty of his family. A letter from a former classmate at West Point informed him that many of his friends were having financial trouble—they also were unable to get jobs and were having a difficult time trying to adapt themselves to civilian life. He was dunned almost monthly by former army friends who had sold him horses or equipment and had accepted his note while he was a major general in the army. He threatened to go to Mexico or out West to try to get a job and restore his finances. But Pierce knew that he could not leave his parents, for the war had virtually wrecked their lives, and they were no longer able to assume the full responsibility of supervising the farm. In addition, the responsibility of his sister and her family made it necessary for him to stay and try to assist, for Louisa wrote on May 6, 1866: "My garden is poor, does not afford me even lettuce and onions yet, but I shall continue to try. . . . I live hard, and am still growing more thin day by day. We generally manage enough corn bread and milk, but I do not know how long we will be blessed, as the bread question is becoming serious."

Conditions did not improve the next year. A severe winter added to the many problems of the poor and impoverished of the South. As a last resort, General Young tried to collect some of his father's old notes but found, as one debtor wrote, that payment did not depend "on my will, but on my ability, solely." He found debtors and creditors to be at a stalemate—one could not pay and the other could not collect.

Knowing that his Uncle Tom had entered the congressional race in the Sixth District of Kentucky, Pierce wrote him about the family financial troubles and asked his advice about what to do. Colonel Jones answered that he had won in the election, but added that it was humiliating to one of Southern pride and blood to see any of the Southern people willing to accept the conditions of the military occupation. He advised Pierce to stay at home and help his family.

On May 26, 1866, while working on the plantation, Pierce received his last letter from Mary Brooks, with an invitation to her wedding to George B. Addison. She asked a last favor: "Do not reply to this letter, and do not forget me entirely. You are forgiven freely but do not seek a meeting for if your feelings are the same you represented when last in my presence, it will do no good and might harm." Pierce made no attempt to see her again. Conditions at home did not allow him time to pine about a war romance.

Hardships and privations at Walnut Plantation continued. And Aunt Mary Thompson wrote from White Oak, North Carolina, on August 27, 1867, that her family was not able to make a decent living. They had the coarsest, plainest food prepared, and it was served in the plainest manner. There were no servants at all and to hire one was too costly because the Negroes were unwilling to leave the town for the country. The community in which they lived had the lowest and poorest people on the earth, and life was harder than their strength could endure. She never saw any decent people, for the whole community was demoralized. "The Union men or rather deserters, robbers and Negroes, are forming what they call leagues all over the country, in which they take an oath to vote only for those men who will go for confiscation. I expect nothing else than to lose the last acre of land, before we are done with the villains. But," she summed up, "for the present we have to submit, being too poor to live anywhere else. . . . ."

Driven by the needs of his family, Pierce again tried to sell land, but there still were few people with money to purchase. Times were unsettled, and he wrote in 1867, "The foundations are overturned and no one knows what to be at or where to settle." After harvesting the wheat in 1867, he traveled to New York in August in an effort to sell the grain to secure cash. His trip was not successful, however, and he wrote his parents, "I am living cheap. . . . The money for the wheat will not pay us out of debt. Wheat will be cheaper."

Pierce's attitude towards his indebtedness was expressed in a letter to an uncle in December: "The worst tyrant on earth is debt and I for one am beginning to feel it worse than any other. If we could get out of debt once, I think I for one would try to keep out for life." Serious illness of his father and sister in the fall of 1867 did not help. In desperation Pierce wrote again in the winter to Uncle Tom seeking advice. The uncle replied that he was sorry to hear of the general embarrassment which existed throughout the South. "It is deplorable indeed but I suppose you are better off than most of our unfortunate friends also having comparatively nothing." The uncle gave him little encouragement to go to Washington to seek a job, for he saw "nothing very inviting . . . to distinguish an uprising young man."

Pierce's interest in politics was not renewed until 1868. When he returned from the war he was too busy trying to make a living to think about politics. Then, too, his political disabilities had not been removed and there was not a united Democratic party in the state. The foundations of the Democratic party after the Civil War were laid in the various clubs whose chief purpose was to unite the opposition of the state against the radical reconstruction program.

Falling deeper into debt and being unable to meet his financial obligations, Pierce, influenced by his former officer friends and comrades, especially those in Cobb's Legion, became interested in having his name mentioned as a possible candidate for Congress from the Seventh District. Having been a major general in the war for the lost cause was a valuable asset—the key which unlocked the minds of those Georgians who had become bitterly opposed to the underhanded policies of the radical reconstructionists in 1868.

Although Pierce and his family had not taken an interest in politics since the war, the political leaders of the state had been trying to organize against those members who had joined forces with the Republicans and had been placed in power by the military forces. Throughout 1866 Georgians, still shocked by the outcome of the war, found themselves in the rather anomalous position of being considered both out of and in the Union at the same time. Thaddeus Stevens, who headed the implacable Reconstruction Committee of the United States Congress, had as his chief purpose the humiliation of the South.

From the end of the war until 1868 most Georgians cooperated or at least acquiesced in President Andrew Johnson's Reconstruction program. A stable organization of each political group developed from the fight to put into effect the Reconstruction program by the calling of a constitutional convention and electing a governor and members to the general assembly. On December 5, 1867, in Macon, the Democratic Party held its first state convention after the war, to consider what should be done. Although there were delegates from sixty counties, there were only seven counties north of the Chattahoochee River represented. Pierce Young was not elected to the convention. On March 13, 1868, the state Democratic Executive Committee, composed of fifteen members, met and named a candidate for governor and four delegates and four alternates to the Democratic presidential nominating convention. In addition word was sent to all county Democratic clubs to call for political meetings. Pierce was gratified to learn that an old army colleague, John B. Gordon, and a Bartow County friend, Warren Akin, were elected as delegate and alternate to the convention.

On March 20 there appeared in the *Cartersville Express* an announcement of a political meeting for "all men who are in favor of a white man's Government and opposed to negro domination; all who are opposed to having our proud old State converted into a second St. Domingo, and who are not ready to see the names of Washington and Jackson blotted from our country's history, and the names of the infamous Bradley and Bentley enrolled in their steads; . . . are requested to meet . . . to select candidates for Legislature, and Delegates to Congressional Convention . . . on 31 inst." This announcement was intended for the voters in the Seventh Congressional District, made up of the following counties: DeKalb, Fulton, Cobb, Polk, Floyd, Bartow, Cherokee, Gordon, Catoosa, Dade, Haralson, and Paulding.

When General George G. Meade, a veteran of Gettysburg, arrived in Atlanta to become the military governor of Georgia, he was honored at a banquet by local citizens, among them General John B. Gordon and General P. M. B. Young. Pierce called to pay his respects to General Meade as soon as he was able for he had been a friend of George Meade, Jr., at West Point, and was surprised to find the junior Meade a member of his father's staff. Pierce described his friendship for George Meade, Jr., as follows: "I had been at West Point one year when George Meade, a young lad, the son of Captain Meade, of the engineers came to West Point; Meade was one of the cadets appointed at large. He was a delicate young fellow, very handsome and rather effeminate looking. The old cadets were disposed to have a little fun at his expense as was the custom. I stood up for the new cadet, and shielded him as much as I could. A warm friendship grew up between us, which the war never interrupted. . . ."

In January 1868, while in Atlanta, Pierce's friends in Fulton County secured a promise from him that he would allow his name to be placed before the Democratic Congressional Convention. He gave his promise but told them that his disabilities would not be removed if he should be elected. Pierce's friends were persistent, for at the time it was difficult to find a man eligible and acceptable to the people of the district. Ten delegates composed of the leading Democrats of Bartow County were selected and they met Tuesday, March 31, with the delegates from the fourteen other counties of the district at the Bartow courthouse in Cartersville. From the first, Pierce's friends, the delegates from Fulton County, led by Captain John Milledge, dominated the convention and were able to have adopted the majority rule, and nomination from the floor rather than by a committee. Immediately after the rule was adopted, J. A. Stewart of Floyd, A. R. Wright of Floyd, Colonel J. D. Waddell of Polk, and General P. M. B. Young of Bartow were nominated. Colonel Waddell declined the nomination and insisted that under no circumstances would he be a candidate. His friends, however, persisted in keeping his name. The result of the first ballot was Wright—15, Young—11, Waddell—10, and Stewart—2. The president of the convention announced the result and declared that by majority rule there was no election.

On the second ballot, Colonel Waddell again tried unsuccessfully to withdraw his name. When the votes were counted, Pierce received 23, Wright 12, Waddell 4, and Stewart none. The president's announcement that the ballot gave the nomination to General Young was received with cheers, and a motion to make the nomination unanimous was carried. A committee was appointed to inform General Young of his nomination and escort him to the convention hall. Pierce's entry was the cue for uproarious applause, and he acknowledged his victory in a few brief and pointed words.

Pierce's Fulton County friends had been able to maneuver his nomination at the convention; now his own work began. A candidate had to publish his own ballot, finance his speaking tours, and pay for his assistants. For a young man already overwhelmed by debt, this was a tremendous task for General Young. He borrowed money wherever possible, bought on credit, and gambled on his success by promising high rates of interest for loans and his assistance in removing disabilities and securing restoration of pensions and losses for the many people in his district who had claims against the government. And Pierce never treated his promises lightly.

Besides General Young there were two other congressional candidates from the Seventh District—one Republican and one independent—for the general election. The competition meant traveling in every county and speaking upon political issues of the day in the more populous military districts. Announcements of meetings and speeches were made in the county papers and by hand bills. The main appeal of the Democratic party in 1868 was that it promised to keep Georgia from falling into the hands of Republicans and Negroes. Pierce's speeches did not contain the bitter vituperations characteristic of the more radical Democrats. He did not say anything to offend the military governor and the radical leaders of Congress. Yet his subtle appeal was for the Democrats to go to the polls and express themselves against those who were in control in the state.

Pierce's schedule was a rigid one; for example, during the week April 10-17 he traveled and spoke in seven different political ral-

lies in as many counties. Since he could not visit every community, Pierce's friends spoke for him in some places. One of
his most ardent supporters was J. C. C. Blackburn of Euharlee,
Georgia, who rode over Paulding and Floyd counties speaking
in his behalf. In a letter of April 18, Blackburn reported the
progress he had made and added, "I contribute my mite willingly
to promote your interest" against the radicals. Confederate veterans were supporting General Young enthusiastically. And
almost every county newspaper in the district, especially the
larger ones, carried his name on the masthead.

In the general election Pierce received a majority of 3,106
votes over his two opponents, James A. Atkins and Henry G.
Cole. Typical of his unselfishness and of his faith in his friends,
the winning candidate wrote that his success had been made
possible by his many friends throughout the Seventh Congressional District.

The next big hurdle was to have his disabilities removed.
In his 1893 articles for the *Atlanta Constitution,* Pierce wrote:
"I was ineligible when we started to the convention, but was
nominated and elected. General Meade was then in command
of the military district of Georgia, and it was by his influence,
backed by other officers of the army of West Point men, that
I was capable to get congress to remove my disabilities, and to
take my seat in the house of representatives. Both houses of
congress were overwhelmingly republican, the feeling toward the
South very, very bitter and but for the influence of these West
Point men I could never have entered the congress of the United
States. . . ."

Writing several years later Pierce described in more detail his
experience in overcoming the hurdle of disabilities. "On one
occasion, a few days after I was nominated for congress, I was
at General Meade's to dinner. He said to me, 'I see you have
been nominated for congress, Young. Will you be elected?' I
responded, 'Yes, but I will, I fear, never be able to get my seat.'
He said, 'Never mind about that, get elected, and we will get
you in.' "

General Meade was as good as his promise, and on June 3, 1868,
he wrote several letters to some of the most influential men in
the nation and gave them to Pierce, who left for Washington to
get his disabilities removed. One letter, addressed to General
U. S. Grant, read: "General Young commanded a brigade of
cavalry in Lee's army, and his name and feats were very familiar

to me during the war, but since I have been here it gives me pleasure to say I have derived great satisfaction from my intercourse with him. I wish you to talk with him and you will find he is all right—and it is just such men as he we want down here—as their influence and example are more powerful. I should like to see Gen. Young's disabilities removed and him be allowed to take his seat in congress. Not that he would be a republican—tho' I don't know that he is not, but I know he is loyal to the Union and will do as much to uphold it and the flag as if the rebellion had never existed. Hope you may have it in your power to aid him."

General Grant endorsed the letter: "I write with General Meade in recommending the removal of all disabilities in the case of P. M. B. Young, to the end that he may take his seat in Congress." He sent his endorsement and the letter to H. Wilson, Chairman of the Military Committee of the Senate. To it was added the endorsement of approval by I. M. Schofield, Secretary of War, Major General W. H. Emory (who knew Pierce personally), and Major General O. O. Howard. (Another letter was addressed to Thaddeus Stevens, the radical leader of the House of Representatives and the representative from General Meade's home district in Pennsylvania.) Meanwhile Pierce had arrived in Washington. Encouraged by the letters of General Meade, he tried to see Congressman Stevens. Unsuccessful, he rented a room at the Metropolitan Hotel and waited. On July 26, he wrote General Meade about his inability to get an interview with Stevens and about how despondent he was. He asked the General to write Stevens and also to see that his certificate of election was mailed immediately. General Meade was in Alabama when the letter was delivered; so C. D. Emory, a member of Meade's staff and a close friend of Pierce, replied that the matter requested had been taken care of.

Pierce's one ambition was to remove his disabilities. He was finally able to get an interview with Stevens, and described it as follows: "Thad Stevens permitted me an interview on July 29 and soon began to play with me as he sometimes did with those whom he intended to make his victims. He said:

'You are a graduate of West Point, I believe?'

'Yes, Sir.'

'Educated at the expense of the United States, I believe, which you swore faithfully to forever defend?'

'Yes, Sir.'

'You went into the service of the infernal rebellion.'

'Yes, Sir.'

'You were brigade commander in the raid into Pennsylvania, which destroyed the property of so many of my constituents?'

'Yes, Sir.'

'It was a squad of men under your direct charge, and under your personal command, that burned my rolling mill.'

'Yes, Sir,' I replied meekly."

Seeing that Stevens had information about him which he did not dream the old veteran knew, Pierce found it impossible to deny the truth of the questions. Stevens roared out, "Well, I like your d - - d impudence. I will see that your disabilities are removed. Good morning!" The next day the bill passed the House and the Committee on Elections recommended that Pierce be admitted to his seat after taking the oath which Congress had prescribed by the Act of July 11, 1868.

Pierce's credentials were presented by John A. Bingham, a Representative from Ohio, and they were referred to the Committee on Elections on July 25. Two days later Dawes reported that the disabilities of Simeon Corley of South Carolina and P. M. B. Young had been removed by an act of Congress and the Committee recommended that they be admitted to their seats on taking the prescribed oath.[2] Pierce and Corley took the oath of office. The same day Pierce wrote his mother, "I have postponed writing to you that I might write good news in my first letter. It has been long coming, and mighty hard work, but thank God —and good strategy—I am now finally seated in the U. S. Congress. Just one hour ago I was sworn in and took my seat. My heart sank often in me during the struggle but I came to the attack with renewed vigor. After I got everything fixed as I thought, I ran over to New York to the convention, and whilst I was there a bill to remove my disabilities passed the House but when it got to the Senate some senator had me struck out of the bill, so I was even worse off than I was at first. Uncle Tom told me on last Thursday when I got here from New York that he thought I was lost, but not I, I went to work and got a bill passed the Senate with my name and two others on it. I carried it to the House on Saturday and it was rejected, but they agreed to leave it to a conference committee formed of the Senate and House which recommended me, and the bill passed at 11 o'clock Saturday night and today at 11½ o'clock I was sworn in—merely taking the oath to support the constitution—and now I am a sure enough

M. C. Both houses adjourned at noon till September. I have no
idea they will meet till December." Then Pierce added, "I fully
intended to return and bring you to New York, to the Democratic
Convention, but Uncle Tom and others thought it would be
disastrous for me to be absent so long. . . . You were most fortunate in not being in New York during the convention; everything
was crowded and miserably disagreeable. . . . I will be at home
in about eight days."

On July 31, the editor of the *Cartersville Express* voiced the
opinion of a majority of his constituents, when he wrote, "We are
rejoiced to learn that Gen. Young's disabilities have been
removed, and he is allowed to take his seat in Congress." Then
he added, "He is a young man of fine ability and of commanding
personal appearance, and we hope and believe will make as
efficient representative of the people of the 7th Congressional
District of Congress, as he did a General in the army. He is a
Southern[er] of the truest steel. Long may he live to represent his
constituents in the council of his people."

Pierce did not get an opportunity to participate in Congress,
but it was significant that he, a Confederate major general in the
war, had so quickly had his political disabilities removed. To
his supporters in the Seventh District he represented the first step
toward complete restoration of the Empire State of the South
to the Union. But such hope was dashed aside when Georgia was
placed again under military rule the next year.

Political events moved rapidly in Georgia. The capital was
moved from Milledgeville to Atlanta when the new Constitution
was ratified on April 25, 1868. The legislature met on July 4,
and on July 21 both houses ratified the Fourteenth Amendment,
required by the Congressional Act of June 25, 1868, as a qualifi-
cation for readmission to the Union. The editor of the *Atlanta
Daily Constitution* in an editorial expressed the opinion of many
Georgians when he questioned the wisdom of the ratification.
The state Democratic convention met in Atlanta on July 23.
There were 1009 delegates from 108 counties and almost every
leader in the state was present. One historian described the time
as one never more heated in Georgia politics. The convention
"was a solid assemblage of the leaders of public opinion in the
commonwealth, with one conspicuous exception, . . . ex-Gov.
Joseph E. Brown. . . ."[3] The convention ratified the nominees of
the Democratic Convention, adopted the platform, and elected
presidential electors. Pierce heard about the convention while

he was still in Washington and rejoiced at the stand of the Democrats of Georgia.

He began to receive requests from his constituents asking for assistance in the removal of their disabilities. Many congratulated him upon being permitted to take his seat in Congress and praised the Georgia legislature for not electing Joe E. Brown to the Senate. The Conservatives nominated Alex H. Stephens and H. V. M. Miller, while the radicals supported Joe E. Brown and Foster Blodgett. After the first ballot, in which no one received a majority, the Conservatives and Moderate Republicans united on Joshua Hill, who defeated Brown on the next ballot. As William F. Graves of Marietta wrote, "I begin to hope that there is yet a brighter day for Georgia."

On August 28, the *Cartersville Express* carried an account of the meeting of the state Democratic executive committee in Atlanta on August 23. A resolution was adopted that recommended that the congressional districts in the state hold a convention as early as practicable to nominate candidates for Congress, and suggested that the convention in each District be held on the 8th day of September. One of the candidates was General William T. Wofford. On September 4, the Democrats of the various militia districts elected delegates to the county convention to be held at Kingston on September 9. The *Cartersville Express* for September 18 reported that the delegates at the county convention adopted a resolution that this was "no time for strife and contentions among Democrats. Let our delegates go uninstructed, and do what they think is best to be done and then let the Democracy of the Seventh District stick up to these."

At the Seventh Congressional District Convention, which met at the Methodist Church at Kingston on October 2, all counties except Chattooga and Dade sent delegates. Both Wofford and Young addressed the delegates. The newspaper account described the latter's address as "chaste and pointed," and went on to tell how Pierce informed his friends that he was a candidate for renomination and "Should esteem it a great compliment to receive it, but he stood ready to yield his personal desires to the best of his party, and should stand by the nominee of the convention and do all in his power to procure his election, feeling assured that the action of the convention would be shaped in reference to what they consider the good of the party." No other name was proposed, and Pierce was unanimously nominated by acclamation.

On October 16, the editor of the *Cartersville Express* ran the name of General Young on the masthead and promised that he would give him his earnest support for Congress, in the approaching February election.

Pierce wrote to the committee on October 7 thanking them and the convention for their kindness and expressing his profound sense of obligation for the distinguished honor conferred upon him. He explained that his pleasure because of the event "was not unmingled with a solicitude of painful character. To me it is clear that American politics have reached a point in the downward track of decline and corruption, which leaves it barely possible for the true friend of liberty and law to inaugurate recovering measures. Our deception capacity as a people for the acts of the demagogue, and our toleration of the pranks and insolence of tyranny are most astounding. Today, in less than 80 years of a political existence, we are forced to our election between the best and the worst of government in the experience of mankind.

"I say the best government, because the world can bare [*sic*] witness to the universal freedom and happiness of our people, under the twenty-seven years of Democratic and Constitutional Government which preceded those sad days. I say worst, because throughout our unhappy South we are so trampled upon and outraged that we can almost declare that any change whatever would be a mercy. And now, right now, we are all put to our elections. The last day of next Nov. will find this once glorious heritage a prey to a most remorseless party, or government once more in the firm grasp of the law-abiding and law-loving Democracy. If once again this glorious old party, which made America what she was in her palmy days, shall be firmly stated in authority, our very enemies themselves shall bless the day we hurled them from power. But if God in His awful and afflictive providence, shall suffer us again to be leased out to the misrule and venality of a corrupt party for four years more, then, to my hope the book is closed, and all the glory that could be recorded for us is already written." In concluding, he requested the cooperation of each Democrat in the district to help hold high the glorious banner of the South. He promised to do his share in leading them.

As a congressman Pierce was not idle. He visited his constituents whenever he was in Georgia; he sent them congressional reports, papers, and seed. He kept a long mailing list of friends in each county, and whenever possible he engaged in speaking tours in the districts of each county. It was a time when grand political rallies were held and free barbecues were given in order to attract the people. Leaders such as John B. Gordon and J. D. Waddell were often at the rallies and often spoke for Young when he was in Washington—in an effort to arouse the Democrats against radicalism.

VIII

◊◊◊
◊

A Champion of Southern Rights

POLITICAL events kept moving rapidly in Georgia. On July 28, 1868, the state was removed from military rule and returned to the Union fully reconstructed with statehood regained. Early in September the predominantly white general assembly expelled the Negro members by declaring them ineligible, and then filled the vacant seats with white opponents. Such action enabled the Republican leaders of Georgia under General Rufus Bullock to appeal for assistance to the radicals in the national government. In addition, the appeal was supported by reports of mistreatment, abuse, and outrages directed against the Negroes of the state. When Congress met in December 1868, Governor Bullock presented a letter to the Senate claiming that Georgia had not been admitted to the Union because a properly organized legislature had not ratified the Fourteenth Amendment as the Reconstruction Acts demanded. On January 25, 1869, the Senate Committee on the Judiciary recommended that Senator-elect Joshua Hill of Georgia not be allowed to take his seat, because Georgia had failed to comply with the requirements of the Omnibus Act, and therefore was not entitled to congressional representation. The report of the Judiciary Committee was not acted upon, so that Georgia's status was left doubtful.

When Congress met on Monday, December 6, 1868, Pierce answered the roll call. He wrote his mother that he believed he would never forget a portion of Chaplain C. B. Boynton's prayer that morning, ". . . and we beseech Thee to impart unto them a wisdom that shall enable them to plan and execute all such measures as may tend to produce universal and stable propriety and peace."

Two days later Pierce wrote his father that all the Congress-men from Georgia were fearful that Bullock and his cohorts would "cause the state to be remanded back to a territorial gov-ernment—our senators [Joshua Hill and Dr. H. V. M. Miller] are not yet admitted and I fear they will not get in at once, as Bullock, Blodgett and others are here working against the admis-sion of our senators. . . . We will yet have some trouble I fear about our state; the more rabid radicals are very indignant at the Georgia legislature putting out the Negroes." Aware of the family's ever-present need for money, he assured his father that if he got in "a pinch" he would send money or whatever else was needed at home.

The first bill Pierce introduced in the House of Representatives was on December 14, to relieve Nathan Land and J. A. Howard of Bartow County from their legal and political disabilities. The same day he introduced a bill to relieve the disabilities of Varney A. Gaskill. Five days later he introduced another bill to relieve the political disabilities of five other Georgians.[1]

The anxiety of Pierce and his friends about the status of Georgia increased, for the radicals of Congress viewed with alarm the political events that had been taking place. They did not believe that Georgia was being reconstructed according to their plans. The Senate did not allow Hill and Miller to take their seats. In December, Charles Sumner introduced a bill for a further reconstruction of Georgia. The implacable Reconstruc-tion Committee of Congress took the Sumner bill and throughout 1869 heard extensive and conflicting evidence on conditions pre-vailing in the state. On March 18 the Georgia general assembly voted against the ratification of the Fifteenth Amendment, and then adjourned.

Meanwhile, early in February Congress decided not to count the electoral vote of Georgia, if it affected the results. On February 10, Pierce rose on the floor of the House in protest of such action and gave his first speech. "Mr. Speaker, I rise to inquire whether it would now be in order for me to enter my solemn protest in behalf of the people of my State and in the name of the Con-stitution and laws of the United States against the action of this House in thus excluding from the Electoral College the State of Georgia. That State, Sir, has a full delegation on this floor; her Representatives, of whom I have the honor to be one, were admitted without contest or question. Georgia has performed all the conditions strictly required of her under the reconstruction acts of Congress, and although she is divided, upon mere technical objections, in her representation in the Senate, she has vested rights in this House, and she is again a State in the Union, with all the rights and privileges—so far at least as her voice may be heard in this matter—of any other State. To deny her now and her citizens the dearest right of freemen, the elective franchise, and especially for the Chief Magistrate of the people, is to strike down the great object and principle of republican government, and foreshadow and promote consolidation and despotism. I reiterate my solemn protest against such action." The Speaker answered that the remarks would be recorded in the *Globe,* but continued, "a protest cannot be entered on the Journal as a matter of right; the consent of the House is necessary to grant the privilege."[2]

Working tirelessly against the opposition of radicals, Pierce tried to get assistance from his fellow congressmen. Although he had many friends and army comrades, he was able to do very little. On January 29, 1869, he wrote a close friend, "You may not be immensely surprised to hear that Congress is radical, but it is now more radical than ever, and I regret to note the probability that the Negroes will be reinstated in our legislature, a measure high handed in the extreme, but against which my exertions have been powerless, I fear, so also, it appears that no more political disabilities will be removed for some time. You will see from this that the political aspect is bad. Such is the fact, but I am not altogether without hope of a better time, and not very far off. The darkest hour is just before day. . . . The pressure is so great that we will have to make exertion for the wide dissemination of democratic principles, and while I shall do my part, I shall hope (not against hope I am sure) that you will personally aid me in the work."

On February 24, Pierce wrote an article entitled "Reconstruction in Georgia," in opposition to Congressman Ben Butler's reconstruction plan to place Georgia back under military rule. The article was incorporated in the *Congressional Globe.* In it Pierce said, "I see around me to-day stern and unrelenting faces, men with uplifted hands, ready for another stab at the heart of my poor country, which this narrative would soften.

"But it is useless to hope for the truth. A theory must be sustained at all hazards. A party erected on sectional enmity must not be allowed to die at the hands of fraternal unity and love, and in our politics it has come to be regarded as a vital principle that a sectional war must be waged by one portion of our country against another. Indeed, this startling assumption has been formally made in a public speech by one of the foremost leaders of our political world.

"Is this exaggerated language? Let him who says so read the very first section of the bill now before us. By that section all enactments and proceedings of the last Legislature of Georgia are declared to be inoperative, void, and of none effect. What is there throughout the whole scope of this bill to soften the terrible effect upon more than a million of Americans of such savage legislation? If the 'enactment and proceedings' of the last Legislature of my State are 'void' of course they must also be 'none effect,' and the franchise already vested must be withdrawn, the prison must give up its criminals, the gibbet its felon, and for a space, let it be long or short, society must be in a state of chaos."

Pierce reminded the Republican leaders that they were to blame for the expulsion of the Negroes from the general assembly. He also reminded them that the father of the doctrine that Negroes could not hold office under the last constitution of Georgia was no less than ex-Governor Joseph E. Brown, who laid down the doctrine that "by the Constitution of the State and the laws consistent therewith, the Negro was not eligible to hold office." Then Pierce added, "A legislature notoriously packed in the interests of the majority in the House were the real perpetrators of this heinous offense against liberty and human rights, for which a whole State, an empire within itself, is to be summarily punished."

Congressman Young reminded his fellow congressmen that although it was legal for Negroes to sit in their state legislatures, very few were ever elected. He warned that future history would condemn the action taken, and tried to appeal to the conscience of the radical members. He concluded: "What earthly good can result to the fortunes of white or black from continued exacerbations and this eternal calling for inquisitorial and punitive legislation?"[3]

There was bad news at home as well as in Congress. On January 23, Pierce had a letter from his mother telling of the serious illness of Louisa and of their anxiety about her health. In addition, Mrs. Young told of troubles at Walnut Plantation with the tenants stealing the corn and of Dr. Young's apparent inability to control and administer the plantation. Then she gave the tragic news that Robert's widow and daughter in Texas were "in a deplorable economic condition without friends and means of support." Pierce was very much disturbed that he could not assist his sister-in-law and niece, Josephine and Ida. He had received only two months' pay and the cost of living in Washington was high.

The opinion that a majority of the people of the Seventh District held about General Young was expressed by a correspondent of the *Atlanta Intelligencer,* who signed his name as "Junius Brutus." Writing from Washington, he said, "The representative from the 7th District of Georgia, General P. M. B. Young, is not only the best looking man in either branch of Congress, but he is making a most efficient member and from close attention to his duties and popularity with the controlling members of the government he will soon be able to exert a strong influence in behalf of Georgia. General Young is the only member of Congress from the 'Reconstruction South' who is a representative man of the Southern people. I feel proud to know that the 7th District of Georgia is represented by a Southern gentleman, a gallant officer, a man of dignity and one destined to make his civic as he has his military mark."[4]

"Banquo," a correspondent of the *Rome Courier,* writing to that paper from Washington, also praised Pierce for his devotion to duty and his watchful concern for Georgia affairs. According to him, "No Georgian or other citizen of the South visiting Washington will blush to see General P. M. B. Young representing a white constituency of a southern state. He served the people of Georgia most faithfully and gallantly for 4 years, when confronted day by day with missiles of death; is he not competent to fill the post he now occupies? We answer most unquestionably."[5]

When it was rumored that Louisiana and Georgia representatives were to be excluded from the next House, Pierce knew that trouble was ahead for him and his colleagues. The only hope was in the report that General Grant opposed the unseating of Georgia representatives and attributed the postponement of the Georgia matter by the Reconstruction Committee to the influence of the House.

When the first session of the Forty-first Congress met on March 5, 1869, John Farnsworth, Congressman from Illinois, moved that the six congressmen from Georgia be sworn in as members of the 41st Congress. He stated that Georgia had held the election under an Act of Congress of March 10, 1868, and that each congressman had a commission of election signed by Governor Rufus B.

Bullock.[6] Immediately after Farnsworth made his motion, Congressman Hamilton Ward of New York raised the question of whether the Georgia congressmen should be seated in view of the action of the legislature, and in view of the revolutionary proceedings which had occurred in the state, involving utter disregard of the Reconstruction Acts of Congress. The chief argument was over the fact that there had been but one election in 1868—on April 20—in Georgia; at the election Pierce and the other five congressmen were elected for both the 40th and 41st Congresses. At least that was the impression the people of Georgia had; so no other election was provided for in 1868.

Farnsworth defended Pierce and his colleagues by arguing that the seats were never contested by anyone and that the congressmen were elected on the same day for both Congresses. The Illinois Congressman emphasized that Georgia had met all conditions and there were no charges of fraud in the election.

Despite efforts of their friends, Pierce and his five fellow congressmen were not allowed to take their seats. Instead, their credentials and papers were referred to the Committee on Elections, on March 6. Although Pierce had hopes that the committee would be favorable, he informed his mother that he doubted that he would be allowed to take his seat. He sought aid from Congressman Thomas Jones of Kentucky, his uncle, but the radicals were in control. Their one program was to make Georgia pay for the expulsion of the Negroes from its general assembly.

Then, too, when the Georgia general assembly in March voted against the ratification of the Fifteenth Amendment (many Republicans accused Bullock of withholding the amendment and presenting it in such language that he knew the Democrats would defeat it), Pierce knew that any possibility of taking his seat was lost. Senator Charles Sumner and his cohorts were seeking revenge, and they controlled congressional leadership. Pierce, as well as most Democrats, resented Governor Bullock's visit to Washington, where he appeared before the committee and vehemently denounced the action of Georgia Democratic leaders, declaring that Federal troops were needed to preserve order. He argued for a reorganization of Georgia that would exclude a number of white members from the legislature and reinstate the Negroes who had been expelled.

Pierce was not daunted; he stayed on in Washington renewing his acquaintances and meeting with his friends. He sought advice from political leaders of both parties and even frequently visited

President and Mrs. Grant at the White House. Never had his
West Point friends been more loyal. They tried to heal the
wounds created by the Civil War. General Young was treated as
though he were a full-fledged member of Congress. He enjoyed
the social life; meeting the young ladies helped him to forget the
problems created by the political enigma in Georgia. His political
life seemed like a web, the thread of which began in the Seventh
District and wound around the Democratic leaders of Atlanta
and stretched into the halls of Congress. Being unable to take his
seat was not considered as a personal punishment by Pierce but as
punishment for Georgia and her leaders—his friends. Considering
his cause the cause of all Southern Democrats, Pierce was relent-
less in his efforts to gain his seat in the House of Representatives.
He stayed on in Washington until May, feeling that by being
there he could best help his constituents and the cause for which
he was fighting.

Pierce tried to get free agriculture seed samples to send his constituents and his family, for he realized that the South needed
to diversify its agriculture. In sending samples to his father,
Pierce wanted him to experiment with cover crops and diversify
and rotate the crops.

Congress adjourned on April 10, and on the first of May,
General Young went home. As soon as he arrived he took over
the supervision of the farm. As soon as he had completed the final
planting, Pierce moved his brother George's widow and children
—Carrie, George, and Lamar—from Thomasville, Georgia, to
Walnut Plantation.

Throughout the summer Pierce continued to work on the farm.
Whenever possible he used his free pass on the train to visit his
constituents and discuss what had happened in Washington.
While on a visit to Rome, he met for the first time a young
associate editor, Henry Woodfin Grady. From the very first the
two men became friends. Pierce knew that Grady was from
Athens, the home town of his close friend in Civil War days
Thomas R. R. Cobb. Since Grady was also an admirer of Cobb,
the two men drew close together and remained friends the rest
of their lives. Grady supported Young throughout the latter's
career; in fact, Pierce learned to rely very heavily upon the
young newspaper man, who proved to be a valuable friend and
supporter.

On September 21, Pierce went to the Greenbrier Hotel, White
Sulphur Springs, Virginia, to attend a press ball, a big affair with

more than eight hundred guests. Among the guests were some of his former friends of the army—General Robert E. Lee, General P. G. T. Beauregard, General R. Lindsay Walker, Colonel Robert Ould—and many Southern belles.[7] At the dance he met a very witty young lady, Mattie Ould, from Richmond, Virginia, whom he found attractive.

The crops in 1869 were almost a failure in Georgia and South Carolina because of the drought. Again the Young family felt the economic pinch of poor crops and low prices. Pierce was embarrassed to receive a dun from a former army friend, James W. Watts, of Laurens District, South Carolina, for a $1,025 note which Pierce had signed in September 1864 for a horse and saddle. Watts explained that for $150 in greenbacks he would cancel the note since he had a family of eight children. Pierce replied that he would be unable to pay until later, for he had not received any money since March, and the crop was almost a failure.

Discouraged, he asked his Uncle Tom, who was visiting Walnut Plantation, if he should not get out of politics. Congressman Jones regretted Pierce's unfortunate experience and bitterly condemned the action of the radicals in Congress and of Bullock and his supporters in Georgia; but he encouraged him to run again for Congress. Pierce took heart from his uncle's advice and continued to meet with and talk to the people of his district.

Not until the second session did Congress agree upon its treatment of Georgia, and on December 22, 1869, the state for the third time was placed under military jurisdiction under the Acts of 1868; there it remained until July 15, 1870. Pierce was in Washington when he heard the news. He wrote his mother from the Arlington Hotel of his disappointment and of his inability to prevent Governor Bullock's success. But he did not remain downhearted. He participated in Washington's social life, and met many friends and enjoyed their company. He described to his mother the elegant dinners with friends. Aunt Mary Jones wrote Mrs. Young that she had seen Pierce at numerous balls and parties—"Pierce is a great favorite amongst the young ladies— indeed with everyone—I met him at the President's levee and also at a large party; we left at two o'clock and they had just begun the German."

Lacking money, Pierce again had to return home, where he worked toward his election. He won the confidence of men like Colonel W. L. Goldsmith of Atlanta, who promised to give him all the assistance in his power. He renewed his friendship with John B. Gordon and often visited him; if he failed to go by Gordon's office when in Atlanta Gordon would write a note wanting to know the reason.

During this time Pierce frequently received complaints from Georgians about the Radical control over the state. Typical was Paterson Stewart of Baldwin County who included in his letter a clipping showing "what villains" were managing the affairs of Georgia. He explained the fight was between two "Bullockites" and that the rental of the Western Atlantic Railroad was being used to support the families of the supporters of Bullock.

A close friend, O. A. Lochrane of Atlanta, wrote Young, describing in detail Bullock's return to the legislature and how the members took another per diem and went home to renew their strength like the eagles for another foray. But Georgia kept "a high head and stout heart, looking hopefully to the future, and proudly to the past. She may have a thousand afflictions, but not one regret. She may have surrendered everything, but her sentiments, these are not subject to capture. . . . Give negroes their full rights under the law—educate, enlighten, elevate them, but let the social structure of the state remain, for the honor and purity of the Republic, intact." Lochrane declared that he would go to the last inch of ground left to stand on with full justice to the Negro, "but to upset our institutions and have them believe they are too good to hire to white people, too good to work and their wives have to play lady in pulling down the fabric to overwhelm with ruin and disaster, every element of social existence. If this is progress, down with progress. I want to go back and see old times not of slavery, but of service."

Lochrane wrote again on June 8, 1870, telling Pierce of his value to the Democrats and saying that the state had no man so respected. "We have literally no one but you, and all over the state we look to you for kindness and attention to interest."

Because of his friendship with the veterans, Pierce's influence was widely recognized by leading Georgians. Thomas G. Simms, a former postmaster of Atlanta, wrote him on May 13, 1870, that a high authority "in the Radical wing intimated that Pierce could do more . . . than anyone else, and do it through a gentleman, who I believe is very friendly to you. I allude to General Porter, of the President's secretaries." Simms had leased a place and with his own money established a post office in 1866 for public convenience, but the government refused to reimburse him. He asked Pierce to assist him in getting "the infernal thing settled if possible." In return Simms promised he would fight for him, and "I hope to hear that you are seated—where I intend to keep you to the extent of my ability so long as you want to go to Congress."

Early in March 1870, Pierce went to Washington to oppose Governor Bullock and his friends who were trying to keep Georgia under military rule. By June nothing had been done. After receiving money from home, Pierce wrote that he would stay on in Washington until the Bullock affair was settled—"I've been here so long that I think our people expect me to stay until the matter is settled." A month later he repeated in a letter to his mother that everyone begged him to remain until the Georgia business was settled or until there was no hope of favorable settlement. But, "I believe there will be no action in the senate and on the Georgia bill, so we will still remain out of the Union."

Hearing that certain of his constituents were questioning his prolonged stay in Washington, Pierce wrote a letter to the editors of the *Atlanta Daily Constitution* on July 10, 1870, stating his position in Washington. "I came to Washington, in March, at the earnest solicitation of certain distinguished Democrats of my district; and from the day of my arrival I labored incessantly to bring to a successful solution the troubles and issues incident to the Georgia case."

His opinion was that the people of Georgia had elected the present delegation to the Fortieth Congress, and "it is a fact well known to many members of the Georgia Legislature that I have been most urgent and anxious for the election for the Forty-first Congress, and that I have urged from time to time an enabling act should be passed by the Legislature for that purpose. I still hold to my original opinion, which I advocated a year ago to the Democrats of the House of Representatives and no matter what construction may be placed upon the law, I believe that the people expected an election and that they have a right to that election under the law. I shall be the last one to give my countenance or consent to any act that will deprive the people of my State of a single right or liberty guaranteed to them by the Constitution of the United States or by the Constitution and laws of any State: I shall therefore never take a seat in this congress unless directed by my constituents."

It appeared that Pierce was not keeping up with events in Georgia. Although Bullock had tried again in Washington to use his power to keep Georgia under military control, he and his

Republican leaders had over-extended their luck in returning
Georgia to military rule. The corrupt and autocratic mismanage-
ment of Bullock's appointees over the state-owned Western and
Atlantic Railroad and the corruption of the Bullock-controlled
legislature became too offensive for even the radicals of Congress
to accept. After a bitter fight led by some of Pierce's closest
political friends, a law was passed on July 15, 1870, re-admitting
Georgia into the Union.

The role of Pierce in the defeat of Bullock was revealed by
one "H. D. C.," Washington correspondent for the *Atlanta Daily
Constitution,* who wrote on July 16 that the people of Georgia
were "mainly indebted to the indomitable zeal and diplomacy
of General P. M. B. Young, the representative elect from the 7th
District, for this result. I have been assured from Republican
authority that the bill which passed the House some time since,
. . . would have passed the Senate but for the interposition of
General Young." He explained that all of the members elected
to the 40th Congress except Pierce favored the House bill
because it gave them their seats. He commended the Georgia
representative for having the courage to withstand the possibilities of personal gain and for not making application for his seat
unless ordered to do so by his constituents. The correspondent
continued, "His straight-forward, frank, manly bearing had won
him friends among all but the mean narrow minded puritan who
hates gentility and Southern manhood from the native instinct
of the animal—while the proverbial energy of the General and
his disinterested course has saved Georgia from absolute ruin."
The success of Pierce's friends made him jubilant.

Although the act ended Congressional action upon the state,
Governor Bullock and his associates did not plan to be thwarted
in the control of the general assembly. On July 6, 1870, the governor communicated to the legislature the act admitting Georgia
but added that the United States Congress had adjourned without
having admitted the Georgia senators and congressmen; therefore, section five of the Reconstruction Act of 1867 was still in
effect. This made the actual admission of the senators and congressmen a condition precedent to the abrogation of military
authority, which would last until Congress assembled in the
winter.

Not to be defeated in his efforts to keep Georgia subjugated,
Governor Bullock set out to control the fall election so that he

would not lose. He had his "controlled" legislature to resort to a scheme used in 1866, to hold elections for three days and allow the voter to transfer his vote around. The scheme has been described by one historian as "one of the most extraordinary election plans ever devised, combining the grotesque tyranny of a bayonet machine with the more puzzling novelties of a metropolitan packing jugglery." Governor Bullock, with the advice of the senate, was to appoint the three election managers and the ordinary—two for each election precinct. These election officials were subject to a fine of $100 for failure to serve. The plan provided that the managers did not have the power to challenge a voter and could not refuse a ballot. In addition only one man at a time could be at the polls and others were required to stay at a distance of fifty feet. During the election the sheriff of each county was placed under the absolute control of the election managers, who had plenary powers of arrest and could fine a sheriff $100 for contempt of their orders.

The Democrats were unsuccessful in trying to defeat this procedure in the election. Pierce, with other Georgia Democratic leaders, vehemently condemned the treacherous plan and set about to defeat it. He traveled throughout the Seventh District urging Democrats to go to the polls and vote.

The Democrats held a convention on August 17 in Atlanta. General Young was one of the 300 delegates from 109 counties of the state. There he became a friend of leaders such as Alfred H. Colquitt, who assisted him in later years in his first appointment to the foreign service. When Linton Stephens, who agreed that none but eligible men should run for state offices, wrote suggesting that "for Congress some ineligible candidates," such as an ex-Confederate officer who could not take the oath, should be nominated, Pierce joined with the Democratic leaders and a majority of the press in condemning the idea. With his experience in Congress he knew too well the difficulty that even an eligible candidate had of gaining his seat under the Radical congressmen.

Immediately after the adjournment of the state Democratic convention, the delegates from the Seventh Congressional District met in the room of the state house of representatives and passed a resolution calling for a district convention of the Democratic party in the courthouse in Cartersville on Tuesday, September 13, for the purpose of nominating a candidate for Congress. It was resolved that the basis for representatives in the convention should be two delegates for each member of the house of representatives.

Henry Grady wrote Pierce, "In Tuesday morning (Atlanta's) *Intelligencer,* will be found a card asking you whether or not you indorse Linton Stephens' position—if not I have strong reason to believe the *Intelligencer* will at once drop your name and fight against you to the end of the chapter. If I may take the liberty of advising you, I would strongly urge you not to answer the question—for before the race is over we will need *every* man we can get. You will have strong opposition and many *lukewarm* friends. I am an humble but industrious Democrat and I *know* the sentiments of the people of this end of the District better than any one man in Rome. There were too many aspirants for the position for you to have an easy race. . . . Wrecked ambition and envy are the strongest, as well as the most dangerous, passions of the human mind. When I see you, I can show you letters from men who you believe to be your friends that will open your eyes. I speak in no carping spirit. I speak for the good of the Democratic party and of your own good as God is my guide. I would give one thousand dollars to see Georgia send an entire *Democratic* delegation to the next Congress—and she can do it if she will. Hence I wrote to post you. It is possible that the card may not appear. If it should, I would say, (in substance) I stand upon my record and right for the triumph of Democratic principles and appreciate the necessity of avoiding minor and distracting issues. This would satisfy every body and compromise no one."

Grady assured Pierce that Floyd County was all right and that there were not five Democrats in the county who would not support Pierce. He promised that Chatooga County would also vote for him because half of the inhabitants were subscribers to his paper and they would have "the right faith preached to them."

An editorial in the *Marietta Journal* on August 26 carried a reprint from the *Atlanta Daily Intelligencer* which expressed the wishes of many Democrats. It urged Democrats everywhere to heed the advice of congressional committees and see that the candidates for Congress were men who, if elected, could qualify for admission. Throughout September in Georgia the county and congressional district Democratic conventions met and published their platforms and nominated candidates.

As agreed upon in Atlanta, Democrats of the Seventh Congressional District held their convention in Cartersville. Pierce was nominated by acclamation, because of the fight he had made for Georgia in Congress and in Washington. Again Pierce's friends in Fulton County had been able to get his nomination, not, however, without the first murmurings condemning the politically controlled convention as a method of nomination. From Floyd County came rumors as to whether General Young would have to take the test oath. In Cobb County there were murmurings that Young was not the man for the time and would not be able to cope with men such as Butler and others in the national Congress. Much of the opposition arose from discontented constituents who felt that Pierce was playing favorites with Fulton and Bartow counties. Also he had created political enemies by leaving unanswered petitions for mail services, failing to secure the removal of disabilities for some constituents, and failing to get political appointments for certain citizens. But Pierce took the advice of Grady and ignored the opposition.

As he had done in the election of 1867, but this time less extensively, Pierce traveled throughout the district, making speeches condemning the actions of Bullock and his followers. He had two opponents—George P. Burnett of Floyd County, nominated by the Radicals in a convention at Kingston, and Henry G. Cole, nominated by the Conservative Republicans. Although the Radicals tried every political trick to win, they were defeated. Pierce won the election, held on December 20, 21, and 22, by a majority of 8,539 votes. He was gratified for he realized that his friends were fighting to restore Democratic control in Georgia; he knew that he was only a small cog in the total movement. He was determined more than ever to fight for his constituents and his state as soon as he arrived in Washington.

In an editorial, the *Cartersville Express* of January 13, 1871, said: "Today this commonwealth presents itself as fully accepting the situation, and it will be a perilous work, we may assure the Republican majority in Congress, to reject the vote just cast." The editor urged that the Georgia election should be allowed to remain undisturbed. "Attorney General Akerman has done his best, the administration has put forth its strongest powers, the reconstructed state government has exerted itself to the uttermost; it has been in the words of Andrew Jackson an entire victory for democracy and must remain so."

On January 16, 1871, Congressman H. A. Paine of Wisconsin presented to the House of Representatives the credentials of

Pierce, and of three other Georgia congressmen from the Third, Fourth, and Sixth Congressional Districts, and moved that they be sworn in. Pierce, Colonel W. P. Price of the Sixth, and Marion Bethune of the Third were immediately sworn in. Jeff Long, a Negro from the Fourth, was sworn in a few hours later.[8] The other Georgia congressmen elected were not allowed to take their seats. However, on January 24, Pierce presented the credentials of Stephen A. Corker, who had been elected from the Fifth Congressional District of Georgia. Immediately Congressman Benjamin Butler of Massachusetts opposed, and presented the credentials of Thomas P. Beard, a Negro from the same district, charging that illegal tactics had been used by the Democrats in electing Corker.[9] Remembering his promise, General Young threw caution aside and defended the election of Corker, who was commissioned by Governor Bullock on January 11, 1871, in one of the outstanding addresses of his career. Even Congressman Butler complimented Pierce, saying that the gentleman from Georgia had presented the case with his customary fairness.

Pierce argued that Corker should be seated on the *prima facie* evidence, for his credentials were precisely the same as those upon which he and other Georgia congressmen had been admitted to their seats. Corker won by a majority of 6,000 votes in his district. Pierce exclaimed, "You can throw out the county in which the managers of election have been arrested, you can throw out a half a dozen other counties, and still the gentleman will have a majority!" Then Pierce gave a brief history of the election in the Fifth District and remarked that the Republican accusation of falsification was untrue. He appealed to the Republicans to seat Corker.

When the final debate came on January 24, Pierce's reply to Butler was rapier-like. ". . . I cannot believe that this House, in view of its past action in contested-election cases, will refuse to give him the seat to which he has been elevated by the voters of his district. The arguments that have been advanced do not meet the point. The gentleman from Massachusetts talks of intimidation and outrages that have been committed in Georgia. Mr. Speaker, for the last few years this House and the other end of the Capitol—nay, Sir, the city of Washington and the whole North—have been surfeited with the eloquent recitals of the wrongs and the outrages committed by the people of Georgia.

"Sir, in reply to all these charges, so wantonly made, I desire simply to state that the pictures that have been drawn in the heat of debate upon this floor are creations of the imagination, and do not exist in point of fact. That there have been irregularities, that there have been indiscretions on the part of some of its people, I do not pretend to deny; but when we remember the condition in which the State has been placed, when we recall the legislation of Congress with regard to the State of Georgia, and the unconstitutional acts of its State Legislature, are you, Mr. Speaker, or the members of this House, surprised to learn or hear of occasional irregularities or indiscretions? But, Sir, are we to base our action upon the case now before the House upon such flimsy pretenses? . . . Are we to condemn without trial? Are we to disregard the broad seal of the State? Would it not be wiser, better, and in accordance with established precedent to admit Corker to his seat and let these questions be settled by contest? I trust and I believe such will be the action of the majority of this House."[10]

Pierce received support from Congressmen from Illinois, Indiana, and Massachusetts, who spoke against the injustice of Butler's tyrannical attempt to seat a Republican who had not won. When the vote was taken, Pierce's motion to seat Corker was passed by a vote of 148 to 42. Immediately Pierce's friends congratulated him upon his successful fight and upon the fair manner in which he conducted it on the floor of the House. In addition he received many letters congratulating him upon his fearless leadership. One letter that Pierce prized came from a former friend, Captain George D. Ramsay, Jr., of the United States Arsenal at Charleston. He congratulated Pierce upon his election to Congress, and added, "This morning I saw in the papers a short account of your little tilt with Gen. Butler and I was glad to see that you had the best of the discussion with so able an opponent."

Meanwhile Pierce was again almost swamped with petitions from Georgia leaders requesting daily the removal of their disabilities or requesting aid in getting postmasterships and pensions restored or seed to start their gardens. He encouraged the farmers of his district to raise turnips, oats, peas, clover, and other cover crops. He tried to get the farmers to experiment in raising sheep and cattle in an effort to raise the standard of living of the rural people of north Georgia. Using his franking privilege, he sent government documents and pamphlets on farming to his friends.

On February 11 Congressman Young was not so successful in his support of Nelson Tift against R. H. Whitely for representative from the Second Congressional District of Georgia. He supported Tift and delivered a scathing address on the floor of the House against Governor Bullock, whom he accused of willfully neglecting his job and using every subterfuge to evade his duty in giving the certificate to Tift. General Young further accused Bullock of offering Whitely the congressional seat after the latter was unable to secure a Senate seat. Then he explained why Whitely should not be seated and used historical precedents to prove that in many instances persons had appeared before the House with regular "certified certificates and yet been refused admission to seats because there was . . . testimony showing fraud or wrong . . . particularly in the issuing of the certificates." Despite Young's support of Tift, he lost.[11]

After numerous requests from citizens throughout the South, Pierce introduced a bill [H. R. 3020] on February 13, for the removal of all legal and political disabilities from "all persons who are now citizens of the United States." It was placed in the hopper, and later died in committee, despite the fact that Pierce exerted every pressure to have it brought on the floor of the House.[12]

Congressman Young was very busy during the third session of the 43rd Congress. He spoke on the House bills on rivers and harbors, civil rights, and appropriations. In addition he introduced several resolutions. He was too occupied with congressional duties to have much social life, and when his mother wrote teasing him about his lady friends, he replied, "I have been so busy that I have not gone in society much. . . . There are many pretty girls here this winter but I am not running with them much as heretofore."

There were the usual troubles at home. Mrs. Young, on April 1, wrote to her son that she wished that he could be at home. She told him, "Your father says he is very much annoyed by his debts and if you could spare him another hundred dollars you would oblige him very much." Since his father's health did not improve, more and more Mrs. Young had to assume the responsibility at the plantation. And other members of the family were having trouble. Aunt Mary Thompson was also in unfortunate financial circumstances. She wrote Pierce on March 18, asking for a loan of six or seven hundred dollars in order to save the property she had inherited from Grandma Jones. Aunt Mary wanted to leave her inebriate husband and move to Georgia near Louisa and her family. Pierce was unable to assist his aunt, for the needs at home were too great and immediate.

Early in March, Colonel Henry Jackson of Atlanta wrote General Young about the possibilities of getting a government building which would house a post office, a custom office, and the federal court. Pierce liked the idea and began at once to make plans to introduce a bill for the purpose. On March 20, 1871, he introduced a joint resolution which provided that the mayor, the postmaster of Atlanta, the judge of the United States Court for the district of Georgia, the president of the Board of Trade at Atlanta, and eleven outstanding citizens be appointed as a commission to select a proper site for the building and to report their findings to the Postmaster General and Secretary of the Interior as soon as possible. The resolution was referred to the Committee on Public Buildings and Grounds.[13] General Young was on the Committee of Mines and Mining, but he had a very close friend, Representative Walter Sessions of New York, on the Public Buildings Committee, who agreed to see the resolution through.

Before the Congressional Appropriations Committee Pierce made a passionate plea by describing how Atlanta had "arisen from the ashes" of the Civil War and how the increased population made it necessary to have a suitable government building. Pierce described further the inadequate space being used—the court "is held in the third story of an ordinary brick building, in a small room, totally unfit for the purposes of a court room, being hardly large enough to accommodate a jury and bar. The Post Office is now in the basement of a building whose walls are cracked, and is not considered safe." Then the General emphasized the cost to the United States government in rent, repairs, and furnishing the offices. He explained that the city had given to the government free of charge a costly lot in the center of town on which to construct a building, and that he proposed attempting to prove the wisdom and necessity for its construction. Pierce quoted the amount of revenue from the Post Office in 1871, and the amounts received in the money order department and from internal revenue. He concluded his plea by saying, "I have voted for subsidy after subsidy to aid in building up and improving other sections of our country, but never *one cent* has ever yet been given to aid and encourage

our struggling people of this young and flourishing city. May
I hope, Gentlemen, the time has come at last when Atlanta
can tender you her thanks?"

Obviously, then, Pierce believed in the future of Atlanta and
saw the necessity of planning for its growth. However, it was
not until the next session that Congressman Sessions was able
to bring it out of the committee, despite Pierce's efforts to rush
the resolution. The bill was enacted into law.[14]

On March 22 General Young rose on the floor of the House
and asked to be allowed to make a personal explanation of a
matter. His request was granted, and then Pierce had the clerk
read a paragraph from a news story by the Washington correspondent on the *Augusta Chronicle,* in which he made dis-
paraging remarks about the Georgia congressman, saying "He
says he would like to charge through the House with a company of cavalry to shoot and to kill [the Republicans] and I
believe in truth he would." Congressman Young explained that
he would not have dignified the paragraph with any notice had
not his attention been called to it by a distinguished Republican
friend. "The allegation is simply preposterous, absurd, ridiculous," he said. "I have never felt or given utterance to sentiments that could warrant such a statement. From the day of my
admission to the Fortieth Congress in 1868, to the present moment, I have met with nothing from members of this House
but uniform kindness and courtesy, and I have never for a moment entertained feelings for any member of the House other
than those of kindness. . . . Like the people whom I have the
honor to represent, I desire and intend to obey the laws of my
country and to do all in my power, both in my private and official
capacity, to promote its peace, prosperity, and its glory."[15] Pierce
hated any form of misrepresentation, and he felt that in fairness to his friends in Congress who had been so kind to him
he should not allow such a statement to go unchallenged.

By this time the Georgia congressman had received so many
letters from his constituents condemning the enforcement of the
Fourteenth Amendment that he delivered on April 4 before
the House of Representatives an address entitled "Enforcement
of the Fourteenth Amendment." When the House was considering
H. R. No. 320, to enforce the provisions of the Fourteenth
Amendment, he stated that he stood as a "Representative of a
people whom I believe to have been grossly wronged and oppressed; a people who, after four years of a bloody, devastating

war, laid down their arms and intrusted their liberties to your generosity. There never was an army disbanded after so long and so violent a struggle with such quietness as were these armies of the confederacy. Worn, weary, hungry, shoeless, and almost naked, and bleeding at every pore, but gallant and still true to their honor, they surrendered to what they believed to be the magnanimity or, if you please, the mercies, of whom, sir? Not to the armies of a foreign prince, not to the purchased hirelings of an invading despot, but to the armies composed of their own countrymen; men of their own flesh and blood, in whose honor, in whose magnanimity and sense of justice they believed they could trust."

Pierce commended the kind treatment shown by General Grant at the surrender of General Lee. He denounced the reconstruction in progress, for states were required to establish state governments in the face of and in defiance of their own constitutions and laws. Congress required states to frame and adopt constitutions which stripped them of the right dearest to every American citizen, the right to vote and hold office. "You not only required them to renounce these rights, but you required them at the same time to clothe with all the rights and immunities of American citizenship the ignorant black man who had so recently been their slave, and then in many of the States of the South placing the black man in government and authority over the white man whom you deprived of his political rights. You sent your Government officers into these States to collect the revenues, and for months and years while the revenues of those impoverished districts were flowing into your Treasury, you persistently refused them in violation of the Constitution, you refused them representation though they were daily praying for admission to Congress and to be permitted to participate in the Government even under the proscriptive restrictions you had forced them to accept."

Continuing, Pierce explained that armed forces were used during an election to keep the white people from going to the polls; yet the Southern people "have borne with forbearance and Christian fortitude all of these wrongs." He described the cost of the Republican-controlled legislature and their abuses in Georgia and South Carolina, and how the wrongs had been magnified to cover up the wrongs and abuses of the Radicals. Then Pierce proceeded to chide the congressional leaders for their stern reconstruction which violated every principle of individual right and liberty. He pleaded: "We want peace; that peace you have so long promised us, that peace which is guaranteed by the Constitution, and which today is enjoyed by the people of every State in the North and in the West. . . . Restore to us our old Government; we wish to be citizens of none other. We want no other Government; it is the Government of our fathers and yours; it is the Government we desire to transmit to our posterity."[16]

Pierce sent a copy of his talk home and his mother wrote later that they thought it good and his father had heard it complimented in high terms. Mrs. Young added, "Your father's health is tolerable good, but you know he complains a great deal and says he suffers very much." Pierce worried a great deal about his father's health and continued sending him money to be used in financing the farm. To his mother he sent clothes, believing that he could buy things cheaper in Washington than she could in Cartersville or Atlanta.

Personal finances worsened. Throughout 1871 Young received monthly numerous duns from clothing companies, grocerymen, printers (for ballots), and former creditors at Augusta. In order to relieve his financial burdens he borrowed money and invested in real estate with a friend, A. R. Shepherd of the Board of Public Works of the District of Columbia. On September 27, he received a check for $2,000 for his share of the property sold on Massachusetts Avenue. Seeing how easy the money was made, General Young invested as heavily as possible in real estate in Washington. On November 11, he again received from Kilbourn and Latta a check, this time for $8,814.22, for lots sold by them.

General Young had not been able to forget the charming and witty Mattie Ould of Richmond, whom he had met in 1869 at a ball at the Greenbrier Hotel in White Sulphur Springs. Throughout 1871 he spent every spare weekend in Richmond, whenever he could slip away from Washington. In his letters home he told his mother that he was in love with Mattie. Mrs. Young wrote Louisa in 1871, "I do believe Pierce intends to marry the Virginia girl, but," she added confidentially to her daughter, "there is no telling what he will do; he is the fullest of business of any man I ever saw [sic]. I wonder he is not crazy."

Mattie Ould was young, pretty, vivacious, carefree, and spoiled. Her mother was dead, and she and her sister lived under the supervision of their maternal grandmother. Pierce loved the young Richmond belle and was jealous of her and her friends.

On November 13, 1871, he wrote a friend, C. H. Phinizy, of Augusta, who had been attentive to Mattie, inquiring as to what news he had about Mattie, and especially if she was engaged to someone else. Two days later Phinizy replied that he had not had any communication from Mattie, for he had broken off with her. He wrote that Mattie was supposed to be engaged to one "Hoozier" Donans and advised Pierce not to get involved with the young lady for she was so lovely that he might fall in love with her. Phinizy's advice was ignored. For the first time Pierce was really in love. He visited Richmond the weekend of November 18. The following Saturday Mattie wrote to him, saying that she loved him. She described how at his request and suggestion she had reduced her weight to 125 pounds and was beginning to take music to improve herself. She candidly expressed her love with all of her heart, concluding her letter by saying, "It is foolishness to feel as I do. . . . You know that you have my whole heart and that I love you better than anything else."

Congress adjourned on Thursday, December 7, until the following Monday, and Pierce immediately left for Richmond to spend the time with Mattie. After he left she wrote Mrs. Young: "I have been waiting and wishing for some time for an excuse to write to you and now that I have one I shall not lose much time in fulfilling my wish." She said that Pierce was always regretful of leaving Cartersville because of his mother, but that she would be a mother to him. Then she told of the amusing incident in which she tried to treat General Young as her son. When Pierce arrived at her house, he told her that he was sick with pneumonia. Mattie tried to convince him that he was mistaken and finally persuaded him to consent to see her doctor. "In the meantime there was much groaning and tribulation in the back parlor of No. 223, Gov[ernor] Street. Presently Dr. McGuire, an old army friend of the General's and our physician, made his appearance and I discreetly retired to the front parlor, and waited his decision. There was a profound silence for the space of five minutes, I began to feel a little frightened and just as I was about to express my fears, I heard the grave voice of the Dr. declare General Young's 'pneumonia,' to be [a] 'crick in the neck.' Well, Mrs. Young I wanted to laugh heartily, but I dared not, for strange as it may seem I am rather inclined to be afraid of the General. However, it [is] a good thing for he can manage me completely, so I went into the parlor and sympathized with him until he left."

Although General Young was much in love with Mattie, he was jealous and afraid that she did not love him. Consequently he frequently asked in his letters for reassurance. On December 21, Mattie wrote: "You are a strange person—'Do you love me Mattie?' Love you! You know I do, better far than my own salvation." She frequently repeated how much she loved him and hoped that she was worthy of his love. "I do not care but for two things in the world—and they are your love and approbation my darling, and I am happiest when you tell me you are satisfied with me. For the first time in my life I have an object. To be worthy of you, and with God's help I mean that you shall be proud of me some day."

Mattie Ould was much younger than Pierce; she was lively, exuberant, and popular. She was not self-effacing—she had no secrets and frankly told or wrote about everything that happened. Her naiveté led to behavior that often upset the Southern gentleman of Georgia, who had definite ideas about the decorum of young ladies. Pierce tried to set up rules for her to follow. She had to get her picture from a former suitor. She had to retire at eight o'clock each evening when he was not with her—this her friends could not understand. She gave up opera, plays, and parties unless he was her escort. She wrote, "I almost believe it is a sin for me to love you as I do, for it is better than anything or anybody in the world, and I am never perfectly happy unless I am very close to you." She explained that a cousin thought she was "the most lovesick creature she ever saw." She begged Pierce to take care of himself, "for if anything should happen to you, you know what would be my case—I should die, I know, for you are all that makes this world anything to me." Pierce gave his sweetheart gifts, sometimes mailing them and sometimes presenting them in person when he visited her. It pleased him when she squealed with delight on seeing what he had brought her. On January 18, 1872, Pierce wrote his mother upon his return to Washington from a visit home that he had stopped for a day in Richmond with Mattie. "She looks remarkably well and sends much love to you." He asked Mrs. Young to write Mattie.

As much as he loved her, Pierce at times became exasperated with what he considered Mattie's fickleness, as when she talked or looked around in church. So Mattie wrote in February of attending preaching services at Monumental Church to hear Dr. Woodbridge and she remembered "almost all of it and I did not look around the church more than twice, so you see I am thinking of you everywhere. . . . Grandmamma says I am a perfect study to her that she never expected to see me so utterly subjugated and dependent on you for happiness." The gay and fun-loving Mattie was known among her friends as a wit. Quick and sparkling in repartee she teased her friends constantly, and in turn she was teased. Because of her efforts to follow Pierce's rigid discipline, and her refusal to have any other dates, her friends teased her about General Young and her moving to Georgia to become the mistress of a plantation. After one of his visits, when a friend chided Mattie about seeing her head resting on Pierce's shoulder, she quickly retorted, "It was just an Ould head upon a Young shoulder."

In March Pierce confided to his mother that he loved Mattie very much, but was undecided what he should do. Mrs. Young wrote to him, "We will be glad to see you married or not married. We will try and do the best we can for you. From your letter I believe it is hard for you to make up your mind as to matrimony. Suit yourself. . . . Let us know of any arrangement you want made at home." Pierce asked Mattie to marry him, and she accepted. She wrote him about their engagement: "I will say that I would give my life to be able to say how much I honored and loved the gentleman who asked me to be his wife, for I do indeed with my whole heart. . . ." Throughout 1872 Pierce kept up his courtship, by letters and by visits, but no definite marriage date was set. Mattie wanted to wait a year after her father's re-marriage, and until her grandmother's health improved. She confessed that she was jealous of Pierce's devotion to his congressional duties and wrote him that she considered Congress one of her "most formidable rivals, for it certainly leads you into temptation or rather surrounds you with them."

General Young continued to lavish Mattie with beautiful and expensive gifts—he even gave her a horse and carriage—and visited Richmond at every opportunity. On a visit to her in July, Pierce found that a mutual gentleman friend was sick at his boarding house, and he planned to stop in and visit him when he and Mattie went promenading. However, the two had so much to talk about that Pierce was unable to make the visit before he had to leave for Washington. He was amazed and shocked when Mattie in her next letter wrote that she had visited the sick friend herself—had gone to the gentleman's room unaccompanied, unchaperoned. Such violation of decorum was unheard of—a young lady did not act with such impropriety. Pierce had considered Mattie on a pedestal, above any reproach, and she had committed an unpardonable breach of proper womanly behavior. He became so enraged that he wrote her a letter denouncing her action as a disgrace, and breaking the engagement. Immediately Mattie wrote him, "Please come to my house if only for a few minutes. I *must see you*—I ask this as a great favor. I did not mean to displease you and I am distressed to death." She was broken-hearted over the angry action of her handsome fiancé. She wrote him later that her friends wanted to know if everything was off between them.

Pierce's rigid standards for the girl he loved can be explained by his general attitude about how a gentleman should regard womanhood. A woman was to be loved, admired, defended, protected, and treated as a fragile and delicate flower. The reasons for his later actions may be explained in some degree by the close relationship between him and his mother—he was mamma's son; and although she told him that she approved of Mattie and his marriage to her, Pierce was afraid of marriage; he enjoyed celibacy too much to give it up although for the first time he was really in love. He never forgave Mattie for what he considered her indiscretion and the breach was never healed. Many of the presents he gave her are among the family mementos at Walnut Plantation. In 1876 she married Oliver J. Schoolcraft, an editor, at Salem, Virginia. She died of childbirth within a year. Pierce always loved her, and kept her pictures and all the clippings about her. Yet years later he was to deny that he had ever loved Mattie Ould.

IX

❖❖❖
❖

The Democratic Standard Bearer

THE YEAR 1872 saw the political pot boiling with fury in Georgia. In addition to local elections, there were elections for governor, congressmen, and president. To the Democrats it meant the final triumph over the Republicans and scalawags who had been in power since the war. Young men's Democratic clubs were organized throughout the state and held meetings at which leading Democrats were invited to speak. The county and district Democratic committees met and nominated county officers. Georgians were more interested in the election of their county and state officials than in the election of national officials. The majority of voters were determined to restore the Empire State of the South to its honored place of prewar days.

General Young continued to take advantage of his franking privilege to communicate with his constituents. He hoped to be returned to office without serious opposition. His interest was more than mere vote getting, for he believed that Georgians should experiment with diversification of crops, and he continued to send out government seeds. However, the weather in the early months of 1872 was unusually bad, and it was not a crop year.

By the middle of March, Pierce began to hear the first rumors that he would have opposition in the next election. On March 21, he wrote Henry Grady that he could not return to Georgia until June, "and as I hear several aspirants are beginning to make combinations against me for renomination, I write asking you to take charge of my interest in your section—as I know the weight of your influence I shall rest easy in knowledge that you are looking out for me, and interesting yourself in my behalf." He explained that he was "no intriguing politician, and I hope I shall never become a political trickster. I have found in my life that an honest, bold, and fearless course is the best policy; it goes farther and lasts longer than chicanery and dissimulation." Then Pierce stated that he supposed there would be a convention in August, "in which I hope you will give me your support. I hope I can say, without egotism that I am beginning to be of some use to my constituents. It requires some time to become acquainted with the way and running of the 'powers that be,' and to learn the rules and usages of this body; I trust I have not labored in vain, and that ere long the oppressed people will be restored to their rights under the constitution and to those liberties of which they have been so long outrageously deprived. After a long and cheerless night the day begins to dawn and with the cause of the righteous, with a firm purpose, and hearts true, we may confidently hope for the next contest for the presidency that our flag of Democracy will be unfurled over a field of glorious victory." General Young's friends rallied to his support.

With assurances from friends throughout the district, Pierce remained in Washington trying to look after the interests of his constituents. He wrote on May 2 to Alexander H. Stephens, asking his view on a bill to refund the cotton tax and expressing the opinion that it was not a good bill, for it would not correct the wrong imposed by the government upon the cotton producers. "I should be greatly obliged if you would draft such a bill as you think would be acceptable to the class of persons who have been robbed of so many millions of dollars." He had high respect for Stephens and his ability.

Stephens replied that he did not like the details of the bill and that it was not the type of bill that he would like to see passed. But he stated that he would vote for it "as it stands rather than run the hazard of getting nothing by insisting upon one that would come nearer my views as to what it ought to be. In view of the fact that this has been drawn up after a great [deal] of consultation I think it would be useless to offer a substitute. . . . If it passes an amendatory act will stand more chances of being carried than an amendment to it at this time. If it is lost then the whole subject will still be open for further exertions to get [it ad]justed." Then Stephens turned to public affairs, and expressed his gratification at Pierce's vote upon the question of the fraudulent amendments to the Constitution. "That vote will stand in honor to your memory long after the time serving 'tricksters' of this day will be consigned either to oblivion or infamy." He went on to warn that the tricksters had not "played out. Their purpose was not only to get the Democracy to drive the nails in their political coffins by sanctioning the next unscrupulous usurpations by which these amendments have been attempted to be incorporated in the fundamental law but by art, deceit, craft, and treachery to transfer the whole Democratic party to Radical policy and Radical men." He concluded with the hope that there "will be nerve enough, patriotism enough, and statesmanship enough among the Democrats in congress to stand to their colors and principles in this crisis. If they do and will enter in the canvass with the right spirit and conduct it as it ought to be conducted a most signal and glorious victory will be achieved by them."

When Congress adjourned, before leaving for home Pierce wrote a friend that he felt certain that nothing would be done to relieve the country of the distress with which it was burdened, because Congress had not made the necessary appropriation. He explained that he had heard about a few sharp politicians in the district forming a "ring" or combination to farm out different offices as gifts to their friends. "Cooperations have already begun against me, I am told and misrepresenting me to the people to push me out of place, before I can return to my district." He hoped his friends would "deal frankly with me, and if the people are tired of me I am willing to retire, but I am not willing to be duped by a set of unprincipled demagogues."

Back again at Walnut Plantation, Congressman Young busied himself trying to straighten out tangled farm affairs. He found that his father's health had not improved and that his mother was assuming more responsibility in supervising the farm. He did take time out to help organize the Etowah Dragoons, an organization composed of veterans. He was unanimously elected captain and was appointed as one of a committee of four to draft a constitution and by-laws and to select representatives from each district.

On July 13, the Democrats of Bartow County were called by the chairman of the County Democratic Executive Committee to meet at the courthouse. They selected General Young, with nine other fellow countians, as delegates, uninstructed, to the state convention to be held on July 24. Many people thought

that General Young not only would have opposition but also
that he would not win the nomination. An example of public
opinion at the time is shown in a letter that Thomas G. Simms
of East Point, Georgia, wrote to Dr. James F. Hambleton at the
Exchange Hotel in Washington, D. C., July 22, 1872: "I learn
that there will be much and very formidable opposition to our
friend the 'Earl of Etowah' in the approaching convention and
the chances of [his] being nominated very much against him.
It would be a heavy and serious blow to him if he should be
defeated and I predict he will be."[1]

During the remainder of July General Young talked with the
people of the district. On August 8, the *Cartersville Standard
and Express* placed at the top of its masthead the name of General P. M. B. Young as its candidate for congressman of the
Seventh District. Meanwhile, the Democratic Executive Committee of the district met at Kingston to make arrangements for
the congressional election. A number of names were mentioned
for the nomination, which was to be made later. The editor
of the *Standard and Express* reported that Daniel S. Printup
had already "taken time by the forelock and publicly announced
himself as an independent candidate. Dunlap Scott appears also
in the Rome paper for the same office. . . . We are authorized
by many of the friends of General Young to state that he also
is in the field, and will contest his position as the present
representative against all comers. They can see no good reason
why he should give place to anyone else, having already discharged all of the duties of his party, the good of the state,
and with distinguished honor to himself, acquiring for himself
the undoubted character of being the ablest Representative in
Congress from the state of Georgia. Energetic and watchful of
the people's interest and personally influential, he carries with him
power in Congress which anyone else could hardly attain. General Young is before the people, and attending to his political
interest. On Tuesday last we understand that he made a telling,
eloquent speech before the people of Cherokee, reflecting great
honor upon himself as a public speaker, and winning the admiration of all the large crowds who heard him. Take care, gentleman aspirants! You have no easy task before you when you seek
a place of honor and preferment now held by the gallant Young
who led his fellow Confederates on a hundred bloody battle fields,
and who, having discharged his duties in Congress to the satisfaction of all, is still acceptable to the people of the District."

On August 17, the Bartow County Democrats met at the court-house to select delegates to represent the county in the congressional convention in Cartersville on September 5. The delegates were instructed to vote for General Young for Congress. Before adjournment, Pierce addressed the delegates, thanking them for the honor conferred on him and urging them to keep party unity and harmony.[2]

Opposition arose in Cobb County. On September 5, several citizens petitioned in the paper that the voters write in to select their ablest and best man to represent them in Congress, one "who may be admired for his commanding talents, respected for his virtues, and in all emergencies and in every crisis worthy to be relied on for his wisdom for unswerving integrity."

Although General Young and his friends used strategy and managed to have the congressional convention in Cartersville, they were not able to get him the nomination until the forty-fifth ballot. Dunlap Scott of Rome, J. A. W. Johnson of Dalton, and J. D. Waddell of Marietta were close contenders up to the forty-third ballot, when the last two were withdrawn and George N. Lester of Marietta was proposed. On the forty-fourth ballot Johnson withdrew his name from the ballot and the friends of Pierce were successful in getting him nominated.[3] The vote was Young, $21\frac{1}{2}$; Lester, $12\frac{1}{2}$. Then the nomination was made unanimous.

Henry Grady claimed in the *Rome Daily Commercial* for September 7 that Young possessed all the attributes of a gentleman soldier and would die before betraying the humble trust his people bestowed upon him. "He is our standard bearer and men who love the flag will fall into line, and march sharp up to the music of the charge. The column of the *Commercial* and the pens of its editors are freely offered to the good cause, and we trust that for the next thirty days thousands of honest men will echo back to McConnell, Leland, Whitworth, Head and Wood the battle cry under which they fought so gallantly. 'Two votes for Y-O-U-N-G!' "

A week later the editor of the *Standard and Express* congratulated the Democrats of the Seventh Congressional District "upon the nomination of the gallant soldier and devoted Georgian whose name heads this article." He thought that either of the other gentlemen whose names were brought before the convention would have made a worthy representative in the federal legislature, "but General Young's course on Congress reflects the highest credit upon him. He was one of the most useful and influential members of either house from Georgia. A true Democrat, attending to business and courteous to all, he generally succeeds in carrying through what he undertakes. He is bound to play a conspicuous part in our future policies."

Realizing that the battle for election had just begun, Pierce planned his speaking tours to include each county of the Seventh District. The lack of travel facilities made campaigning hard. Pierce was often fatigued, but he attended rallies, barbecues, and miscellaneous meetings, and spoke whenever the opportunity was given him. His speeches were described generally as forceful, argumentative, and impressive.

In the general election Pierce defeated his Radical opponent, Colonel James F. Dever, by a popular vote of 7,918 to 4,331.[4] From all over the state Pierce received congratulations; he went to Atlanta where he received the plaudits of his friends and discussed with them the success of the Democrats in Georgia. He believed that never again would the Republicans gain control. With other Democrats he regretted that the Democratic candidate for President, Horace Greeley, was defeated, and determined more than ever to fight for the South and the Democratic party in Congress.

When General Young returned to Washington he found his mail full of the usual petitions, requests, applications, and duns from all over the state and the South. From Walnut Plantation reports kept coming from his parents about loss of tenants, sickness of the farm animals, and lack of money to pay debts.

Pierce wrote his sister on January 30, 1873, that he was extremely busy with his public duties. He emphasized that it was difficult to get the floor of the House because every member had his pet measure he wanted to get through.

Throughout this year Pierce together with various leaders, including Atlanta's postmaster, James L. Dunning, tried to hasten the construction of the post office, but the building was not completed until 1874.

In February 1873, the House of Representatives had under consideration the report of a special committee appointed to investigate the alleged Credit Mobilier bribery, the most tremendous legislative scandal in American history. The investigating committee's report accused seven House members of being involved in this scheme to defraud the government of millions of dollars, and recommended expulsion from Congress for two and punitive measures against the others. Pierce spoke opposing the resolution to take action against the accused house members, saying in part, "If they are guilty now, they were guilty five years ago of the acts for which they are arraigned here today, and after the committal of which they have been by their constituents returned to two separate elections as Representatives to this capitol. And we are asked by the committee to expel two of them and punish the others. Is this a common court of justice, to investigate, pry into, and arraign for trial the representatives of the people for acts they may have committed long before they were elected by their constituents to represent them in the Forty-second Congress? Is this a high court sitting here in judgment over the acts of the people? Has it come to this, that you shall dictate to the people whom they shall not elect as their legal representatives?"

Pierce warned his fellow congressmen to be careful, for the House of Representatives was "the House of the people; its members are the creatures of the people . . . from whom it derives all of its power. . . ." He advised his Southern friends not to support the resolution because it might set a precedent for future representatives in expelling "any members for any cause that to them may seem proper."

Dr. Robert Young's health gradually worsened and Mrs. Young wrote Pierce frequently of conditions on the plantation, especially about the unreliable labor and the frequent changes of workers. Except for the cook and yard man, white tenants had been hired—much to Mrs. Young's disgust. Each time Pierce replied he enclosed money to be used on the plantation. Meantime he tried to live as economically as possible at the Willard Hotel. Always mindful of the financial drain upon him Pierce continued to speculate on real estate in Washington. Through Fitch and Fox Real Estate Brokers he purchased several lots, hoping to make money on them. He was still beset with requests from his constituents; finally, in April 1873, he had placed in the *Atlanta Herald* an outline of the steps necessary to take in order to collect claims against the government. He believed that if his constituents would follow the procedure he prescribed, it would save him time.

On April 16, Governor James M. Smith of Georgia invited the governors of the Southern and Western states and delegations from the larger cities in these states to meet in a convention in Atlanta on May 20, to consider the "proper steps to

secure the construction of the great trade artery." He asked
Pierce to attend and serve as chief adviser. Later, on July 19,
Governor Smith authorized Pierce to make "any and all requisi-
tions, either by law, or by the regulations of the Ordinance
Department . . . to enable the state of Georgia to receive the
Ordinance Stores to which she [is] entitled under the acts of
Congress, and to do any and all other such acts in the premises,
as I might by law and regulation do, if I were personally present."

Throughout the summer of 1873, Pierce was at home supervising the plantation. His mother had written that he was needed
at home, for his father was not able "to attend to his business
and no one will take any interest in it for him." He tried to
instruct his nephew George, who was staying with his grandparents, but found that George was not interested in farming.
Early in August Pierce went to Washington to see about his
investments and to try to get his back pay for the years 1869-1870,
when he was not allowed to take his seat in Congress. He returned
home to be faced still with the problems of finances. In October,
Kilbourn and Latta, Real Estate and Net Brokers, wrote Pierce
that the First National Bank of Washington had failed. They
stated that their firm had advanced some $9,000 to meet pay-
ments for the Real Estate Association, of which Kilbourn was a
trustee, and the failure of the bank compelled the trustee to call
upon the parties in interest "to make the necessary advances to
meet these payments." They asked Pierce to remit $2,000 to meet
the obligations. In addition the real estate brokers stated that special taxes "to quite an amount" had to be provided within sixty
days. To meet his obligations Pierce immediately wrote N. G.
Ordway, Sergeant-at-Arms of the House of Representatives, to
pay his monthly check as a member of the House to Edwin L.
Stanton, Receiver of the First National Bank.

General Young found that he did not have a monopoly on
financial difficulties. He received from John B. Gordon on
October 7 an urgent request: "Can't you lend Colquitt and
myself some money? We will give you the acceptance of the
Southern Life Insurance Company [an insurance company
organized by Gordon as president and Colquitt as vice-president with assets of $1,534,483.97], making it safer than any bank.
[We] are willing to pay you for 30 or 60 days loan any reasonable
interest." And upon his return to Washington he discovered that
there was great distress in the large cities because of the money

panic. Although President Grant had said money would be plentiful in sixty days, Pierce did not believe it.

Early in 1874, General Young received a request for assistance from a former Confederate officer, P. G. T. Beauregard of New Orleans, for congressional documents dealing with the improvement of the mouth of the Mississippi River. General Beauregard advised Pierce and his Democratic colleagues not to let the depression make them "rash and impudent—permanent relief cannot be had for the South until 1877 when with a conservative Congress and Executive some of the damages of the last ten years may be repaired and the South delivered forever, I hope, of the accursed carpetbag rule."

The family financial situation did not improve with the next year. The crisis reached a peak on April 16, when Dr. Young wrote that he was mortified by a visit from the sheriff; "he has levied on three of my wood lots; it is advertised for sale on the 1st Tuesday in May. . . . You know I have no possible means to pay the debt; nor to stop the sale; the judgment amounts to near four hundred dollars." He had been compelled to try to borrow money from the bank. General Young mortgaged some of his real estate in Washington to meet the financial obligations at Walnut Plantation and told his father to draw on his account.

In Washington General Young was able to get an appropriation for the United States Engineers to examine the Oostanaula River from Resaca to Carter's Mill. He believed that the major rivers of north Georgia could be developed into waterways for cheap transportation.

Throughout the winter the first rumblings of congressional elections were heard in the Seventh District. Dr. William H. Felton, a preacher, doctor, and farmer of Cartersville, had let it be known that he would run as an independent for Congress. Dr. Felton bitterly opposed the Democratic oligarchy, which he declared was Bullockism in Georgia, and condemned bossism, which he felt had "filled every office in the state for nearly thirty years, except in a few notable instances."[5] Pierce's name was mentioned as early as April 1, as one of the candidates to stop Felton. He opposed the Democratic caucus, believing that it was too easily controlled by political bosses. However, he thought a convention had the same weakness and believed that the people themselves could make as good a selection as any convention could.

The first attack on General Young came from the *Rome Courier,* which accused him of being negligent in caring for his district's affairs and implied that he had been engaged in real estate scandals in the District of Columbia. Immediately Thomas Hauck wrote a letter to the *Atlanta Constitution* in defense of Young's record. He called the attack "a piece of cool impudence" that was "wholly destitute of truth." Then he condemned the paper for its ignorance of Pierce's record in Congress.

On June 24, the *Standard and Express* announced there were many aspirants for Congress in the Seventh District. It argued that since the convention had been so odious in the past a primary election should be held, and there was a need for unity of action and harmony in the ranks of the Democratic party at all levels of government; otherwise the party should disorganize. The editor believed that the Seventh Congressional District was on the eve of the most exciting congressional election since the war. He warned: "Unless there is some wise and honest plan, by which the people may have a voice in choosing a standard bearer— our colors will surely be lost in the struggle and some Republican will take the seat now occupied by the gallant Young."

Meanwhile, the leaders of Rome carefully watched Pierce's efforts in Congress to improve the Oostanaula River. They feared that his chief interest in opening the river was to make it a feeder to Joe Brown's railroad rather than to help the people of Rome. Although political opposition began early, Pierce stayed on in Washington and left to his friends the responsibility for his interest in the district.

General Young's worries and responsibilities were increased on May 2, with the death of his sister-in-law Ginnie, George's widow, for she left two sons and a daughter at Walnut Plantation. Because his parents were too old to care for them, Pierce knew that the children would be mainly his responsibility.

While the country was being rocked by the Credit Mobilier Scandal, the American people became excited, and saw fraud in many activities that they had not formerly considered suspect. Congress enacted on March 3, 1873, in the last days of the session, the famous "Salary Grab" Act, which increased the salaries of the President, Vice-President, Supreme Court Justices, Speaker, Senators, and Representatives; and the law was made retroactive to the Congress just ending. Immediately people throughout the United States vehemently protested. Although the succeeding Congress repealed the obnoxious law so far as it related to senators and representatives, constituents condemned those congressmen who had been active in Washington. Pierce had joined with his fellow congressmen in voting for the law.

Few political figures wholly escaped the bitter vituperation of some constituents. Pierce did not. The real estate scandal of Washington, which created criticism throughout the country, was attacked by the editor of the *Rome Courier,* who took special delight in associating Pierce with the infamous real estate pool. He condemned General Young for having engaged in unethical tactics, and expressed the opinion that either Young was naive for being taken in or he was a willing investor, intimating that the latter was more likely. He further insinuated that Young had duped his constituents and that he had received $50,000 from the pool.

Pierce denied the accusation and declared that he had never had $50,000 in his life. He explained that at some time during the first part of 1871 he called upon William S. Huntington, cashier of the First National Bank of Washington, and requested his advice on how to invest an amount of his salary. He said that he and Huntington had been intimate friends for more than a year and that he had made several transactions by which he had received a good interest for the small amounts that he was able to raise. Huntington advised him to purchase real estate in the northwest part of the city of Washington and agreed to invest Pierce's funds—five thousand dollars. Since Young was very busy in Congress, he did not call for some time on Huntington, who died two months after the agreement. Pierce explained that he did not know where his funds had been invested, having been told only that his money had been invested in real estate in the northwest part of the city.

Later General Young found at the bank that the fund had been turned over to Kilbourn and Latta for investment. "I called upon them and they informed me that they had purchased some real estate for me in the NE part of the city, and would at some convenient time give me an account of it." General Young repeated that he did not have any knowledge of the investment deal until 1874 when he saw an article in one of the New York papers announcing the "District Real Estate Ring." He reported that he went to Kilbourn and proposed to sell his interest in real estate which they held in part for him. They paid him the price he had paid for it; they returned without interest the money he originally put in their hands. Pierce declared that "no person

ever attempted in any way to influence my vote in the District
affairs in congress directly or indirectly, and . . . to the best of
my knowledge and belief nearly all if not all of my votes will
be found to be against the appropriations for this District."[6]

Pierce's friends came at once to his support. They asserted that
the accusation was so obscure that "no fair minded man would
say he believed it, for it would require a strained and perverted
construction of language and an illogical deduction from facts."[7]
His friends described him as one who was "constantly, honestly,
faithfully, and zealously watching and advocating the interests of
his defamer and the rest of his constituents, and being honest
himself he did not doubt the honesty of his agents for at that
time he had no reason to do so, and it was no part of his business
to investigate the character of the citizens of Washington good
or bad."[8] Moreover, as to the accusation that he was unpatriotic
in not investing his money in Georgia, General Young's friends
claimed: "This feeble *ad captandum* thrust will fall far short
of its mark, for the people of Georgia have too much generosity
and intelligence not to accede to every gentleman the time-hon-
ored right to do what he pleases with his own . . . they have sense
enough to know exactly how much or how little the temporary
investment of five thousand whole dollars would benefit the
state."[9]

Pierce's friends denounced the Rome editor for his lack of
sagacity and his prostitution of the truth—"his base purpose
becomes too patent and he publishes himself as being guilty of
a degree of moral depravity which far outstrips the grasping
avarice of the salary grabber. . . ."[10] But his friends did not
defend his indiscretion in voting a rise in salary for himself.

General Young publicly denied the charges of his accusers.
He sent to the leading newspapers of the district a statement
that he was not a member of the "Real Estate Pool" and that
the accusation was a malicious falsehood. Later he replied in
more detail to a question put by a writer signing himself "Justice," in the daily *Herald.* "As to the 'Salary Grab,' I supported
with my vote the bill to increase the salary of senators with
one exception; I voted for the increase, because under all the
circumstances which surrounded it I believed it to be my duty.
I am of the opinion now, and I am confident, when the matter
is truthfully represented to my constituents, they will fully and
entirely indorse my course."

Pierce concluded that the people knew him to be "no half

and half Democrat; not one who runs with the hare and hunts with the hounds! I do not belong to any 'ring' in Washington or in Georgia. I never sought to lobby for Bullock, Blodgett or Kimball, nor for any of their enterprises. That I have made mistakes, I frankly admit, yet I have never deserted my colors. The object of the attack made upon me . . . is to break me down, not for what I have done, but to advance the interest of others. I will only add that if the people desire a change, any good Democrat, fairly nominated, shall have my free, full and hearty support."[11]

Under such a cloud of charges and counter-charges, the meeting of the Democratic Executive Committee of the Seventh Congressional District was held at Cartersville on July 15. A credentials committee of three was appointed, and each county was allowed two delegates for each representative in the general assembly. Calhoun was selected as the town for the convention, to be held on the first Wednesday in September. In addition the committee asked that each of the aspirants for Congress attend the meeting for the purpose of electioneering for his nomination.

On August 5, a call was issued by the editor of the *Cartersville Standard and Express* for all the Bartow County Democrats to meet at the courthouse on August 15, to elect delegates to the congressional convention. The independent candidate Felton was excluded from the convention. The chairman, A. P. Wofford, called the meeting to order and stated that the object of the meeting was to select delegates to attend and represent the county at the congressional convention at Calhoun on September 2. After organizing, the delegates then proceeded to ballot for a candidate. It being apparent that the sense of the meeting was decidedly in favor of General Young, John W. Wofford moved to declare him elected by acclamation. The motion was unanimously adopted and General Young immediately nominated delegates to the convention.

The chairman appointed a committee to select three suitable persons to constitute the executive committee for Bartow County. Before the convention adjourned, it passed a resolution that a primary election for the county officers be held at each militia precinct on the second Saturday in November. This was initiated by Pierce, who several months before had expressed a distrust of the convention.

On September 2, the district convention was held at the courthouse at Calhoun. Five counties nominated their favorite sons on the first ballot. Pierce was nominated from Bartow County, James R. Bowen from Cherokee, D. S. Printup and Nathan Bass from Floyd, and J. D. Waddell from Cobb. Each was warmly supported by his friends. The reporter for the *Standard and Express* explained that Bartow County was "strongly and enthusiastically in favor of the nomination of General Young, not only in consequence of our pride in him as a county man but more especially because we are satisfied that he is the most popular man in the District, has already achieved reputation which has made him historic, and is admittedly one of the most influential members of congress from the whole South." However, Floyd County demanded a less controversial person and advocated a compromise candidate acceptable to all. Fulton County had been lost to the Seventh District when Georgia was redistricted on July 20, 1872, and the county was transferred to the Fifth Congressional District. The transfer cost Pierce his chief support.

The political situation in the Seventh District demanded that the Democrats secure to oppose Dr. Felton the best available candidate, one who would not be vulnerable to any scandal. On the seventeenth ballot L. N. Trammell of Dalton was selected to face Dr. Felton. Pierce congratulated Trammell and promised him his full support. He appealed to the delegates to fight for Democratic unity against the rising independent insurgents. The Democratic delegates returned home determined to win the election. The conduct of the convention was described as fair and honest, with no cause for criticism. The *Rome Courier* in reporting the convention called attention to Young's magnanimity in withdrawing his name after the third ballot, since he knew that a number of delegates were stoutly opposed to his nomination. Realizing that divided into factions the Democratic party could not win, he wanted the nomination only if it was unanimous. More than anything, Pierce wanted the Democrats to win; therefore he was willing to step aside for someone who could lead the party.

Immediately after the convention Dr. Felton attacked the method by which Trammell had been elected, and went on to attack his entire political record. Although the Democratic nominee retaliated with firmness and fervor, Dr. Felton forced Trammell to admit in a debate that he had received $9,500 from the manager of the Western and Atlanta Railroad. Trammell wrote at once to the Democratic Executive Committee offering to resign for the good of the party. The committee then proposed to Dr. Felton that both men retire as candidates and let the party settle the contest. When Dr. Felton refused, the executive committee called Colonel Trammell and told him they had decided that he had to continue in the campaign. But Trammell insisted on withdrawing, the while branding Felton's accusation as falsehood.

At once the *Rome Courier* began to advocate General Young as the man for the crisis, the editor saying that he believed Young to be a man who had been faithful to his trusts, whose record as a "brilliant soldier, a good citizen and a faithful representative of the people in congress, will bear the test of the most rigid and exacting scrutiny." He sketched the life of Pierce as a soldier and described how his bravery, gallantry, and noble bearing had won for him the admiration of his own people in the South as well as the esteem of those who were his enemies in war. He emphasized that in Congress Young had been made a member of the Military Committee of the Lower House of Congress and a member of the Board of Visitors to West Point, positions conferred upon no other Southern man since the War. "These distinctions alone," said the editor, "indicate the high esteem in which he is held by those he fought so bravely, and to whom he has not yet made a single concession of principle or of devotion to the South, in regard to which there is not the shadow of a doubt resting upon the mind of a single Southern man. His is a character that reflects the true chivalry of the South and illustrates our beloved old State as it was in the earlier period of our history."

The editor reminded the people that it was as a civilian that General Young should be remembered. He had been elected three times to Congress; he had given his attention especially to the material interests of the Cherokee section of Georgia, seeking and urging most persistently every measure in Congress that would, in any manner, promote the material development of the country. It was because of his untiring efforts in Congress that the improvements upon the rivers were begun.

He reminded the voters of the district that one of the grandest objects for their immediate section was the establishment of an arsenal in Rome, "a measure of which he is the especial champion and for which he has already secured the most favorable consideration. General Young's influence as a military man and his prominence as a member of the Military Committee, together with his influence at the War Department on account of his great popularity as a West Point man, all combine to invest him with an influence that but few other men can bring to bear in favor of the establishment of the arsenal here in close proximity to the best iron for ordnance purposes there is in the world." The editor warned the people that such a plant would cost $350,000, but reassured them by prophesying that it would bring into the district money from four to five hundred employees. "For these reasons alone, the people of this section should feel an intense interest in returning General Young to Congress that he may complete, if possible, the great work he has inaugurated, and upon the success of which, in part, hangs the destiny of this city and of this section of the country."

In concluding his article the editor advised the people that it was always best to retain faithful public servants, "especially when experience in the process of legislation at the Federal Capitol is so important to the success of great and momentous enterprises involving so much of the material prosperity of this country. There are other good men in this District," admitted the *Courier,* "but it would require at least two years for a new member in Congress to make his influence felt for his constituents. General Young is known and appreciated there, and his return to Congress would be . . . a strong endorsement by his people of his efforts to advance their material interest. . . . The failure to reelect him would be taken as an indication that the services he has rendered in the great work under discussion are not appreciated by us because they are not worthy of our attention and support."

The *Courier* ended with an appeal to all voters—soldiers, farmers, veterans—to send delegates to Rome with instructions to nominate the faithful representative for reelection "whose record as a soldier, and as a member of Congress has demonstrated that he is one of you—fought with you and has served you faithfully—one who was foremost in the conflict for your liberties and has stood by your rights in the halls of Congress and defended your honor after you had been beaten and your enemies sought to oppress you."[12]

The committee called for another congressional convention to meet at Rome on October 19 to nominate a new candidate. All of the counties of the district, except Dade and Cherokee, sent representatives. Although the delegates tried to pressure General Young to accept, he declined, and refused to allow his name to be used. Colonel William H. Dabney of Floyd County was nominated by acclamation.[13]

The editor of the *Rome Courier,* in reporting on the convention, entitled his report "General Young's Magnanimity." He described Pierce's conduct at the convention as deserving "especial mention and praise for the promptness with which he peremptorily refused to allow his name to be balloted for, though his action was a source of much regret upon the part of his friends, who were confident of his nomination, which would have doubtless been secured on the second or third ballot, if not on the first." He explained that General Young was aware of this fact but also realized that a number of delegates were opposed to his nomination. Pierce did not desire the nomination unless it came cordially and without opposition. He was not willing, in such a crisis of the party's interests, that his name should, in any manner, produce a scramble. "He wanted the nomination to be unanimous and to go out with all the strength that unanimity could give it that the organized Democracy should be maintained in its integrity, and succeed to signal triumph."

General Young's friends had canvassed his chances with great care, and "they knew that his nomination could be effected, and they believed, that he would be the strongest man before the people if nominated." At this moment, Pierce, if he had said the word, could have been nominated again for Congress; but "he magnanimously telegraphed to his friends 'not to ballot for me, but go for Dabney.' This he did that there might be no cause of the slightest want of harmony in the nomination." The result was that Young's friends threw their support to Colonel Dabney "as a compromise upon whom all conflicting preferences might unite, thus giving to Colonel Dabney, through the advice of General Young, a splendid send off for Congress."

The editor concluded that the "Democracy of this District could not fail to recognize and appreciate this manifestation of self-abnegation and magnanimity of General Young, and it should never be forgotten. And what makes this episode in our political troubles more agreeable and pleasant is, that on the previous day, Colonel Dabney said to a few friends that he did not desire the nomination, but that he thought that General Young was the proper man to be nominated."[14]

The political battle in the Seventh District grew hotter, and Pierce joined with his friends John B. Gordon, Governor J. M. Smith, and Tom Hardeman to stump the district for the new candidate. These men planned their strategy to defeat the fighting doctor-preacher. They visited every town and county speaking against Dr. Felton, who was like nothing seen in Georgia politics before. "He held religious services on Sunday, and spoke politics on week days, and played perilous work generally with personal antecedents."[15] Despite the effort of the Democratic leaders Felton defeated Dabney by over a 200-vote majority.

Although General Young was not seeking reelection and would retire from Congress on March 4, he continued to work for his constituents. People throughout the South still wrote letters to him requesting assistance. He was able to get an additional appropriation to remove obstructions from the Oostanaula and Conasauga rivers, for which he received a note of thanks from the city council of Rome. What many people thought of him was best expressed by the editor of the *Cartersville Express*: "Suffice it to say that thus to be sustained, honored, and loved by the whole people of his native county, by the old and young, is to one of generous mood like himself, of far more value than gems or gold or rubies, and bespeaks for him every admiration, even in the hearts of strangers. In the mouth of every one, 'We have never seen the like before,' and to close this narrative of this remarkable affair we have only to say, that whatever others friends or foes, may have to think or say of him, P. M. B. Young as a soldier or civilian, friend and citizen, stands first in the regards and affections of the good people of Bartow County."

Pierce did not neglect the interests of his party. He wrote his father on January 11 that Congress had opened with a lively discussion on the Louisiana question, and that he wished for Democratic success. Meanwhile he considered applying for Clerk of the House so that he could stay on in Washington. A very close friend, J. Lindsay Johnson of Rome, wrote on February 11, offering his services, saying that "for you either there or here I am at your service." More optimistic friends wrote asking for jobs under him as clerk. He returned to Cartersville on March 12.

Nevertheless Pierce's enemies were not content until they had the last say. The Washington correspondent of the Augusta *Constitutionalist* wrote on March 6, 1875, "The poor congressmen! I am so sorry for some of them. . . . Poor Young! I am very sorry for him for I believe he really would like to stay in Washington, or to come back next winter. It is rumored that he intends to be a candidate for the clerkship of the next House, nobly resolving, if he cannot serve his country as a congressman at the rate of $5,000 a year, to devote himself to her in a clerkship.

"And then, besides, isn't it better to be in Washington as a clerk than not to be in Washington at all; and moreover, it is a little hard for a man—and such a young man, too—when he has been drawing his thousands yearly from the public treasury to be cut off before he has drawn more than forty or fifty thousand dollars.

"But, alas! Pierce M. B. Young—Pierce M. B. no longer will be a sometime gay and sparking Brigadier, with an immaculate shirt front and a flowing necktie, with well greased, slick and shining hair, a dark and a rolling eye, and a huge mustache—'take the shadow of a great sorrow'—loll with the delicious abandon in a congressional easy chair, and ogle congressional female galleries; no more, ah! Never more—but, why pursue the mournful theme—why longer muse in melancholy mood upon the cimmerian gloom of the future of the last name on the roll call of the Forty-third congress?

"Wear tearful eyes and tremulous lips, let us bid an eternal farewell to the sad-eyed congressman as he reluctantly steps down and out, bids a long farewell to all his greatness, and goes to join the innumerable caravan of back-pay grabbers and petticoat congressmen which throng the dusky road to political oblivion."[16]

Pierce did not answer the criticism.

X

❖❖
❖

The Price of Politics

GENERAL YOUNG went home to resume supervision of
the plantation. He saw that the crops were planted and
repairs made on the fences and barns. But it was not long before
he grew restless. His mother wrote Louisa in late April that
Pierce was "going it all the time seeing to the work. You know
that he cannot be still and think; farming is too slow a business
for him."

While still a member of Congress, Pierce had received passes
for railroad travel from Thomas A. Scott, president of the Pennsylvania Railroad Company. Early in May he left for Washington
to inspect his business interests; after seeing to them, he traveled
to New York to visit friends and to buy various articles for the
house. While there he was guest of honor at a dinner given by
a leading New York merchant, and was asked to speak. After
a few remarks of thanks, Pierce emphasized how important it
was for the national government to remain armed and at the
same time to seek peace. "Let us frown down sectionalism and
all marplots who would keep alive the fires of discord. I hold
it to be the duty of all good men, North and South, East and
West, to labor for the glory and prosperity of our common
country."[1]

In New York General Young contracted to be agent in the
South for an engineer who had been with him at West Point.
Upon returning to Georgia, however, Pierce was unable to bid
successfully upon any engineering work. Undaunted, the ex-
congressman sought other work in order to improve his finances.
Throughout the summer and fall he traveled, using his railroad

pass, seeking employment, and all the while, he went deeper in debt. In the winter he wrote to Louisa that he was greatly troubled by his and Dr. Young's financial condition. "I have been very run for funds to pay the small debts about home. George's children are becoming expensive and money was never so scarce I think." Unwilling to explain to his parents the details of the financial crisis throughout the country, Pierce became deeper involved in financial embarrassment. When Mrs. Young wanted wool and carpet for the house, instead of telling her that he lacked the money, he bought the material, giving a draft on an Atlanta bank. A week later he received a letter from the proprietors of the mill demanding immediate payment. For assistance he turned to his friend Edwin L. Lawton, Receiver of the First National Bank of Washington. Lawton gave Pierce sufficient support by allowing him to draw a draft, provided he would make it good within two weeks.

His father's illness throughout the winter of 1875 added to Pierce's financial burdens. Early in March his name was mentioned along with others in several articles in the *New York Sun* concerning the investigation of the "Real Estate Pool" in Washington. Deeply concerned, Pierce wrote at once to I. W. Glover, a friend in Washington, asking if there was a possibility that he would be called to testify. On April 12, Glover replied that if the committee deemed it necessary to have his own testimony, it would promptly subpoena the General; however, he added, "I do not anticipate such a necessity. Kilbourn can give all the necessary information if he will."

Knowing that his enemies would publish the accusations of the New York papers and that his friends would need to know the truth, Pierce wrote an article for the hometown paper, the *Cartersville Express,* in which he reiterated his explanation of 1874. On April 15, editor B. F. Sawyer of the *Rome Courier* attacked and ridiculed General Young's statement, charging that the only reason Pierce withdrew from the real estate venture was that he feared a scandal. "He announces that he is ready to vindicate his record whenever it becomes necessary, and expresses the belief that Kilbourn's testimony will exonerate him from all blame attempted to be attached to his conduct." The editor pointed out that in two respects General Young's report looked "a little shady," viz., the carelessness with which the General handled his money "and the length of time, over two years, it required him to find out the character of his confederates." He also thought that General Young's patriotism, if not his integrity, was in question because he had invested his surplus money among thieves while his downtrodden country so badly needed it to recuperate. Sawyer emphasized that Pierce was a Georgian, honored, trusted, and exalted by his neighbors. All he had in the way of official preferment he owed to them, and a pure patriotism would have suggested that out of the abundance of his salary he should remember his people, who were appealing to strangers for capital to reconstruct their waste places, rather than invest it abroad among those who would be glad to see the South sunk in hopeless ruin. The editor concluded: "It looks as if he cared no more for the people who made him what he was than the butcher cares for the dumb cattle he drives to the shambles. But, however, we suppose the money he let the thief, Kilbourn, have was a part of his ill-gotten salary grab, and as he incurred so much infamy in getting it, he ought to have the right to put it where it will do the most good surely."

As soon as the *Courier* published its diatribe, Young's close friend, G. H. C. Willingham, editor of the *Cartersville Express,* came to the General's defense and asserted that the charges were "ill advised and unjust" and that his previous statement "of a simple array of facts" clearly vindicated him from the charges that he was an operator or partner in the real estate scandal in Washington under "Boss Shepherd." Then Editor Willingham concluded: "Now let the *Courier* howl at Gordon, Norwood and other Democrats."[2]

Such a defense, far from assuaging the Rome editor, added more fuel to his efforts to defame General Young, for in his next edition he pointed out one by one and emphasized the weaknesses in the defense article. Sawyer took delight in trying to prove that Kilbourn was the ringmaster of the pool and that Pierce was a joint partner with him in the purchase of a piece of real estate. The editor explained that the object of the investigation in Washington in 1876 was to connect President Grant with the ring and if his connection was "established as clearly as General Young's own 'simple array of facts' establishes him, we may expect every Democratic paper in the land to open on him in torrents of patriotic and virtuous indignation." Sawyer explained that it was not his purpose to detract from General Young's good name, for "We have too much state and southern pride for that." He stressed that he would be glad to place the name of General Young "high above the possibility of reproach; and if it is tarnished by the slime of the infamous Washington Real Estate Pool, he has no one but himself to blame for it." He referred to the salary grab because it was "ill-gotten, ill-starred and carried with itself a curse." If Pierce had not obtained the money, he would not have had the opportunity to speculate and forget "his high southern birth and position and consorted with thieves."

Mrs. Young worried about her son's reaction to Sawyer's attempts to embarrass him. She told her daughter of her anxiety, and Louisa immediately wrote Pierce advising him "to keep cool" and not let the Rome editor "get under his skin." Throughout the year the *Courier* continued to vilify the former congressman, who, although chagrined, refused after his first statement to reply to the allegations. He was grateful to his friends throughout the state for their defense of his reputation. In the face of Sawyer's continued charges the Democratic leaders of the Seventh District elected Pierce as a delegate to the National Democratic Convention at St. Louis, Missouri, on June 27. Pierce realized that his election was the result of the support of his friends, such as Governor James M. Smith, R. E. Lester, and J. W. Wofford. At the convention he was active in the successful fight for nomination of Samuel J. Tilden, whom he had met the summer before in New York and had learned to admire. After the convention, he returned to Georgia enthusiastic over the prospect of a Democratic success in November.

General Young felt that one of the best ways he could help in the campaign was through "The Volunteers," a military organization of young men and veterans of the Civil War. He had helped to organize the Etowah Dragoons in 1872 and had been elected captain. When at home he took an active part in the organization. The general assembly of Georgia passed a resolution on February 25 authorizing Governor Smith to appoint a board of officers to study the volunteer military organization of the state and make a recommendation. The following day Governor Smith appointed General Young, along with eight other Georgians, to the board. Young worked untiringly with the members and at the same time spoke at every opportunity for the Democratic party and its nominees.

Using his railroad pass Young went to Washington to talk with the Georgia Representatives and leaders. Later he went to New York and Saratoga Springs, where he met many friends, among them Governor Tilden's sister and several of his relatives. On his way back to Washington Pierce went by way of Albany, for a conference with Governor Tilden. He agreed to go on a speaking tour for Tilden in Vermont, and spent the last week of August traveling through that state speaking for the Democratic candidate. He wrote his father on September 1 that "We have no hope of carrying it [Vermont] but we want to reduce the [Republican] majority."

At home once more, Pierce devoted every spare minute to Tilden's campaign. So sure was he of Democratic success that he wagered some of his real estate in Washington to Alex R. Shepherd that New York would not give the Republican ticket a majority of ten thousand in the election. When the Democrats won by an overwhelming majority in the Georgia elections in October, General Young thought the victory was an excellent indicator for the November election. Part of his enthusiasm resulted from the fact that he had worked closely with the Democratic leaders of Georgia. He participated in the nominating convention in Atlanta on August 2, and he knew that his friend Alfred H. Colquitt had refused to allow his name to be used as a nominee for Congress and the Senate despite the solicitation of Democratic leaders. Pierce knew the respect that Georgia leaders had for Colquitt and also something of the affection that many people of the state had for him. Therefore he united with the other Georgia delegates in successfully getting Colquitt elected president of the State Democratic Convention.

When the question was raised in the fall and spring of 1875-1876 as to whether Governor James M. Smith would run again, Pierce along with other Georgians began to encourage the consideration of General Alfred H. Colquitt, the "hero of Olustee." Ex-Governor H. V. Johnson, Banker John H. James, and ex-Confederate officer Thomas Hardeman, Jr., were ambitious political leaders who also sought the gubernatorial honor, encouraged by personal ambition and the flattery of friends throughout the state.

It is difficult to evaluate the extent of Pierce's encouragement and aid in the effort to have Colquitt elected governor by the Democratic leaders; but throughout August, he worked indefatigably with friends at the Colquitt headquarters in the Kimball House. When Colquitt was nominated and made a stirring speech Pierce knew that he had supported the right man for governor. Later the overwhelming popular vote for Colquitt (111,297 to 33,443) over the Republican candidate Jonathan Norcross confirmed his belief.

In November Georgia more than doubled its Democratic majority for the Democratic candidates Samuel J. Tilden and Thomas Hendrick, and the first returns throughout the country augured national Democratic success. However, there was a delay in determining the final result, for there were disputed votes in the election in South Carolina, Louisiana, and Florida, and of one elector for Oregon. Great excitement prevailed. Returning boards were appointed in these four states to pass on the disputed returns. As soon as General Young heard that the special board for Florida was meeting in Tallahassee to count the Florida votes, he went with Joe Brown, Henry W. Grady, and others and worked hard to prevent the fraudulent nullification of the Florida votes. Pierce earnestly felt that Tilden's election was certain and that he had to be inaugurated to relieve the South and save the Democratic party. As soon as the Florida board adjourned, General Young, disgusted, went to Washington with the hope that he could exert some pressure upon his friends in Congress to insure the legal election of the Democratic presidential candidate. Discouraged, he returned to Atlanta to attend the inauguration of Colquitt and the inaugural ball at the Harkham House.

All was not going well at Walnut Plantation. General Young tried to get his nephew Lamar to assist his father but soon found that such a plan would not work. Lamar was too young and restless and did not want to be tied down to the plantation. Somewhat disheartened and almost sick, Pierce wrote his sister in February that he "had to do everything . . . in the way of business . . . without aid, so it keeps me going . . . and worried no little, unless I can sell some land I shall be embarrassed very soon by Father's indebtedness." He also worried about his brother-in-law, Dr. Jones, who was ill and seemed to be frittering away his education "upon the rabble that swam around that little town."

Louisa Jones seldom complained of her husband's poor health and of her hardships. Although burdened with the responsibility of a growing family, she followed her brother's career with pride. When the *Atlanta Constitution* in February 1877 carried a diatribe against him, Louisa wrote her mother: "The hounds are after Pierce again. I allude to the testimony of ex-Congressman Eldridge. I had hoped that the matter had all been settled and left Pierce's name fair, but since Eldridge swears that Pierce and himself were members of the ring, what will the world say of Pierce? I wish he had never been a congressman rather than his honor and veracity should be doubted." Then Louisa for the first time expressed contempt for Pierce's successor, "Old Felton is at the bottom of that thing and still keeps stirring it."

Although until the last moment General Young had hopes that Tilden would be inaugurated, Rutherford B. Hayes took the oath, under a cloud of doubt according to many people throughout the United States. Pierce commented to his mother on March 10, "Well, the farce is over and Hayes is in." Disheartened and somewhat baffled by the rascality he penned bitter letters of disappointment to his friends. One Northern friend replied that not only Southerners but also Northerners could sympathize, "for Tilden had some mighty strong advocates in the North."

A few weeks later while in New York Pierce wrote his mother that he had visited Governor Tilden, and he had found him broken very much since he last saw him. "I think it will kill him yet. Too much ambition is a bad thing."

Returning home, Pierce learned that L. N. Trammell, who had professed friendship and support, had been among persons instrumental in keeping the real estate scandal before the public. Trammell had urged the editor of the Dalton paper to republish the article from the *Rome Courier* abusing Young and accusing him of complicity with the Washington ring. S. Fouche, a friend in Rome, confided in Young that there seemed to be "a pretty good understanding between Felton, Trammell, Underwood, etc.; at least, there are indications of the formation of an alliance ring with these individuals at the hub. . . . They are aspirants of unbounded greed." Pierce now knew why the accusations were being made again; the Felton crowd in an attempt to be reelected would not stop at anything. However, he was unable to understand the actions of Trammell, who had supported him, and in fact had been instrumental in aiding his election to Congress in 1870 and 1872. When Pierce decided not to run again in 1874, he turned to Colonel Trammell of Dalton as the logical Democratic candidate, and even traveled throughout the district to speak for him. However, when the railroad bond scandal was revealed by the Feltons in 1874, Pierce agreed with Trammell that he should step down in favor of Dabney for the good of the Democratic party in the Seventh District. From that time Trammell became embittered and felt aggrieved, claiming that his former friends were disloyal.[3] He accused Pierce and other friends of not supporting him. When Pierce did not deny the charge, Trammell took it for granted that he was guilty and began to look for some way of embarrassing him.

Trammell found support for his plans from the editor of the *Rome Courier* and a few of the more acceptable supporters of his former opponent, Dr. Felton. At Trammell's insistence, Sawyer reprinted every few months in the *Courier* his charges against Pierce in the "salary grab" and the Washington real estate scandal. Although Trammell asked Senator Norwood to check the scandal on Pierce's congressional record, the Senator replied that he knew nothing of such a scandal. Young's "public record . . . contains nothing which renders him vulnerable. At least I have never heard of anything he said or did in congress on which you could assail him. On the contrary you knew that he has been very circumspect in his course in the House," he replied. This information seemed to inflame Trammell, who even joined with the Dalton ring and his political enemy Dr. Felton to defame General Young. In 1876 Trammell threatened to retire from the Georgia political arena when he found that Democratic leaders like Norwood, Gordon, and Joseph E. Brown supported his political Judas.

Young followed with interest the efforts of certain Democratic leaders of Georgia to hold a constitutional convention, and rejoiced with them when the people voted for the convention on the second Tuesday in June. Although he was not a delegate to the convention, held on July 11, many of his close political friends and former army comrades were leaders in it. Pierce intentionally avoided state politics, feeling that his future would be better served in the national government.

Early in August Pierce went on business to Washington. He became ill and had to stay longer than he anticipated. On October 8, his mother wrote him in distress that they had been expecting him for several weeks. "You are sadly needed at home," she told him, explaining that the workers had been taking advantage of Dr. Young, who was so forgetful that he could not be relied upon. Never had the future seemed so dark. Conditions at the Plantation seemed to have reached a new low, and the health of Pierce's parents was failing. There seemed to be no employment for an ex-Congressman. What could be done to decrease the burdens? This was the vexing question he must answer.

XI

◇◇
◇

The Trying Years: 1878 to 1884

AN UNEXPECTED bit of financial luck came to Pierce
Young on November 13, 1878, when William Lambert of
New York sent him a draft of $100 for six weeks' expenses for
checking the presidential election returns in Florida. In his letter
Lambert said that he had political influence and hoped to be appointed as commissioner to the Paris Exposition, if "all good
Democrats" helped him. Pierce, a good Democrat, rejoiced over
the news, and hoped to go to Europe with Lambert, if his parents'
health improved.

On December 15, Congress by joint resolution approved the
United States' participation in the International Industrial Exposition in Paris in 1878 and appointed Richard C. McCormick
as commissioner-general to represent the country there. Under the
supervision of the Secretary of State, William M. Evarts, Mc-
Cormick made the necessary rules and regulations. He was given
full authority to select his assistants, who were to be paid from
the congressional appropriation made for that purpose. Each
additional commissioner was to be paid $1,200.

William G. LeDuc, Commissioner of Agriculture, wrote General Young on December 21 that he was presenting his name to
President Rutherford B. Hayes "as a proper person to represent
the agricultural interest of the South at Paris." Then he added,
"I hope that you may receive the appointment but at this time
nothing can be said to it." Mrs. Young told her son that he must
not let anything stand in the way of his accepting the
appointment.

On February 6, Pierce received the announcement from Commissioner LeDuc formally appointing him as a commissioner to Paris to represent the Southern states. LeDuc also specified his duties—to travel through the South to make collections of products peculiar to the section, to be sent to the Exposition. LeDuc at the same time asked Colonel Barbour, President of the Orange and Alexandria Railroad, to give Pierce a pass to travel over the railroad, since he would not receive any pay for collecting the material.

Soon after General Young received his appointment he was glad to learn that Sam W. Small of Macon, Georgia, was appointed one of the secretaries. The two men immediately began to select samples of Southern agricultural products, with special emphasis on cotton. Pierce secured letters of introduction from friends and traveled throughout the South collecting the exhibits and sending them to the temporary office located in Atlanta. He wrote LeDuc that he had been very successful in collecting samples. Working diligently, General Young and his assistants got the necessary produce ready by the end of March for shipment to the Exposition.

Commissioner LeDuc wrote General Young to use his discretion as to the time of leaving Cartersville for Paris. However, as soon as he could make his plans at home and get his business in order, Pierce left for Washington and then journeyed to New York. He sailed on the *Britannia* for England on April 20, with a small book of addresses and letters of reference which he planned to use. One of the prized letters of introduction was written by Commissioner LeDuc to General Charles F. Stone, Chief of Staff, Egyptian Army, Cairo, Egypt. Another to General Stone was written by General William T. Sherman of the United States Army endorsing General Young as an honorable man and a graduate of the United States Military Academy. Because of the emergency, Pierce was issued a temporary passport by Secretary of State Evarts, which allowed him to travel "without let or molestation" and extended to him all friendly aid and protection "as would be extended to like officers of Foreign Governments reporting to the United States." The temporary passport was to be used until the regular passport arrived. In the same letter the Secretary sent Pierce one half of his salary ($600); the other half was to be paid at the close of the Exposition.

After a few days of sightseeing in London, Pierce went on to Paris, where he took a room a short distance from the Exposition. At noon on May 1, he attended the opening ceremonies at the

Trocadero Palace, with a great assemblage of dignitaries from all parts of Europe. Marshal McMahon, the President of France, declared the Exposition open. He was impressed by the presence of the Prince of Wales, the Crown Prince of Denmark, and other distinguished visitors. General Young enjoyed the brief visit of the dignitaries and cheered with the other Americans as the Marshal inspected and complimented the United States sailors and marines drawn up in line to salute him.

Although Young found his duties arduous, he had time to enjoy the social functions given by the French. Nevertheless he did not neglect to write his friends and especially his family. He wrote about his experiences to the editor of the *Cartersville Courier*, and described in detail the historical places he saw in Paris, especially his visit to Notre Dame. Each letter he received from home he carefully kept. He had to smile at his mother's complaint that Secretary Small never wrote anything about her son for the papers but wrote all about "General McCormick's laborious works, etc."

Early in July Pierce asked and received permission from the French president to travel in central France and study farming in the region. Wherever he stopped on his tour, and whenever the opportunity came, Pierce spoke as an ambassador of good will. In Marseilles, he expressed the wish that the men of the two countries could work together to reach an agreement so that American products would be cheaper for the French to buy. Back in Paris he enjoyed the social life, and was entertained by persons such as Madame Downing, her daughter Madame Moir, and Dr. Thomas W. Evans. At one of the dinners Pierce, ever the diplomat, responded to a welcome by offering his "profound thanks" for the kindness that had been extended to him and his comrades in France. "We have secured the warmest welcome from the French authorities, and from the moment I set foot upon French soil I have known nothing but welcome and the most lavish hospitality." General Young expressed his admiration for LaFayette and his hopes for a long life for the republic of France. Despite all the social entertainment, Pierce by August 2 was homesick for Walnut Plantation and wrote his mother that he would like to sail for home on September 5. He thought Paris was beautiful, "and all the curious things interest me very much, but I do not like it as well as I do my home. . . . I am tired of going to the Exposition but I see something new every time I go, and I do so wish you could all see how grand everything is."

But plans to return home did not materialize as Pierce thought they would, for he was sent with letters of introduction to Italy, to inspect the olive oil business and to interest Italians in Southern produce, especially cotton. The trip to Italy delayed the Walnut Plantation correspondence. Anxious because he did not hear from home, Pierce wrote a friend in Atlanta to visit his parents to see if they were well.

Before there was time for a reply he heard from his mother, who in turn indicated great anxiety at not having received letters from him. "You are sadly needed at home, for I fear that these negroes will take the advantage of your father, though he is doing the best he can." A few weeks later she spoke of the yellow fever epidemic in Chattanooga, with many refugees scattered all along the route to Cartersville. "The cars only go to Dalton and return." Pierce fretted a great deal about affairs at home, but he sent encouraging letters to his mother and gave long descriptions of his tour of the Mediterranean coast.

In October Mrs. Young sent distressing news of her grandson George, who had been seriously injured by some Mexicans in a fight in Texas while hunting buffaloes. George had written that he never expected to see any of them again and asked his grandparents' forgiveness for all of his misdeeds. The family never heard from him again.

Even in Europe Pierce was dogged by debts. When he failed to pay the taxes on his property in Washington by the end of June, two of his lots were sold at auction. Fortunately, a friend, William L. Davis, took up the notes and sent him the bill for $250. In addition he received other duns throughout the summer. He was glad, therefore, to see the formal close of the Exposition on Tuesday, November 10, 1878, and immediately began arranging for his return home and for shipment of the exhibits back to the United States. After a pleasant trip at sea he arrived safely in Washington on December 13. He wrote his mother that he had already begun to compose his final reports, and planned to be home by Christmas if possible. "I am never so happy anywhere as I am at home with you and Father." Then he added that he had no idea of marrying very soon, and that in any case he would not marry unless his mother approved of the lady. His major business in Washington was to gain approval of his claim for collecting the exhibits. He wrote his mother on December 20 that if he succeeded in getting the money it would "relieve us entirely of all our debts. It is hard to know what to

do, but I think we will get out all right somehow. . . . I will never
be happy till I can pay our debts and come and live all the time
with you and Father, but I feel it would be cowardly to go there
and sit down and let the land be sold when there appears to be a
chance to save it by trying to raise the money here, and I am
doing all I can I assure you."

Throughout the fall and winter financial conditions at the
plantation did not improve. Cotton was sold for seven cents—not
enough to pay the taxes. Almost daily demands were being made
on notes Dr. Young had signed, and Mrs. Young was distressed
that she was unable to control the financial matters at the farm.
She wrote Pierce on February 12, "We want to see you at home
very much, to guide and direct." However, Pierce remained in
Washington trying to obtain financial relief. When Congress
adjourned on March 4, President Hayes called Congress into
session to enact some appropriation bills that it had failed to
pass earlier. General Young explained to his mother that he did
not get his relief bill through "for want of time" but hoped to
have it passed early in the coming session. He said that he would
return home as soon as he could make a loan on his property,
"for you know as soon as I get home everybody will jump on
me with those little debts, and I dare not come till I get some
money which I hope will be in a very few days. . . . I am determined to do so before the crop is put in, but I must get some
money—you know that it is intolerable to be constantly dunned
without the means to pay."

Mrs. Young replied in part, "We want to see you very much,
money or no money; it does not make all the happiness in this
world, at the same time it is a good article to have plenty of. How
few now a days have a surplus." When he did not return by
April 26, his mother asked, "What detains you so long in
Washington?"

The family creditors increased their demands on General
Young. Some requested immediate payment, adding such reasons
as "Am compelled to raise some money this month or be ruined,"
or "I have to raise some money by the first of May to pay off a
judgment," or "I would not call on you but am compelled to
raise it by some means."

On May 7 Mrs. Young informed her son that some Northern
people were coming to Georgia to purchase land; she wondered
if they had better advertise the Resaca land for sale and try to
stop the interest on that debt. "God knows that we are very sorry

and grieved that you should be injured in your property for debts that have never been any advantage to us. . . . It seems that God smiles on some people and blesses them very good and with bright sunshine. I pray that it may be your lot. . . ." She advised her son to take care of himself. "There is no telling now a days who are your friends, every man will swim himself and let you sink if it is to his advantage, that is the theme the wide world over. At the same time you have as many friends I suppose as any man of your age; be watchful of all; don't trust too far."

William G. Devoe of the Department of Agriculture notified Pierce on June 9 that his request for the expense in collecting the exhibits for the Paris Conference had been put in the hands of the Secretary of State. Ten days later he stated that Pierce's account could not be paid because the services were performed after his appointment as a commissioner to the Exposition and that consequently, under the statute creating the commission and providing for its maintenance, there was no appropriation available by which the Department could remunerate him for his services.

Disappointed, Pierce confessed to his mother on June 10 that he was sick and tired of Washington and was glad Congress would adjourn within a week. "I think I'll come home to be dunned to death. I am sure there is no pleasure in this world to a man in debt without the means to pay. God grant that I may find a way out. I am yet working alone and able to do but little." Delayed, he mailed a note to his mother a week later that he was leaving Washington for home.

As soon as he arrived General Young immediately assumed the chores of the plantation. He wrote his sister on June 30 that he had been so busy since his getting home that he had not been able to leave for any length of time. He found conditions at home pressing. His father's health had reached a state where a doctor had to be called in to see him frequently. By November 26, General Young telegraphed his sister to send her husband to see their father. "We are uneasy about him though there is no cause for immediate alarm."

Depression was on the land; there was little money; interest rates were high. Pierce had borrowed until he could no longer repay, and he could no longer face his creditors. In December Robert's widow in Texas desperately sought a loan of $600; without it, she would lose the land her husband had left her. But Pierce was unable to assist her. He was momentarily relieved by being called to serve on the grand jury in the January 1880 session of the superior court. At least the *per diem* would amount to a small sum.

Dr. Young did not respond successfully to medical treatment, and on January 13, 1880, at eighty-two, he died. He was buried in the cemetery at Cartersville. The local paper that reported his death eulogized him as one of the "old land marks" of Bartow County, possessing "qualities of head and heart that endeared him to all who came in contact with him. Sterling worth, kindly and hospitable manners, and charity were eminent in his character."[1]

Pierce now took over completely the administration of the plantation. Throughout 1880 he worked prodigiously to pay the indebtedness incurred by his father. He sold farm produce, and as a last resort sold the land at Resaca to meet the heavy indebtedness. He sought new renters who could be trusted and who had the initiative to farm without too much supervision. Often he was so tired and depressed that he would have given up if his mother had not encouraged him.

While he was trying to bring Walnut Plantation to a solvent status, he familiarized himself with state politics and renewed his political acquaintances in Georgia and in the Seventh Congressional District. When the Bartow Democrats met in a convention at the courthouse in Cartersville on June 1, he was elected chairman. He and three other neighbors were elected delegates to the State Democratic Convention to be held in Atlanta on Wednesday, June 8. At the convention he took an active part. He nominated A. O. Bacon of Bibb County as permanent president. Pierce wanted and moved for a plurality vote to be used in nominating delegates for the national convention, but his motion was defeated; a motion for a majority count won. In the nomination of four delegates-at-large from the state, Pierce was nominated by a good friend from Whitfield County and was successfully elected on the first ballot (180 votes) with General A. R. Lawton of Chatham County (271 votes), George T. Barnes of Richmond County (256 2/3 votes), and E. P. Howell (214 1/3).[2] When interviewed immediately after adjournment General Young stated he was for David D. Field and C. N. Potter, the Democratic candidates for President and Vice President.

On June 18, the Georgia delegates to the National Democratic Convention left Atlanta for Cincinnati. Pierce was gratified to see his fellow Georgians, but he was almost overwhelmed with emotion when General Joseph Wheeler and the Alabama delegates boarded the train at Boyce Station. The two ex-Confederate officers embraced each other like old school chums.

Immediately upon their arrival at Cincinnati, the Georgia delegates found that rumors were flying in every direction, especially about whether Governor Tilden would again be a candidate. On June 22, Pierce was placed on the Credentials Committee and later elected chairman. Henry W. Grady in a news story about the delegates said: "Pierce Young is the showiest man in the Georgia delegation."[2] When Grady polled the Georgia delegates on Tilden he reported Pierce's predicting, "If Field is not nominated on the fourth or fifth ballot a New York or Indiana man will be rushed through. . . . I am for Field, but I can never vote against Tilden."

When Tilden's letter declaring that he would not be a candidate was made public on June 22, Pierce, according to Grady, reported that he had gone to Tilden only a few weeks before, promising him the Georgia delegation if he would permit his name to be used. Tilden refused point blank to make a single move to influence the delegates in the state, asserting, "My cause is well understood and, if it does not plead for itself, I will not." Throughout the next day the members of the Georgia delegation were bombarded with telegrams from leading citizens of the state urging them to go for Tilden. Pierce received telegrams from Mark A. Cooper and many other friends urging him to support Tilden.

On June 24, General Young was granted one of the highest privileges of the convention, giving the report of the Credentials Committee, which had worked through the night to have the report ready. There were three contests among the delegates: one from Massachusetts, one from Pennsylvania, and one from New York.

He closed the report with a ringing speech in which he said, "Samuel J. Tilden is not before the convention. I only wish to God that he were and had his ovation from the whole house." He received thunderous applause. His handling of the contested delegates from New York won him praise for tact and parliamentary ability. By the second ballot, when Pierce realized that Winfield S. Hancock and William H. English would be the Democratic candidates, he persuaded the Georgia delegates to vote unanimously for them.

When the Georgia delegation returned to Atlanta on June 25, they were given a grand reception at the railroad station. Across the arch of the passenger depot was a banner that read, "Hancock and English. Georgia Delegates, Welcome, Thou Good and Faithful Servants." A large crowd with a brass band met the delegates. Various members spoke, and Dr. H. V. M. Miller echoed the sentiment of leading Georgia Democrats when he declared that the people of Georgia endorsed the action of the delegation and were united for Hancock and English. Senator B. H. Hill's estimate of the delegates was that it was the best delegation Georgia ever sent anywhere, and many agreed with him.[3]

As soon as General Young investigated affairs at home, he began making plans to aid Governor Colquitt in his campaign and also to defeat his political enemy, the independent congressman, Dr. Felton. His plan for the latter was to nominate a candidate for Congress by militia district primaries. The executive committee of each county in the Seventh District would appoint three election managers for each voting precinct of the county, and each manager would be required to take an oath before a justice of the peace to make true returns. Then Pierce proposed that immediately after an election the returns should be forwarded to the *Daily Constitution* for publication, and the candidate receiving the highest number of votes was to be declared the nominee of the people of the Seventh District. Additionally, no man would be allowed to vote in the primaries until he had pledged himself to support the nominees. General Young claimed that his plan would do away with the convention system and would end the cry opposing rings, for the nomination would be made directly by the people. The editor of the *Daily Constitution* wrote that the "sore dissensions" in the Seventh District had brought discord and bickering in almost every district of the state and he desired that "there should be some sort of accommodation or compromise that would give harmony once more, and end the feuds in what should be Georgia's banner district."[4] Whether this would come through the plan proposed by General Young, the editor would not say; but he believed if it was tried many factions would be "avoided." The editor of the *Marietta Journal* opposed the plan.

Announcing that several influential men in the district had already signified their willingness to adopt his new plan, Pierce submitted it to the district Democratic Executive Committee which met in Dalton on July 16. However, he was not able to get his plan adopted, though it was recommended for consideration by the state committee whenever it was practicable to select delegates by the militia district primaries to send to conventions.[5]

Throughout July, there were reports that a canvass of the leading men in the twelve counties of the Seventh District indicated decidedly that General Young was the most popular candidate to run against Dr. Felton. The *Daily Constitution* stated that the paper's source of information maintained: "there is no man in the district who has done more for the party than Pierce Young, and he has never been beaten before the people."[6] The article continued: "We are not advised as to whether or not General Young would consent to make the race, but he has never yet failed to lead his legion or his party, no matter what the dangers or troubles were. And if they put the standards of the organization into his hands he will carry it—in our opinion."

As soon as General Young heard about the rumor, he denied it and did everything to discourage the use of his name. He realized that if Felton was to be defeated it must be by someone new in politics, someone whose public record could not be questioned by the doctor and his shrewd wife, who herself took active part in her husband's campaigns. Thus, Pierce set out to unite the Democrats of the district in nominating the one man who he thought could defeat his archenemy.

On August 4, the State Democratic Convention with three hundred and fifty delegates met at the Capitol in Atlanta to nominate a gubernatorial candidate. Pierce was one of the delegates from Bartow County and the only one who favored Governor Colquitt's renomination. Under advice from Colquitt and other party leaders he introduced a resolution to adopt the two-thirds rule for nomination of candidates. Speaking to the convention delegates, he claimed that he rose in "no captious spirit" but only to bring harmony in the convention. "We are here in the interest of the democratic party and of no men or set of men. This rule is the time honored rule of the party and I want it adopted here and now, not that I think it so right, but because I think it is in the interest of peace, prosperity and harmony."[7] The two-thirds rule was adopted for the convention then in session, with the proviso that majority rule would be used in later conventions.[8]

Alexander Stephens thought adoption of the two-thirds rule was a mistake. General Young soon found that Stephens was right and he was wrong. Although the Colquitt delegates were in a majority, and confident of victory, claiming they were certain of more than two hundred votes, they were unable to amass the two-thirds vote necessary for nomination. The anti-Colquitt minority was able to consolidate and hold the control, so that no nomination was pos-

sible. The followers of Lester and Hardeman let it be known that
they would break up the convention or defeat Colquitt.[9] After the
thirty-first ballot on the fifth day, when Colquitt led by thirty-four
votes over a majority but lacked twenty-four votes for the required
two-thirds, Pierce rose on the floor and appealed for a nomination
before the convention adjourned.[10] He tried to pressure the anti-
Colquitt delegates to change and vote for the incumbent Governor.
One of the young delegates opposing such a move was Thomas E.
Watson from McDuffie County, who offered a motion that, for
the sake of party harmony, a committee of two from each candidate's following should retire and select a person from the list of
names exhibited, or any other good Democrat in Georgia, to offer
the convention. The motion did not carry.[11]

This was the longest Democratic State Convention in Georgia's
political history, lasting for seven days. It was the first major test
of the Bourbon triumvirate, Brown, Gordon, and Colquitt. General Young continued to support Colquitt for two main reasons.
One was to save the Democratic party in the state and keep it under the leadership of the ex-Confederate officers; the other was to
use the triumvirate to build his own political future.

After thirty-two ineffectual ballots, the convention by a majority
vote recommended Colquitt as the choice of the Democratic
party.[12] Once other state officers were nominated, the convention
adjourned. Pierce admitted that he did not approve but favored
remaining until a two-thirds choice was made. "But since the
matter has come to what it has Governor Colquitt can beat any
man by 50,000 votes. He is sure to be elected," he prophesied. He
agreed with the *Daily Constitution* that the convention was "one
of the most extraordinary political bodies ever assembled in Georgia. It is the outcome of an extraordinary canvass and . . . it has
precipitated a campaign which has had no parallel in the state
since the war." Furthermore, Pierce would agree that the whole
purpose of the minority had been to assail the character and de-
stroy the reputation of Governor Colquitt. "Their personal prejudices and preferences they deemed of more importance than party
harmony."[13] Pierce would also have agreed with the editor of the
Columbus Daily Times that the convention had been very un-
skillfully arranged.[14]

When the majority, or Colquitt delegates, adjourned, the minority delegates remained and organized, with Thomas M. Norwood as chairman. They passed a resolution that the recommendation for Governor Colquitt was not binding and that the minority

should have a candidate for governor. After several days of wild rumors, the newspapers reported that the minority faction had telegraphed Dr. Felton asking him to enter the gubernatorial race. Because of his interest in the congressional race, he declined. At last the minority leaders, consisting of nine men, announced that Norwood would be their candidate in November's general election.

In August, Pierce was again mentioned as the strongest man to become the Democratic congressional candidate from the Seventh District. Yet although his friends strongly urged his candidacy, he refused to let his name be used. When the district convention met at Rome on August 19, he was able to get J. W. Robertson of Cobb County nominated. Three days later Robertson declined the nomination because of a disinterest in politics and a desire to devote full time to his business. Consequently on August 26, the convention reassembled to nominate a candidate. Colonel Judson C. Clements, a thirty-five-year-old native of Walker County and a former state representative from the county and senator from the 45th District, was unanimously nominated on the first ballot. General Young, happy to find such an attractive neophyte to run against the old doctor on November 4, pledged the young man his support against Dr. Felton.[15]

Clements, knowing the ability of Felton to assail the personal records of his opponents, followed a new strategy. Instead of engaging the doctor on the platform, he carried on a quiet dignified campaign, free from personalities. He won the people by his sincerity. Pierce began immediately to assist in organizing campaigns to aid Colquitt and Clements. The gubernatorial campaign was one of the bitterest in Georgia history. At first Norwood wrote Colquitt proposing that they both retire from the race. Colquitt refused on the grounds that his own candidacy was the choice of nearly two-thirds of the party, while Norton was the nominee of a committee of nine. There followed a campaign composed of bitter debates, and charges and counter-charges of slander between the two candidates and their followers. General Young, with others, spoke for Colquitt on the same platform with a follower of Norwood.

On August 28, Pierce met with other Bartow supporters of Colquitt in a political rally at the courthouse in Cartersville. During the month of September he undertook a speaking tour for the governor. At Hampton on September 7, he was booed by the anti-Colquitt followers, but the following day at McDonough he gave

"an eloquent and ringing speech for Colquitt. The speech had
fine effect, and covered the general with glory."[16] Pierce traveled
up and down the route of the Seaboard Railroad speaking for his
friend. At every opportunity he went to Atlanta. Because Bartow
County was not overly enthusiastic about the Governor, Pierce's
real accomplishment was in having Governor Colquitt speak in
Cartersville on September 22.

The gubernatorial election proceeded as Pierce had predicted
at the convention. Colquitt defeated Norwood by 55,539 votes,[17]
but the latter carried Bartow County. The Governor was vindicated. The people had spoken and the triumvirate was not to be
questioned again. Many people who were tired of the campaign
of slander Norwood's followers had conducted voted for Colquitt.[18] But Pierce's real joy was in the defeat of Dr. Felton by
young Clements, who received 11,572 votes to Felton's 10,727.
There was wild enthusiasm in Cartersville, with Pierce leading
the celebration.

Although he devoted himself primarily to the congressional and
gubernatorial races in Georgia, Pierce followed the presidential
election as assiduously as time permitted. The success of the Democrats in Georgia and in the Seventh Congressional District did not
carry over into the presidential election. General Winfield S. Hancock, the Democratic nominee, received few votes outside the
Solid South. There was much dissatisfaction in the Democratic
ranks, even in Georgia.

General Young spent most of the year 1881 at Walnut Plantation. It was during this year, 1881, that he received a medal from
the Paris Exposition authorities in the Department of State for
the services he had performed at the Exposition. In the name of
the Commissioner General, Edward H. Kinglet commended Pierce
for the excellent work he did in France. In September his friends
tried to persuade him to become a candidate for the secretaryship
of the United States Senate, but he discouraged them, although
the South Carolina delegation in Congress promised to support
him.

In September 1881 Pierce received a letter from B. H. Warner,
a real estate broker in Washington, indicating that he had a party
interested in buying certain lots on O Street if the General was
interested in selling. Pierce agreed to sell and went to Washington
in January 1882 to see about his real estate. He needed money to
pay past debts and to live on; so he asked his friend Alexander H.
Stephens to help him get the money owed him for his election to

the Fortieth Congress. Stephens replied that he doubted if he could obtain payment by an amendment to the appropriation bills but thought the proper remedy was to send a petition to Congress stating all the facts of the case.

Unsuccessful, General Young returned home. Having serious trouble in paying taxes on his real estate in Washington, he borrowed $100 from his close friend Senator M. C. Butler of South Carolina, who requested repayment and also a loan from Pierce in December. The senator was financially embarrassed also.

Although General Young held no political office, he still received letters seeking his assistance in writing or speaking to the President of the United States or to some congressman, and in September 1882 Pierce again actively participated in Georgia politics. Joseph E. Brown, president of the Western and Atlantic Railroad, sent him a pass for the rest of the year so that he could campaign for Alexander H. Stephens for governor and Judson C. Clements for congressman from the Seventh District. Although General Young did not have the flash of Gordon, he enjoyed speaking, and the sincerity and power of his common touch won for him friends wherever he went. In the campaign he opposed Feltonism and all who would break up the Democratic party. Always in his speeches he praised the Confederate soldier and the sacrifice he had made. Both of his candidates won, and on November 4 he attended the Governor's inauguration in deGive's Opera House.

General Young again rejoiced over the defeat of Dr. Felton. Mrs. Felton wrote years later that nothing human or mortal could have won against the combination opposing her husband, and that she could not understand how he was elected the first time, since the Bourbon triumvirate was in full authority and had an abundance of campaign money.[19] Pierce did not receive any money for his services in campaigning; a pass on the railroads was all he ever accepted.

The day after Governor Stephens' death on March 4, 1883, James S. Boynton, president of the senate, took the oath of office and assumed the duties of the executive. Ordering an election to be held on April 24, he summoned the state legislature to meet in a special session three weeks later to count the votes and install the new governor. On March 13, Pierce received a letter from William T. Newman to the effect that Acting Governor Boynton was expecting Pierce to help in the campaign by carrying Bartow County for him.

General Young agreed to support Boynton (whom he had

known in the army), and discredited certain letters that were
supposed to have been written in 1869 by Boynton to Colquitt
indicating that he had not been true to the Democratic party. He
did this despite the fact that his friends Gordon and Colquitt
were in favor of A. O. Bacon, speaker of the Georgia house of
representatives. Pierce was a delegate on April 11 to the gubernatorial convention at which Boynton, Bacon, and Henry Mc-
Daniel were the candidates for nomination. Efforts to nominate
Bacon were unsuccessful and the convention deadlocked. The
impasse was finally broken after the chairman, Judge Charles F.
Crisp, upon a resolution introduced by Dupont Guerry, appointed a conference committee composed of the supporters of
the candidates according to their strength. General Young was
appointed one of the six representatives on the committee for
Boynton. After considering the candidates for some time, the committee agreed to recommend a compromise candidate, Henry D.
McDaniel of Walton County. The delegates received the recommendation with considerable enthusiasm and on Pierce's motion
the nomination was made unanimous.

In an effort to secure money, Pierce in the summer of 1883
joined his friend H. C. Glenn in a project to raise watermelons
for the market. The venture was only partly a financial success
for the seeds and guano were expensive and labor was exorbitantly
high. It was a bad season and many seeds failed to germinate. For
his labor and effort he received approximately three hundred
dollars. A second business venture at this time, raising turkeys for
market, returned less money than the watermelons—no failure
but no major financial success.

Pierce had purposely remained near Walnut Plantation because
he realized that his mother's health was failing. After he and his
sister took her to Atlanta in April for a medical examination Mrs.
Young began to improve. Her strong will to live abetted her
recovery. By August Pierce felt that he could leave his mother,
but he hired H. Barton Leake to stay at night in the home. He
went to Washington to renew his notes and to lobby in the
election of Speaker of the House. Finding that his creditors in
the capital were in need of money and trying to collect, he was
forced to sell several of his real estate lots.

Although he hoped to finish his business in order to be home
for Christmas, Pierce was delayed. In an effort to meet his notes,
he wrote Goode and Fontaine, land and loan agents of Atlanta,

to negotiate a loan on the plantation. He found that his friends were financially as desperate as he. The financial crisis of 1883 was threatening the small merchant, businessman, and farmer. Credit was hard to obtain. Pierce then turned to his friend John B. Gordon, but Gordon was unable to assist him financially. As a last effort he offered to sell the "Square North of Square No. 189" in Washington to J. V. N. Huyck for $5,000. The necessity of paying his debts and the financial demands at Cartersville made the sale unavoidable, but the transaction took so much time that Pierce was unable to depart for Cartersville until February.

When Pierce arrived home, he was grieved to learn that his sister's youngest daughter had died after a brief illness on the anniversary of their father's death, January 12. He also found that his nephew, Tom Jones, Jr., had been seriously ill; so he felt that he must assist financially his sister's family.

After taking care of personal and plantation business, and re-assured by Mrs. Young's doctor about her condition, Pierce again journeyed to Washington to talk with the Democratic leaders. He believed that the Democrats would be successful in electing the president in November. After several conferences in Washington with Brown, Colquitt, and others, General Young found that Governor Grover Cleveland of New York, whom he had met several years before at Niagara, was being suggested as the Democrat hope. He went on to New York to meet and talk with the leaders there. However, realizing that his mother was very feeble, he wrote home often to let his sister know where he was, and he insisted that he be telegraphed if Mrs. Young became critically ill. Returning home, Pierce was glad to find his mother greatly improved.

Senator Colquitt wrote Pierce to come back to Washington on the first of May. Mrs. Young insisted that he go. He agreed, provided that his niece Carrie Young, who made her home with them, would write every day and would telegraph if his mother should suffer another attack of "colic." While in Washington Pierce sold another lot and paid Senator Butler of South Carolina the $350 he had borrowed the previous year. Then he returned to Walnut Plantation to stay with his mother—a personal decision about which he was always grateful. For on May 25, Mrs. Young had a fatal attack of "colic," and on May 26 she was buried alongside her husband in the family lot in the Cartersville cemetery.

Pierce was always close to his mother and her death was an irreparable loss. He grieved for her, but he realized that at her age she could never have been restored to her former health. With the death of his mother he became much closer to his sister Louisa, to whom he remained devoted all the remaining years.

XII

◊◊◊
◊

A Public Servant in Russia

ALTHOUGH the death of his mother was a great personal
loss, General Young realized for the first time his responsibilities would no longer keep him so close to Walnut Plantation. During the first few months at home after Mrs. Young's
death he tried to pay off as much of his indebtedness as possible,
for he wanted to enter public service again. However, when the
Atlanta Constitution announced on July 3 that General Young
would be a candidate for the state legislature from Bartow
County, he vehemently denied the report and when efforts were
made to organize against Congressman Judson C. Clements, he
let it be known that he thought that Clements should have
another term. He also refused when friends asked him to be a
delegate to the Democratic convention in Chicago, replying that
he felt he could best serve the Democratic cause by attending
the convention in an unofficial capacity.

At the national convention General Young worked hard to
help Grover Cleveland secure the nomination. The election was
held on Tuesday, November 4, after a vitriolic campaign between
Cleveland and James G. Blaine, the Republican candidate. The
four days from Tuesday, November 4, to Friday, November 7,
were days of great suspense for Georgians. As soon as Pierce cast
his vote in Cartersville, he went by train to Atlanta so that he
could get the returns as soon as they were published at the
Atlanta Constitution office by his good friend Henry Grady.
When the election of Cleveland was finally confirmed on November 7, Pierce joined with other Atlantans and Georgians in wild
rejoicing in the election of the first Democrat in twenty-four years.

191

Immediately after the celebration Pierce began to approach his
friends about an appointment abroad. Receiving encouragement,
by January 1885 Pierce had made up his mind to seek an appointment in foreign service. In February Henry Grady advised him to
go to Washington, and gave him a letter of recommendation to
present to President-elect Grover Cleveland. Grady testified to
the ability and the long, devoted and unselfish service of General
Young to the Democratic cause, going so far as to say: "From my
position I can hardly help making estimates of what this leader
or that is doing in our Southern field and I do not hesitate to say
that in earnestness and efficiency—in being always ready and
always zealous—no man has surpassed and the very few have
equaled General Young.

"He is beloved of our people and is the ideal of his friends.
I shall have no request to make of you, Sir, and shall esteem all
that I have done or said in your behalf or in behalf of Democracy
more than repaid if you can see it in your way, to merit the
wishes of this gallant soldier and leader. You could make *no*
appointment in Georgia and I speak advisedly, that would be
more popular or deserved."

General Young's request was endorsed also by the two Senators
from Georgia—Joseph E. Brown and Alfred Colquitt. The former
called Young a gentleman of high character and qualifications,
and a leading Democrat, who had served with honor and distinc-
tion in Congress and whose appointment would give great satisfaction to the Democracy of Georgia. Senator Colquitt wrote that
Young was "a gentleman of intelligence, high character and with
an acquaintance with public matters which fit him to discharge
creditably and represent faithfully the interest of this country
in its diplomatic relations."

Although General Young went to Washington with high hopes
of obtaining a position in foreign service, on March 20 he wrote
his sister, "Am very fearful I will not get my place." As other
appointments were made and approved, he became anxious. He
knew that on May 8 President Cleveland appointed George V. N.
Lathrop, a lawyer of Detroit, Michigan, as envoy extraordinary
and minister plenipotentiary to Russia.

On May 27, Pierce wrote Secretary of the Interior Lamar,
telling how sadly disappointed he was, and seeking his aid. Lamar
answered immediately that he had received his letter "with painful emotion," for he knew that inaction of the department "must

be torture to a proud and sensitive and honorable nature" like the General's. Yet Lamar explained that "the causes which delay decision . . . are not necessarily referable to any reluctance on the part of the Secretary [of State Bayard] to recognize your services and your claims to be chosen as a representative of this Democratic administration abroad. . . . I talked with Bayard about it, as I have about other things, and I declare to you that he gives me no indication of a purpose to overlook or disregard or reject your claims. And yet I cannot say that he gives me any encouragement except a sort of gracious courtesy and appreciative way that he had of speaking about you. I wish you knew the depth and extent of my sympathy in this matter, and I wish I could help you."

General Young's anxiety was assuaged on June 17, by the official announcement that he was appointed consul general to St. Petersburg, Russia. He at once telegraphed his sister of his good fortune. The *Atlanta Constitution* on June 28 announced the appointment, calling Young "As brave a knight as ever drew sword," and adding, "There is not a true man in Georgia who will not be pleased that the gallant Young has been suitably rewarded." Pierce's picture, photographed by Kurtz, was in Frank Lester's *Illustrated Newspaper*. Leading newspapers throughout the United States had nothing but praise for the appointment. They reviewed the General's military and political career and predicted for him success as consul general to St. Petersburg. The *Cartersville Courant* on July 23 headlined an article "A Revolution in Russia." After describing Pierce's education at West Point, the article continued, ". . . [he] was a confederate major-general when almost a boy, possesses a dignified bearing and graceful address, and is a man of affairs. Besides all this, he is one of the handsomest men in America, and will be a revolution in Russia."

Immediately Pierce began his preparation for the trip to St. Petersburg. He wrote many friends of his good luck and in turn received many congratulatory letters. A few offered to go with him as a secretary or companion. His South Carolina relatives thought his photograph in the *Illustrated Newspaper* handsome and wondered if he would take a wife with him to Russia. After arranging for his sister and her family to look out for the plantation while he was abroad, Pierce spent several weeks in Washington getting acquainted with his duties. He came to admire Secretary Thayer and was sorry to learn that his wife was an invalid.

He studied the geographic, social, and economic conditions of Russia; he read avidly the data on Czar Alexander III, who had come to the throne in 1881.

On October 16, 1885, General Young sailed from New York. He described his arrival in Russia as follows: "I arrived here about December 1st, and after a pleasant journey, only interrupted by a few days sickness in Berlin, on account of over exposure. I first came into the snow just after reaching the border, a few miles from Konisburg, [sic] and it was snow then all the way to St. Petersburg about 300 miles. I got here in the night and I found the coldest weather I had ever known, though everyone said it was a mild winter. I immediately invested in an overcoat that cost about two months pay, and looked like it had been taken from the back of a young bear. I really did not suffer from the cold, the houses are so warm and I was well wrapped when I went out, but there is an indescribable something in the climate that has the most singular effect upon the system."[1]

Writing in 1888, General Young described St. Petersburg as unhealthy and its lower class as coarse. "The first impression of the traveler on approaching St. Petersburg is of wonder at its size and its position. On every side stretches of what is apparently a low flat marsh, covered with innumerable buildings; the strangest place for a city ever chosen by the obstinate will of man, seeking to dispense with all natural advantages. Peter the Great chose it, it is said, as being 'a window looking out upon Europe,' but surely a site might have been found with an equal outlook and a less desolate and fatal position of water, but which sits on her rocky thrones like a queen above the dangerous element. St. Petersburg lies helplessly at its mercy. In autumn when the Neva is rough and stormy, and in spring, when the ice is breaking up, the danger is greatest. The waves rise to the level of the streets, the numerous canals overflow—guns from the fortress are constantly fired to warn the people of their peril, while the inhabitants seek the upper stories of their houses and the police prepare boats for rescue. Another consequence of the marshy situation is its unhealthy water is undrinkable, and dysentery and similar diseases prevail whenever the friendly frost is not present to turn everything to ice. Peter the Great did not build his capital in ignorance of what he was doing. He laid its foundation upon human lives. For many years, 40,000 men annually were drafted from all portions of his empire to work in this poisonous marsh. Every cart and vessel entering the post was obliged to bring a certain number of stones to pave its streets, and hundred of thousands of wooden piles were buried in its depths. Soil was also brought in in great quantities to raise the level of the place, and massive granite quays built along the rapid river; but nothing has availed to prevent disastrous inundations, seven or eight of which are particularly mentioned since the foundations were laid in 1702. At one time the river rose thirteen feet."[2]

Pierce thought that it was not only the want of elevation and of picturesqueness that was depressing to visitors but also the endless rows of immense buildings, the monotonous gardens, and the general appearance of regularity in the city. "It is evident that there are not enough people to fill its streets, and it is a positive relief to enter a few thoroughfares where business and life is centered, such as the Nevasky Prospect. Of course, in winter, when the court is here the richest come in from summer homes in Finland and the islands. When the sleighing is lively and all the gayeties of the season in vogue, St. Petersburg would show to much greater advantage."[3]

Since General Young had been told about the painful contrasts of luxury and poverty on the streets, he expected to meet beggars on every hand, "but such has not proved to be the case. There are always beggars at the church doors, but seldom elsewhere, and poverty is by no means so obvious and distressing as in many cities. It is not the poverty, but the coarseness, almost brutality, in the lower classes that impresses you most vividly. The men that you meet in their sordid rags or their undressed sheepskins seem not to need or deserve any better raiment. It is suitable for them. Mild of face, with long tangled hair, and inexpressibly dirty, often half drunk, but never cringing. You shrink from rather than pity them. The pictures drawn by Tolstoy are seen to be fearfully realistic. The women are less forbidding, but with little intelligence or good humor. Actually I have never seen a smile nor heard a laugh in the streets since we have been here. Nobody understands or wishes to understand you; the poor are sullen, the well-to-do careless or insolent, and then there is so much that is strange and utterly foreign. For some, to us, unexplained reason the days of the months are changed. You thought it was the 20th of August, you find it is the 8th. The Russian names of the streets and the signs over the shops might as well be

written in Runic. As very few of the natives, however, are better
off than yourself in this respect, the shopkeepers do not trust
to the alphabet for setting forth their wares.

"I have complained of the want of life in the streets. I must
make an exception in favor of the droshkies. These little carriages
fly about in every direction, for everybody rides. You look down
one of the long quays perhaps and see no walkers, no loungers,
but you are sure to see droshkies. They are small, low vehicles,
each holding two passengers, with a driver on a high seat in front
clad in a long blue blouse with a leather girdle and a peculiar
cap on his head. The horses, with their huge arched collars, are
active and gentle and apparently well treated, and if you know
enough Russian to make a bargain, you will find this method of
transit a cheap and convenient one. It is certainly convenient;
you have only to raise your hand, droshkies sweep down upon
you like vultures on their prey, sometimes jostling each other in
their endeavor to reach you first, but as none of the drivers know
a word of anything but Russian, you may not find it very easy
to make them comprehend where you want to go. This difficulty
overcome, however, you will soon be spinning at a rapid rate
over the badly paved streets. You will probably soon notice the
driver snatch off his cap, wave it in the air, and, replacing it,
make a hasty sign of the cross by touching the forehead, breast
and each shoulder in succession. This is when a church is passed,
and such recognition of the sacred edifice and shrine is common
among both walkers and riders.

"There is no nation probably so devoted to religious form as
the Russians—certainly none which believe so implicitly in the
value of sign and genuflexions. It is strange enough to watch the
crowd which fills the church during service time. There are never
any seats; all—rich and poor—stand together, but in place of
standing quietly, or, at most kneeling occasionally, like the con-
gregators in a Catholic church, the whole body of worshippers in
a Greek church are in motion, bowing, prostrating themselves,
waving the arms up and down, continually making the sign of
the cross described above, they resemble a garden tossed by a
great wind."[4]

Soon after his arrival he sent to the *Augusta Chronicle* a description of his trip and of his plans to journey to Berlin or
Vienna and have a "jolly good time." After traveling several
hundred miles he reached the German frontier and was halted
by a squad of Cossacks whose officer demanded his passport.

Pierce replied: "Passport be blessed! I had to get one to enter your effete monarchy, but did not know it was necessary to procure one inside of your land. I have not got a passport and am in a hurry, so please stand aside and let me proceed on my trip. I am consul general too, and don't want any confounded red-tape nonsense."[5] The Cossack officer did not comprehend a word of what was said, but knew the handsome suspicious-looking foreigner did not have the papers required of him. So Pierce was put in the charge of two grim and dirty Cossacks, hustled on a train bound due north, and conducted back to his post. Carried to the Russian headquarters, the luckless consul was after some delay identified. Pierce stated: "Profuse apologies were vouchsafed, but nothing further was done to make amends for 1,400 miles of jaunting to no delightful purpose."[6]

Soon after his arrival the new consul general received his "exequatur," and tried to follow diplomatic protocol. The *Atlanta Constitution,* writing of Pierce's experiences on January 5, 1886, described the Russian spy system and wondered if the new consul general with his "independence and freedom of speech" did not find the regulations and secret investigations irksome. The paper predicted that he would "quickly be on good terms with the military, just as he was with Generals Grant and Sherman after the war."

By March, General Young was able to report about his new post to Secretary of State Bayard. He found that the service heretofore had not been conducted in a manner reflecting credit upon the United States government. The late Consul General Stanton had appointed as engineer J. V. Swan, an English subject, whom Pierce discharged for inefficiency and dishonesty. When Swan demanded his pay, Young investigated and found that Stanton and Swan had moved the consulate to a private home and as partners had an understanding about rent and other financial arrangements. He condemned not only the inefficient manner by which the office had been administered but also the lack of trained personnel. "The American consulate general here is not in good repute, and it is not surprising when men are employed who have been discharged from business firms for dishonesty, and thereafter placed in charge of the consulate general of the United States." General Young enclosed in his report to Secretary Bayard a list of the places he thought should be visited and inspected as possible sites for the State Department, adding that he had not been absent from his post an hour since he took charge on

December 10th except to visit Moscow under orders from the
Department. He also added that he was forwarding his and the
minister's recommendations for George O. Price to be vice-consul
general at the post at St. Petersburg. Pierce described Price as
an American citizen and a man of high standing and respectability, "and I trust you will appoint him at your earliest
convenience."

General Young wrote, "I regret to have to say that I do not like
my position here; my duties are easy and agreeable but the pay
is about half what it should be, and the position of a consul general not high. I am alone, and I live economically without carriage and many other conveniences necessary to the dignity and
respectability of an officer representing the government of the
United States in a consular capacity." He thought that his salary
was too small and living costs so expensive that the office was
a burden on one's private account. He advised raising the salary
or reducing the rank of the post to a consular agency with a
merchant in charge. He thought that "the government should be
liberal to its officers sent to posts of hardships and dangers."

Pierce sent another damaging account of J. V. Swan, for, in
addition to unpaid bills, further investigation showed that Swan
had drawn money for expenses which he did not make. Worst of
all Swan had reported that he made a business trip to Moscow
to investigate a former clerk, Van Ryper by name, and had hired
a lawyer to assist him; investigation by General Young proved
that the report as well as the account for money had been falsified.
Pierce paid the $150 rent which was due on the private home
being used by the consulate and relieved the United States Government "of all obligations to occupy or rent the apartments."

All was not work for General Young. He visited Moscow and
formed some views of Czar Alexander III, who had ascended the
throne in 1881 after the assassination of his father Alexander II.
Pierce liked the Czar, describing him as "a good hearted, amiable
man, but a bold, fearless one. I believe his ambition is to be a
patriot. He is certainly popular. I have often seen him driving in
the streets, attended by only the empress and a man, and always
the people show much affection for the family as well as the
emperor himself. They rush around his carriage to greet him, and
insure great admiration for him. Much liberty in the administration of government seems not always to insure peace and friendly
feeling for the administrators of the law or the laws themselves,
as was demonstrated in the recent revolutionary proceedings of

the anarchists and socialists in Chicago, but it is a matter of much congratulation to Americans that only foreigners were engaged in that disgraceful affair."[7]

Pierce encouraged his friends to visit him "for . . . you will return to your own country with renewed health and renewed patriotism, and you will never cease to be grateful to the Almighty that you were born under a free sky and in a land where you are compelled to bow the head and bend the knees to no man." He did not like the Russian weather, and wrote a friend that he could not sleep for two months after he arrived except for a few hours at a time. The doctors said the air was poison to him. He concluded, "The winter was severe upon me, and I don't think the climate agrees with me."[8]

After he had been at his post for about six months, General Young described St. Petersburg as "the most solidly built city in the world. The houses are very large, and as if intended to stand a siege. There are many hundreds of people living in some of the houses. They are generally not so tall as the houses in our cities, but the walls are much thicker, and they are generally much stronger and better built. The floors are all of oak and laid in square bits of plank, ten inches wide, beautifully polished and they last hundreds of years. The carriages are smaller than ours, but very strong. The Orloff breed of horses in Russia are perhaps the finest horses for cavalry in Europe. They are tall black horses, very symmetrically formed, and are usually fast trotters, fine for harness and for cavalry. The common draft horse of the country is a rather small horse, but very durable and hardy. On the farm, oxen are generally used for drawing plows and carts. They are tall and strong and move quickly. I think for work they are better than the ordinary Georgia cattle, but for milk and butter our Durham and Jerseys are superior to anything here. There is plenty of good milk at all times in St. Petersburg, and cheap, but the town pumps are even used here to aid the cows. Vegetables are not so good as in America, except cabbage, and there is an oversupply of that.

"The most abundant article here is the 'soldier.' He may be seen at every corner and on all occasions, he is largely present at all important gatherings, and it is a great mistake to suppose that the army of Russia is so very costly, for, after investigation, I find it is much the most economically managed army in Europe —perhaps in the world. The pay is almost nothing, and during all the winter months which is more than half the time, the common soldier maintains himself. He is often a mechanic or artisan of some sort, and he has permission to hire himself out as a servant in any capacity he pleases, so long as he can be present on certain days at his regiment headquarters. It is the most self-sustaining army in the world. They are capable of more hard work and fatigue, and live on cheaper diet than any set of civilized men in the world. There are in all about 2,000,000 men in the military service of Russia, in all branches."[9]

In letters to Louisa General Young described in detail the imposing Easter celebration held in Russia. He was particularly impressed by certain rituals—the washing of communicants' feet by the priest of the Orthodox Church, the chanting of the male choir. The custom of church members' kissing one another on Easter Day fascinated the American consul. Another custom during the Easter season that drew his notice was the intemperance of the Russians; "but the fellows under the influence of liquor are very quiet, and never appeared to be imbued with pugilistic proclivities. If half as much vodka had been consumed in any American city as was consumed in Petersburg Easter week, there would have been many a broken skull and bloody nose. The rigorous and speedy methods of executing the laws in this empire have a tendency to cause all persons drunk or sober, to keep a vigilant watch upon their tempers, acts, and language. A quiet person who attends to his business may have an easy, enjoyable time, but a meddlesome person who troubles the affairs of other people and attempts to interfere with officials or government regulations has a hard road to travel and generally leads in the direction of Siberia."

By July General Young seemed to have forgotten the arduous winter; he wrote his sister that he found "the northern country" delightful. The long daylight amazed him and he wrote of reading a newspaper at two o'clock in the morning without artificial light. "It is quite daylight till twelve o'clock and then at one o'clock it is quite light again. In another month it will be daylight all night."

During this month General Young was able to leave St. Petersburg and visit Sweden. He especially appreciated the Swedish cuisine, and sent his sister on the back of a playing card, the menu of one of the restaurants. He enjoyed the friendliness of the Swedes and was impressed by their industry and cleanliness. He told Louisa that he wished she could see the beautiful buildings of Stockholm, especially the churches.

Realizing that for his health's sake he needed a rest from his duties and a change of climate, General Young left his post in August 1886 to return to the United States, and landed early in September. The "Georgia Gossip" column of the *Atlanta Constitution* reported on September 1 that General Young was returning to the United States "about the 15th of September on a ninety days' leave of absence, and that he would arrive in Atlanta about October 1, to shake hands with his friends." As soon as he completed his official business in Washington Pierce hurried to Atlanta to see his friends Henry W. Grady and Governor John B. Gordon. Several days later he arrived at the Jones home near Kingston; he was shocked to see his sister in such frail health.

By November, after talking the matter over with his doctor and friends, Pierce began to have doubts about whether he should return to Russia. He felt that to do so would mean certain death to him—he did not believe that he could endure another Russian winter.

On November 12, Governor Gordon wrote President Cleveland recommending that Pierce be appointed minister to Turkey, to succeed S. S. Cox, who had been elected to Congress. "His high character, his talents, and his recent experience in Russia as well as the high positions heretofore, [indicate that] he will discharge his duties faithfully and efficiently, and will reflect credit upon your administration and the country." Henry Grady also recommended Young's name to the President for the Turkish mission, for he believed the appointment would mean much to Georgia and to the whole South. Grady pointed out that as chief consul at St. Petersburg General Young had represented his country "with a dignity and capability that well merit him for higher honors in the diplomatic service," adding, "A nobler, truer heart does not beat than that of Pierce Young, and his promotion to this important mission would be a deserved compliment to the democratic stronghold of the South."[10]

However, unable to get a transfer or another appointment, General Young wrote his friend Alucire Lothrop, wife of the American minister in Moscow, that he disliked his post at St. Petersburg so strongly that he had decided not to return. He predicted that most Americans living there would die of some respiratory disease because of the severe winters. In her reply, Mrs. Lothrop chided Pierce for his "gloomy forebodings" and stated that she had gotten over her homesickness and was quite content to stay. However, she felt that her husband was wasting his abilities in Russia, "where there is so little of importance to do but," she added, "he seems contented, if not he is wise and says nothing." Mrs. Lothrop said that they had heard Pierce's name mentioned in connection with some post, but did not know what to believe. "When your fate is decided, I am sure you will let us know. Have you really any idea of returning here? I hope we may have the pleasure of seeing you, but feel sure nothing could tempt you to live here."

Realizing by December 12 that he was not going to get another appointment, Pierce wrote a friend, Miss Annie C. Ropes, at St. Petersburg that he was thinking of returning to his post there. She replied that this was the best news of his letter. Then she added: "You were indeed fortunate in being away from here this fall. The weather for three months was simply indescribable. I could not tell you how dreadful it has been without using stronger language that would be unladylike. You can give your imagination full play and you cannot possibly think of it as worse than it was."

Whether or not Miss Ropes' letter influenced General Young is difficult to determine but on December 18 while he was visiting in Washington, he wrote his letter of resignation to President Cleveland, to take effect in thirty days. Pierce explained: "I am impelled to take this step on account of the effect of the severe climate of that city upon my constitution. I have suffered much during my sojourn of a winter and summer in Russia, so much that I am advised by my physician that it would be extremely hazardous for me to return there during the winter months. I had hoped during my leave of absence in Georgia, on personal business, to be entirely restored to my usual strength, but without success. During my term in consular service, I have been treated with the utmost kindness and consideration by all of the officers of the Department of State—for which I desire to express my profound thanks."

XIII

◇◇◇
◇

An Apostle of the New South

IN 1887 GENERAL YOUNG re-assumed his status as a gentleman farmer. He found that his brother-in-law had not been
a success as overseer of Walnut Plantation. The farm was heavily
involved in debt despite the efforts of his sister (now a semi-
invalid) to administer the plantation in her brother's absence
and make it pay.

As soon as he was able, Pierce began to renew his social and
political contacts in Washington and Atlanta. A momentous event
in Atlanta and Georgia was the Piedmont Exposition, initiated
by Henry W. Grady, which opened on October 10. Pierce attended and heard Governor John B. Gordon give the main
address, wildly acclaimed by the more than twenty thousand who
attended the Exposition that day.[1]

But the highlight of the Piedmont Exposition for the South
and especially for Pierce was the visit of President Grover Cleveland and his bride, the former Frances Folson. The presidential
train arrived in Atlanta at 11:25 P.M. on October 17. The rainy,
gloomy weather did not affect the exuberance and joy that
Georgians felt in welcoming a President for the first time in
many years. There were thousands of people in and around the
Union Depot to greet the President and his wife as the train
pulled in. Upon leaving the train, the guests were driven to the
Kimball House, in front of which a squad of the Governor's
horse guard under the command of Captain John Milledge maintained order. General Young, along with Charles A. Collier,
President of the Exposition, accompanied President Cleveland
to the hotel. Henry Grady escorted Mrs. Cleveland.

The next day, Pierce attended the party at the executive mansion given by Governor Gordon, and the elaborate reception for President and Mrs. Cleveland at the Capital City Club.

Although it rained most of October 19, the third day of the Exposition, General Young, as well as thousands of Georgians, felt that it was a great day for the state. For Pierce the day began with a breakfast at the home of Senator Colquitt in Edgewood. Then in the afternoon he participated in the great military parade which began in front of the State House on Marietta Street and ended at the Exposition grounds where a grand review was held. Along the route an incident happened that showed the human and unprejudiced character of General Young. At one point a Negro man "carrying a beautiful golden haired girl of six or seven years rushed into the street moving toward the carriage; a police officer attempted to ride in front of the Negro, calling out, 'Go back there!' General Young, riding in the center of his Gate City Staff guards, who were in full uniform, was immediately behind the President's carriage; he saw a beautiful bouquet in the little girl's hand and called out: 'Let him in!' " The police officer moved away and the Negro hurried to the side of the carriage. President Cleveland reached out and, taking the child by the hand, accepted her gift, to loud applause of the crowd.[2]

Although the rain continued, thousands of people thronged the streets, and the *Constitution* in an editorial on October 21, 1887, stated that too much praise could not be bestowed upon the officers of General Young's staff, "who reported so promptly and rendered such efficient service in the rain during the whole day of the 19th, and the Exposition Company tenders them and the officers and men of the different commands, who participated in the exercise at the grounds, their warmest thanks."

Several days after the Presidential visit was over Pierce went to Richmond, Virginia, to attend the dedication of a monument to Robert E. Lee. There he renewed his acquaintance with former army comrades and friends and later visited battlegrounds that he had not seen since the War.

Returning to Walnut Plantation as the cotton and corn crops were being harvested, he knew that unless he personally supervised the plantation very little money would be realized. No sooner had he settled at home, however, than he became actively engaged in county politics. At a mass meeting held at the courthouse on July 1, 1886, the Democratic organization of Bartow was split between the followers of gubernatorial candidates Augustus O. Bacon and John B. Gordon. The result was the formation of two Democratic executive committees in the county, each faction claiming to represent the Democracy of the county. For two years there was bitter and personal misunderstanding among former friends.

Although a true supporter of the Gordon faction, General Young knew that as long as the Democratic party was split neither side would win, and a major advantage would be given to the Republicans in the eastern part of the county.

Therefore, early in 1888 Pierce encouraged the editor of the *Cartersville Courant-American* to write about the unification of the two committees. This he did on March 2, in an editorial in which he stated that the differences that occasioned the separated organization should no longer continue, for Democratic voters, whether for Gordon or Bacon in the late contest, did not desire further strife or division. Then the editor suggested that the chairmen of the two committees unite in a joint call for a convention to be held at an early date. A week later the editor warned that any man who attempted to thwart the public desire of uniting "runs the risk of incurring public displeasure, and such an action on the part of anyone will result in his personal injury."

On April 3, a committee from each faction met at the court-house to see if differences could be resolved. General Young was one of the three representatives of the Gordon faction. The chairman of each tried to resign, insisting that past differences should be laid aside and that the two factions should come together and act harmoniously as one body. Through his efforts Pierce secured the election of both men as chairmen of the Bartow County Democratic Party. Before adjourning, the Democratic Executive Committee issued a call for a mass meeting of all the Democrats of Bartow County on the first Tuesday in May, for the purpose of electing delegates to the State Democratic Convention on May 9.

General Young participated in the Democratic committee meeting and took an active role in the debate as to whether a state senatorial nomination should be made by a primary election or by a convention of delegates from the various districts in the county. He favored the new system of primary election, although Gordon opposed it in 1880, for he put county welfare first. In speaking for the primary Pierce presented several strong reasons why the method differed from the convention by offering a better opportunity for a fuller and freer expression of the wishes of the people than could be had by a district convention. Although General Young was unsuccessful in efforts to have the primary adopted by the militia districts, he succeeded in having the countywide ballot adopted.

Pierce actively participated at the Democratic mass meeting held in Cartersville on May 1. He nominated the chairman and was himself selected as one of the delegates to the State Democratic Convention. Before adjourning, the Bartow County Democrats recommended that General Young be selected a delegate from the state at large to the National Democratic Convention to be held at St. Louis, Missouri, on June 5.

The State Democratic Convention was held in the room of the lower house of the general assembly on May 9. Pierce was appointed representative from the Seventh Congressional District to the eight-member platform committee, which recommended that one plank of the platform embody the Cleveland principle on the tariff.

The *Columbus Enquirer-Sun* described the state convention as the "most intelligent and determined body of men that ever assembled in the state and the outcome of its deliberations was a fitting conclusion to the recent brilliant campaign for tariff reform." The recommendation of President Cleveland and Senator Colquitt was unanimously endorsed.[3] General Young was loud in praise of President Cleveland and his administration. He was nominated by his friend John Akin of Bartow County as a delegate-at-large to the national convention. Although pleased to be one of the eight candidates, he felt that he could do better by attending the convention as an unofficial delegate, since it was certain that the Georgia delegates would cast the state's vote for Cleveland as prescribed by the convention. Therefore, to the disappointment of his friends, he had his name withdrawn before the vote was taken.

As early as February 24, 1888, there were rumors that General Young's name had been mentioned as one of the candidates in the Congressional race of the Seventh District. The *Cartersville Courant-American,* in reporting the rumor, said: "Should Bartow's gallant cavalier be induced to enter the field, he would make a brilliant campaign and leave his competitors no time to slumber." But Pierce never planned to run for Congress and immediately denied the rumor. Almost at once a second rumor was reported by the *Courant-American* that the General would be "induced to enter the race for the state senate from the 42nd senatorial district; should he do so it will take a swift horse to distance him. Already some of the papers in the state, assuring his election as a foregone conclusion, should he run, have placed him in nomination for the presidency of the senate. And why not? He is a man of distinguished ability and would make one of the best presiding officers that body ever had." Then with a great deal of local pride, the editor added, "With the ex-congressman in the next General Assembly, Old Bartow would proudly maintain her reputation as being one of the foremost counties in the state."[4]

Henry W. Grady, in the *Constitution,* encouraged Pierce to run, and on April 29 wrote: "The cavalier of the State Senate would be General P. M. B. Young, of Cartersville. The Senatorial race is becoming more interesting in that district, and the plot thickens rapidly. Gen. P. M. B. Young is solicited to make the race by many friends, and will probably announce himself." Throughout the state friends encouraged him to make the race. He considered it seriously but realized that he had been too many years away from the local and district Democratic machines. Finally, he became aware that his interest was national rather than state or local. Secretly he still had hopes for an appointment as minister to Mexico or Spain, and, convinced that Cleveland would be elected, he felt that his future would be greater in a national capacity than as a member of the state general assembly. On June 7, Pierce announced that he would not be a candidate for the state senate, and expressed good wishes for the two candidates, J. "Watt" Harris, Jr., and Dr. T. H. Baker.

Always interested in the natural resources of his district, Pierce devoted his time to the plantation and to promoting the development of mineral resources (iron and manganese ore) in Bartow County. Through his efforts Northern concerns were encouraged to invest in the local mining interest, and local citizens were encouraged to organize and to "sell" the county to outsiders.

One of the plans adopted was to invite outstanding leaders to visit Cartersville and to speak at planned rallies. General Young was able to persuade John B. Gordon, the Governor, to speak at the opera house in Cartersville on Saturday, May 5. Later he invited Henry Grady and Joseph E. Brown to Cartersville to speak and boost interest in developing the local mineral wealth. Not able to invest much money himself, Pierce encouraged others, hoping that some mineral would be found on his plantation.

General Young also encouraged the recognition of the Confederate soldier. He never lost an opportunity to speak of the sacrifice and courage of those who died or were wounded in fighting for the Lost Cause. At the twenty-sixth Memorial Day service in Atlanta on May 2, 1889, he delivered the principal address. Before thousands of Atlantans gathered to pay tribute, Pierce praised the valor of the Confederate soldier but added that his behavior in battle was not the most brilliant part of his career. "His record in peace was the brightest jewel in his crown. Notwithstanding the desolation of war, he went to work to rebuild his shattered fortune, and presented to the world one of the grandest spectacles it has ever seen. His success has been phenomenal. . . ." Then he listed the various enterprises that Confederate soldiers had successfully built, and the important political positions they held.

General Young often found occasion to go to the defense of his former comrades-in-arms. In June 1888, when he heard of the death of Captain Pinckney Thomas, an officer on his staff during the War, he wrote the editor of the *Augusta Chronicle*, "He was more than officer to me, for he was my true and loyal friend, as dear to me as my own blood. There was never a soul more replete with modest unselfish patriotism than was his. . . . He was as gentle as a girl. He was as brave as Caesar, and as true a knight as marched under the red cross of Richard to the Holy Land. His death fills my soul with sorrow." So impressed was the editor by the letter that he wrote an editorial entitled "A Noble Tribute," in which he stated in part, "There were few knightlier or more chivalric souls than that of General Pierce M. B. Young. His old comrades are warmly attached to him, and his own feeling for members of his staff and command is deep and tender and lasting. Perhaps this sentiment in the soldier's heart for those who fought at his side strengthens with age, and becomes more sensitive as the men who were spared in battle are, one by one, removed by death."[5]

In 1890, learning that General Wade Hampton of South Carolina was being shunted aside by the newly organized legislature, and concerned about the lack of appreciation of Hampton, Pierce wrote Senator Butler that he did not believe the people of South Carolina could turn their back upon General Hampton. "If it could be so, there would be but one other glaring event of history during the last hundred years that would rival it, and that was the shooting of Marshal Ney by the French people." Young reviewed the war record of General Hampton and described his leadership in the Reconstruction. He told how Hampton helped to restore South Carolina to the union and to place her on the high road of safety and success along which she now traveled, saying that he did not believe the veterans in the South Carolina legislature would repudiate their leader.

The need for money continued to dog General Young and on June 11, 1888, J. W. Waldrip brought suit against him. The judgment was rendered in favor of the plaintiff, and Pierce had to borrow the money to pay. Not discouraged because of his debts, he continued sure in his belief that Cleveland would be elected and that he would be able to get a foreign service appointment. He spent, and borrowed to buy, or bought on credit. He and his creditors alike seemed foolish—he in asking for so much credit, and they in granting so much. The entire summer and fall were a fictional paradise for Pierce. He was so sure of Cleveland's success that he never worried or planned anything for the next year except to be in the foreign service.

On the afternoon of the election, Tuesday, November 6, Pierce went to Atlanta to hear the returns as they were posted by the *Constitution*. All through the night he waited for the good news of Cleveland's success. It did not come. Heavy-hearted, he returned to Walnut Plantation; he could hardly believe that his Democratic world had fallen apart. Although President Cleveland had received a plurality of 100,000 votes, the Republican candidate, Benjamin Harrison, won by an electoral vote of 233 to Cleveland's 168. But General Young could say with Grady that President Cleveland was "as great in defeat as he was in triumph," and that he had made the best president this republic had ever had.

Pierce tried to forget that his world had shattered around him by devoting long hours of every day to gathering the crop and planting wheat and oats. He took stock of his financial and political status and made certain decisions. One was to begin at once to work for the reelection of his friend President Cleveland in 1892, and he believed one of the best ways to do this was to speak at every occasion possible. First, however, he had to recoup his finances. Borrowing as much money as possible from the bank on the 1889 crop in order to plant, Pierce began to explore the possibilities of several jobs.

General Young went to Augusta in December to visit Editor Patrick Walsh of the *Chronicle* and to confer with Senator Butler

of South Carolina. He wanted to discuss with his friends the plans
for the future of the Democratic party in the next presidential
election. In reporting Young's visit the *Chronicle* described him
as one of the most popular fighting officers that Georgia gave to
the Lost Cause and stated that his diplomatic service had in no
way detracted from his good record as a soldier.

An amusing incident happened in 1889 while General Young
was visiting Catoosa Springs, a favorite summer resort of Savannah and Atlanta socialites. One day he saw an old fellow come
up with a basket of eggs and a bunch of chickens for the hotel
people and recognized him as an old trooper of his command.

"Jake," Pierce called out; "Jake Dorridge, how are you?"

"Why, laws a massy, General, how-de-do? I haint seed you since
the wah."

They chatted for a few minutes. "Do you come here often,
Jake?"

"Pooty nigh every day. The folks want my chickens 'n' aigs. I
like to rest my eyes a-looking at some o'those yer pooty gals."

"They are handsome, aren't they, Jake?[1]"

"Deed they are," Jake replied quickly.

"Now Jake," said General Young pointing his hand toward a
group of three young ladies with whom he had been talking,
"tell me which of those three young ladies is the prettiest."

"Aw, General Young, they's all pooty. 'Twouldn't be good manner for me to say ary one was pootier'n tother."

"But, Jake, it will give them a great deal of pleasure to learn
your opinion. They are great friends, and will not feel at all hurt
by your decision. Now, walk right up and pick out the best
looking."

After much solicitation Jake undertook the task. He walked
up and peered closely at the laughing girls. About a hundred
guests had gathered by this time to see the trial. Finally Jake
turned, scratching his head. All three of the young ladies wore
broad sashes around their waists.

"General Young, they's all three so putty it's hard to make a
choice, but still I am forced to say that the one with the yaller
belly band is a leetle the trimmest."

There were ladylike screams, and in a flutter of white dresses
three young ladies with various colored sashes dashed into the
hotel out of sight.[6]

Memorial Day, April 27, 1889, was observed with special pomp
and ceremony in Atlanta. The *Constitution* described the "long

and picturesque procession" which excited the enthusiasm of thousands of people who lined the streets and followed it to Oakland Cemetery, where the exercises were held. It was a colorful parade of marching veterans and cadets accompanied by bands, and carriages filled with attractive ladies who were officers of the Memorial Association, and also the city mayor, members of the city council, and the orator of the day, General Pierce Manning Butler Young. When the General arose to speak, he was greeted with cheers. He spoke under difficulties, for a strong wind was blowing, making it almost impossible for those in the rear to hear him. The newspaper reported that General Young's "oration was peculiarly appropriate and particularly eloquent, one of the most eloquent ever delivered upon a similar occasion." He praised the Confederate veterans and then paid tribute to Southern womanhood and the Memorial Association and the work it was doing in Georgia and the South; he also praised Henry W. Grady for what he had done for Atlanta and Georgia. He declared that the crowning act of Grady's life was his proposal for a Confederate Home, "for he will build it, and it will endear him to every member of every soldier's family in his native state. Long may he live to enjoy their gratitude."

Speaking of the solid South, General Young said: "We are not solid in a bad sense, we are solid in devotion to our country, solid in our determination that the honor and virtue and intelligence of these states be maintained. I would to God we could today forget every bad feeling engendered by the war, that we might live in peace and affection, and march hand in hand, shoulder to shoulder, no north, no south, in pursuit of one common, great and glorious object—the prosperity of our common country."

General Young was selected as the orator for the memorial services at Kingston on May 10. His name "brought out the people from all sections of the country" and they "were delighted and were loud in their praise of the grand speech" which he delivered.[7]

In the years 1889 and 1893 General Young, encouraged by Grady, wrote several articles for the *Constitution*, describing his experiences as a cadet at West Point and as a soldier during the war. These articles were widely read, and many of his former army friends wrote to him after reading them.

December 6, 1889, brought to Pierce the news of the death of Jefferson Davis at New Orleans. Although he did not always agree with Davis while he was president of the Confederacy, Pierce, during his cadet days at West Point, had learned to admire him, and after the war the treatment of the Confederate President by the United States made Pierce look on him as a symbol of all that the Lost Cause stood for. As soon as the news of President Davis's death was announced, General Young was one of a group meeting in the headquarters of the Confederate Veterans Association of Fulton County, at the request of W. L. Calhoun, the President and Commander. He was appointed to a committee of five to prepare memorial resolutions. The resolutions expressed the "honor in which his old soldiers held Jefferson Davis—the high estimate they had of him as a statesman, soldier, patriot, and gentleman, and the love they cherished for him as their old commander . . . [they] proudly point to his brave patient life, his unswerving devotion to duty and truth and his self-sacrificing patriotism. . . ."[8]

General Young was also a member of a committee of ten appointed by the Fulton County Confederate Veterans' Association to attend the funeral in New Orleans. Soon after the committee arrived, Pierce and his friend Dr. J. William Jones visited the casket of their former chief executive. The *Constitution* stated that the two men were overcome with grief, and cried, unashamed.[9]

Later in the day when Dr. Jones visited Mrs. Davis, he mentioned Pierce's name. "Do you mean General Pierce Young?" asked Mrs. Davis with evident interest. When Dr. Jones gave an affirmative answer, she replied, "Why, I knew him when he was nothing but a boy, when Mr. Davis gave him his commission; I remember, too, that he was a dashing officer, and I would like to see him." During the afternoon General Young called to see Mrs. Davis at the Charles E. Fenner House, where her husband had died. The paper described the meeting as "one of full feeling."[10] General Young was deeply touched by the changes in the lady since he had last seen her.

But a greater personal loss to Pierce was the death of Henry W. Grady on December 23, 1889. His grief was profound, for Grady had been a close friend and adviser since his days with the *Rome Daily Tribune*. Much of the early relationship with President Cleveland was through his friendship with Grady— even his appointment as vice consul at St. Petersburg. Although Mrs. Grady wanted a simple funeral, on December 25, the day of the service, streets of Atlanta were decorated in funeral black and white and lined with thousands of silent, sorrowing people. A statement by one of Grady's nearest friends that "He is the last man with whom I would ever associate death," expressed Young's feelings.

The price of cotton steadily declined and reached a new low in 1889. Although Pierce had advocated crop rotation and cover crops since 1868, he knew that many of the farmer's economic ills were caused by his inability to raise his own supplies and stock. So Pierce watched with interest the growth and development of the Farmers Alliance, which gained control of the general assembly of Georgia in 1890. He felt that much constructive legislation was enacted but, fearing that the political control would hurt him in political affairs, Pierce did not join the Alliance. He believed that legislation was only part of the answer —agricultural education and experiments also were essential. So he became a life member of the Georgia State Agriculture Society, organized in 1846, to encourage experimentation in soil improvement and planning. On his plantation he experimented with various cover crops and animal breeding.

For the next four years, 1890-1894, General Young, in addition to his farming, engaged in various business activities. One of these was serving as a contractor to sell lumber, clay, and brick. He bought lumber and brick from several Alabama concerns and contracted with the city of Birmingham and with the village of Asheville, North Carolina, to pave several streets. This venture was not a financial success, as attested by his bank statements during the enterprise. Too frequently he gave checks on Birmingham or Chattanooga or Newnan banks trying to forestall checks which he knew were not good; too often he received a notice from the Alabama National Bank of Birmingham that he had overdrawn and that he must remit immediately. Pierce received so little financial return from his business ventures during these years that his condition was almost penurious, and he was unable to assist his sister.

During the years 1891 and 1892, General Young traveled throughout Georgia and South Carolina speaking to veterans' organizations and at reunions. He supported the "New South" which he had advocated before in his writing and speeches. He did not resent the Negro but tried, as had Grady, to uphold him in his opportunities to work. Exploiting him, whether for political or economic reasons, Pierce bitterly condemned, for he believed the adjustment of the Negro would have to be by an evolutionary process. Both white and Negro had to be educated in what was best for each race. He was in favor of educating the Negro, but he frequently asked his friends, educate him for what?

General Young realized that the poor white, who had also become a victim of the post-war economy of share cropping, was the real problem in the adjustment of the freed Negro because the poor white had to compete economically with the Negro in order to live. Pierce bitterly opposed the appeal to Civil War prejudices by many politicians to keep themselves in office. He condemned the demagogic tactic of clouding every political problem by yelling "nigger."

XIV

◊◊◊
◊

Minister to Nicaragua and Honduras

THE PRESIDENTIAL election in 1892 was held on November 1, and General Young with other Democrats was overwhelmed by the returns. His friend Grover Cleveland with the Vice Presidential candidate Adlai E. Stevenson won the nomination over the Republican candidates Benjamin Harrison and Whitlaw Reed. The *Atlanta Constitution* expressed its exultation in headlines: "Redeemed! The Union Once More in the Hands of Democracy. Cleveland and Stevenson—A Democratic Tidal Wave Sweeps the Country!"

Realizing that the death of Henry W. Grady broke one of his main contacts with President Cleveland, General Young, in 1892, began to renew his friendship with the Democratic leaders in an attempt to obtain an appointment in the foreign service. He recognized that one way to make himself known to the Southern party leaders was to work through the United Confederate Veterans, whose commanding general was Gordon. Pierce accepted the position of major general in the organization and traveled throughout the South organizing local Confederate camps. For a while he acted as a lobbyist for the Florida Central and Peninsular Railroad Company.

By November 1892 the rumor had become publicized that Pierce would receive an appointment as Minister to Mexico. The *Macon Telegraph* opined that the appointment would be but another honor in his wreath of success. "General Young should receive recognition from the president and claim any honor he wishes since he is not only one of the most prominent politicians in the South, but one of the most loyal and lovable of men." The *Atlanta Constitution* reported on December 31, 1892, that the friends and admirers of General Pierce M. B. Young were claiming for him the mission to Mexico. The paper thought that the people were justified in believing that he would be *persona grata* in the ancient Aztec capital because he had already exemplified American diplomacy and chivalry under the rigid poles of Russian palaces. "The United States could have no truer, safer minister in the eruptive republic than General Young, and his appointment to that, or any other befitting post, would be applauded by his wide constituency of admirers in all parts of the union." One of the recommendations for Pierce was signed by several of the Georgia congressmen who wanted for him a first class mission in the diplomatic service of the United States, saying, "He is qualified by long political and official experience, and we ask his appointment to such a position." A few, like Congressmen R. W. Everett and L. F. Livingston, wrote directly to Democratic President-elect Cleveland recommending Pierce as Minister to Mexico. They believed that "his life-long devotion to the Democratic party, his efficient services as elector, his experience and acknowledged ability as a National Legislator, his acceptable services as Consul-General to Russia, his high social standing, his unquestioned ability, integrity and devotion to duty, his dignified bearing and pleasing address, peculiarly fit him for the responsible position sought." On March 4, 1893, Senator Alfred H. Colquitt wrote his commendation that no man could be found more suitable for the appointment. On the same day Congressman Ben E. Russell of Georgia added, "He is one of the foremost men in the South, a man without fear and without reproach."

Five days after his inauguration, Cleveland sent to the Senate the nomination of ex-Governor Gray of Indiana as Minister to Mexico. This meant that Pierce would have to look elsewhere. One of the papers stated that General Young was, however, a close friend of Cleveland and would "probably receive a first-class position in the foreign service. . . . General Young saw the president and secretary of state this morning, and filed his application for a foreign ministership. The application was for no specific office, but he will get a good mission, probably Austria, or Spain."[1]

On March 18 the two Georgia senators, Gordon and Colquitt, wrote the Secretary of State "making earnest and special request for the appointment of General P. M. B. Young for the position of United States Minister to Guatemala or the other mission of Central America."[2] They felt him eminently qualified as evidenced by his education, training, and ability, which would insure wise and efficient administration. Four days later Senator Gordon and Speaker Charles F. Crisp, a Georgian, called on President Cleveland in the interest of a number of Georgians who desired appointments. They supported the claim of Pierce for a foreign mission. The President replied that he had General Young in view and would consider him within a few days.[3]

General Pierce M. B. Young was appointed by President Grover Cleveland on March 30, 1893, as envoy extraordinary and minister plenipotentiary to Guatemala and Honduras. The *Atlanta Constitution*[4] in reporting the appointment stated that the mission was the best of the second class with a salary of $10,000 and an additional allowance of $2,000 for the rent of a residence. The editor said that Pierce's headquarters would be in Guatemala City, which had 4,000 inhabitants and was nearly four hundred feet above the sea. He explained that Minister Young would have much to do, since the reciprocity treaties had been perfected with those countries in the way of increasing the commercial relations of Guatemala and Honduras with the United States. "He will probably devote particular attention to building up a market for our cotton fabrics."

Then followed a detailed sketch of General Young's life. In appraising the new minister, the editor stated that he was preeminently qualified by ability and experience. He believed that General Young's military training would impress "the Central Americans and strengthen their friendship for our republic." He continued: "It is to be regretted that the minister will find a revolution raging in Honduras when he reaches that country, but his positive qualities will cause the revolutionary factions to respect him and his government, and he will see to it that American interests suffer no injury."

Georgians were pleased over the recognition given General Young and believed that he would do an excellent job. One of Pierce's friends expressed in rhyme the general feelings:

> All hail, the gallant Georgian
> Who goes to Guatemala,
> To bear aloft our country's flag,
> And eat the hot tamale!

The nation's interest will be safe
With such a pink of duty,
But ill fare it with the heart
Of some Honduran beauty.[5]

On April 12, General Young was sworn in as minister to Guatemala before the United States District Judge for the Northern
District of Georgia, William T. Newman. He planned to remain
in Georgia a week before returning to Washington, and later to
sail for Guatemala on May 10. Meanwhile he received hundreds
of congratulatory letters from Georgians and friends all over the
South. *Harper's Weekly* of April 13 exhibited a portrait of the
new Minister to Guatemala and Honduras, and of Professor Eben
Alexander of North Carolina, the new Minister to Greece. General Young was pictured in the high fur cap and sables of "his
Russian incumbency as consul general to St. Petersburg, but it
is our same distinguished and gallant 'general' nevertheless."

There were frequent rumors that the voyage to Guatemala
would be a honeymoon. Soon after his appointment there was
printed in the "Georgia Personals" on the editorial page of the
Atlanta Constitution the rumor that General P. M. B. Young
would carry "a charming bride" with him to Guatemala. "When
did cupid catch him napping, and on whose behalf was the archer
out for game . . . ? The gallant general has seen enough genera-
tions of beautiful women in the high society of his native and
foreign countries and the fact of his at last resigning the freedom
of his bachelorhood will be a pretty clear compliment to the
woman he has chosen. . . ."[6] Although Pierce denied there was any
truth in the rumor, the leading Georgia papers continued to
print it.

Immediately after General Young took his oath, he had the
task of attending to a flood of requests from people seeking information or a market for something they had to sell in Guatemala. And added to his problem of making final arrangements
for departure was another worry. In settling the affairs of the
estate with his brother's children, Pierce had to sell a part of
the plantation which had been in his family since his mother and
father came to Georgia from South Carolina fifty-six years before.

Because of the strain incident to the trip, Louisa insisted that
her husband Tom go with Pierce to Guatemala to help him until
he was settled—so she told her brother. Actually she was worried
about his health and did not think he should make the trip alone;
he had lost too much weight and seemed to tire too easily. She

dreaded seeing Pierce go to Central America where one heard
there were such dreaded tropical diseases as malaria and yellow
fever. Louisa remembered the plague of 1890 in Jacksonville, and
how people fled into north Georgia to escape it. She feared that
her brother's life was in danger in what she believed to be a wild
and almost unexplored frontier peopled with savages. At first
General Young opposed Dr. Jones's leaving his family but when
the latter admitted that he would like to go along to have a
vacation, Pierce was willing, and plans were made for the two to
leave for Guatemala. Pierce would go by Washington to receive
final instructions, and he would meet Dr. Jones in New York.
Before sailing Dr. Jones wrote his wife that Pierce was "quite well
and hearty and was delighted that I did not back out as he feared
I would. . . ."

Pierce and Tom sailed from New York on the steamship
Columbia. A newspaper reporter describing the sailing stated
that a party of General P. M. B. Young's friends escorted him
to his steamship and bade him bon voyage to his new home in
Guatemala. He said further that General Young was very popular
with "the southern contingent in New York and the crowd that
assembled at the dock to bid him adieu was only second to that
which received the Spanish Infanta yesterday."[7]

Pierce and his brother-in-law first landed in Panama, where
they were the guests of Colonel A. L. Rives at his magnificent
home "The Point" for a few days. Then they sailed to Guatemala
City where they were "received with every evidence of distinguished consideration."[8] In describing the arrival, one newspaper
reported that a private train beautifully decorated and bearing
the national colors of both countries met the distinguished guest,
"who was escorted to the capital by those members of the legation
famous already for their magnificent entertainments on former
occasions and General Pacheco, former United States Minister,
who had won a place in the warm hearts of the Guatemaltees
now gracefully resigned in favor and welcomed General Young
whose fame as a diplomat and general had long since preceded
him." The reporter added that General Young had been confined to his room with rheumatism since his arrival and had to
decline General Pacheco's invitation to be a guest at his home.[9]

One reporter described in detail the installation of Pierce as
minister. The ceremony took place in "a long hall decorated with
flags, swords, guns and many kinds of arms. At the far end, on an
elevated stage, sat the president, surrounded by his cabinet minis-

ters, and other distinguished dignitaries of the republic. The president was in full uniform. As General Young advanced with the retiring minister, all rose and bowed low. Then the minister of state presented the retiring United States minister, who delivered a brief address and tendered his letters of recall. General Young then moved in front of the president and delivered this brief address: 'Mr. President: In presenting to your excellency my credentials as envoy extraordinary and minister plenipotentiary from the United States to Guatemala I extend to you and the people of Guatemala the good will of the president and the people of the United States. It gives me pleasure to attest the able and agreeable manner in which my distinguished predecessor has labored to foster and maintain those relations of friendship which have so long existed between the two republics. During my official residence in your excellency's capital, it will be my constant effort to render stronger and closer ties which now so closely bind together Guatemala and the United States of America.' "

When Pierce concluded his speech, the president responded with a short address, extending his hand to General Young and inviting him to take the seat of honor on his right. Then a general presentation of the new minister took place. After these ceremonies, the American party reentered the carriage of state, and were driven back to the Grand Hotel.[10] Pierce spent the rest of the day devoting his time to calling on the various foreign legations of the capital.

The new minister enjoyed his sister's first letter; Louisa was happy over his "delightful" and "instructional" trip, and encouraged him to write about his experiences. She concluded: "Now, my dear brother, remember you are all that is left to me of our once happy home circle, and for my sake take care of yourself and come back to see us when this mission will admit." In a letter to her husband she expressed concern for Pierce's health and safety.

Some letters that Pierce received disturbed him. All was not well in the States. Friends wrote expressing grave concern over the economic conditions in the South, where "money is out of sight and still going." During the summer he received a welcome letter from his good friend Senator Colquitt. The Senator wrote on July 8 that the conflict between President Cleveland and Wall Street seemed to have stampeded Congress and the country, but he felt that the reaction would come before Congress met. Then he confessed with much concern: "I am satisfied we have ahead of us the most desperate fight in Congress since the days of reconstruction. Both parties are split, the issue being more sectional than otherwise, and more important than any now before the country. The Sherman Act is in itself a small matter but its repeal is intended to fix the single gold standard upon us, a calamity so frightful that I cannot describe it." He expressed concern for Pierce's health, for he had heard about his illness, and ended by saying "That you are performing your very arduous duties as they ought to be, I can very well understand, and you are keeping up the dignity of the Republic. . . ."

General Young was homesick after his brother-in-law left for the States on July 2. On his way home Tom wrote a letter from each place where the ship docked, and the letter made Pierce determined to return home as soon as he could. He could see already that the Central American climate did not agree with him.

Pierce received a letter from one of the assistant secretaries in the State Department that D. Lynch Pringle, formerly at Constantinople, had been nominated and confirmed as Secretary of the Guatemalan legation. The letter included a good opinion of Pringle's record and a description of him as honest, competent, and faithful.[11] When a letter came from Pringle himself from Washington with information that he had been recently appointed and would report about the first week in December, Pierce was pleased. Pringle specifically requested permission to pass his personal baggage through the customs at St. Jose. The request was granted. Now that Pringle was on the way Pierce began to make his plans to return to the States.

General Young was anxious to hear of Tom's safe arrival at home. He had given Tom to take to Louisa silver worth hundreds of dollars and Guatemalan coins for his nieces and nephew. What he feared most happened. The night before the ship landed in New York, Dr. Jones, after a late dinner, went to bed early, "locked the door, put my pants under the pillow, containing the silver you gave me. My purse containing the Guat coins and key to the valise hung in my vest at head of bed, and behold this morning my pants were in middle of the floor and everything gone; felt in the vest and my watch also was gone; spoke to purser and Capt. about it and all the comfort I got was that I could get a search warrant when I went ashore and have everybody coming ashore searched." Tom further explained that he had lost all of the letters of recommendations which Pierce had sent. "How much I was worried by all this I cannot express, but at the same time, it cannot be helped now. I will do my utmost to restore all these losses to you, my dear Gen., and also to repay your unstinted kindness and generosity." Pierce decided there was nothing to be done to recover the loss. He knew that Tom Jones was not a well man, and suspected that he had forgotten to lock his door.

Although General Young was occupied with his duties in Nicaragua, he still was interested in national affairs in the States. He wrote to Senators Gordon and Colquitt of Georgia, and also to Senator M. C. Butler of South Carolina. The latter replied on August 6, that matters were uncertain in Washington, and "a great deal depends upon the President's attitude on the financial question. If he stubbornly refuses to make concessions, and demands the unconditional repeal of the Sherman Law, there will be trouble. If on the other hand," wrote Butler, "he shows a spirit of compromise, we shall get along smoothly enough. . . . I think the indications are of a reaction—and a falling off of the influences which carried our people so far astray." General Butler explained that everything, however, depended on the Congress.

Letters from Louisa indicated the precarious financial conditions and the fear of farmers in Georgia. On August 21, she wrote: "Times are so hard here that the people seem panic stricken, and fear they may not have even bread to sustain life. The long dry spell has cut off the acreage yield of corn and many have long since given up the luxury of bacon." She reassured her brother that they were not suffering for they still had an abundance of fine vegetables and a good prospect for a turnip crop. In the same letter her husband added a note that times were getting "closer here every day and many good people living on roasting ears alone. No such thing as money or credit for supplies and everybody still cursing the financial part of the President's message." Realizing the financial strait of his sister, General Young began each month to send her money to assist in the family's finances.

From the first, General Young was extremely busy with diplomatic affairs. One of his initial tasks was to move the legation from Number 61 Calle Real to the Grand Hotel until more satisfactory arrangements could be made. In his first dispatch from Washington were data on the case of the steamship *Joseph Otere* with instructions for him to proceed to Honduras and to investigate the matter. Minister Young wrote Secretary of State W. L. Gresham that he would proceed to Honduras as soon as the condition of the roads over the mountains would permit.

Several weeks later he reported that the torrential rains prevented his departure, and that it would require almost a month to make the trip. Just before the time to go Pierce received a telegram from the American vice consul at Tegucigalpa reporting that a yellow fever epidemic had broken out and that the port was quarantined. So he was delayed in his investigation.

After he had been in Guatemala for a month, Pierce wrote to a friend that the people "grow upon" one daily; the climate was perfect, and the people were kind and polite. "I am much pleased with my post. . . . The soil is the richest I have ever seen. No plows are used by the natives, only big hoes and a kind of pick axe. All the vegetables and field crops we grow can be grown here. Corn grows almost without cultivation. Cattle and hogs live out all the year round without being fed, so do horses, and all other animals. It is certainly the land for the poor man for he can live with but little work. There are many fine stores in this city and a great deal of trade—all in cash. Coffee is the great money crop, but everything brings a good price and sells readily. The market is rich in many kinds of fruits and vegetables. His first business report to Secretary of State Gresham was to ascertain whether one Weeks, "a defaulter of New York," had fled to Honduras or Guatemala. He informed the Secretary that the government of Guatemala promised to do all that was necessary if Weeks should be found in the Republic.[12]

Throughout August, Pierce made plans to visit Honduras, but the yellow fever epidemic and the quarantine of the town of Amapala prevented his going. Furthermore, the existing government in Honduras would be only provisional and temporary until an election could be held. Pierce wrote to the Secretary of State on August 23, "There appears to be no doubt that the Provisional President will be elected as I am informed there will be no opposition. I believe it is best for me not to present my credentials until I can do so to a regularly constituted government." He reported that the provisional president had not been officially recognized by any of the other republics of Central America and would not be until after the election. "As soon as the new government is organized I shall proceed to Honduras and transact the business intrusted to me by the Department of State," advised General Young.[13]

After about six weeks Pierce wrote a private letter to Secretary Gresham, giving his opinions of Guatemala, the government, and the people: "I find in this country that to deceive and even

to do that which is the opposite of common honesty is of every
day occurrence, and it is not confined to private individuals but
is practiced by high government officials. Promises mean nothing
but delay and no dependence can be placed in the verbal declara-
tion of any of these people . . . but you cannot depend upon
any practical result unless you back up your demands by a sufficient show of power to enforce your demands. In my opinion
only results will come when you let these people know that you
mean to do them harm unless they comply and they will put
you off to the last moment."

General Young expressed concern over the resolution which
approved a new secretary of legation, for he wanted someone
who had *"never lived in any of these Central or South American
countries"* or, if possible one who had never been in Guatemala.
Pierce thought the ability to speak the Spanish language was of
the smallest possible consequence, for all persons with whom
they had to do business spoke English, and "If there is any
translation to be done we always use a sworn translator." The
most important thing was to have "a man of sterling integrity
and one who is industrious and who has never lived in this
country. A man who has resided here and been in business
here for a few years seems to have fallen into the Latin way
of regarding private honesty, that seems so prevalent in this
atmosphere."

An election was held in Honduras on August 7, and Pierce
reported to the Secretary of State that it passed off quietly and
that on the 15th of September General Domingo Vasquez[14] was
inaugurated President. On that day Vasquez issued a proclamation of general amnesty, "and those of the late revolution party
who had fled from their country are now returning, and there
seems to be a good prospect of peace and prosperity for that
Republic," said Pierce's report.

If Minister Young thought he had been thoroughly indoc-
trinated in Central American affairs, his ability and patience
may have been shaken by an incident that occurred the first
week of September. Marcus Goldtree [Gotlieb], an American
citizen of San Francisco, claimed that when he landed at the
port of Champerico from the steamship *St. Paul,* his goods were
confiscated and he was arrested and thrown into a filthy hot prison
and kept there for eight days, without any change of clothing.
Before he could come to trial Goldtree was released but was not
given his merchandise. He claimed that, under threat of being

put in chains he was made to sign a document written in Spanish. He demanded that Minister Young get "prompt redress" from the government for the great wrong done him, for he "was unjustly imprisoned and most cruelly and inhumanly treated. I have not committed any crime against the people of this country."[15] Goldtree further claimed that his name and reputation, as well as those of his firm, had suffered, and he demanded that Minister Young secure for him redress and a financial settlement of $100,000.

Perturbed by the report of mistreatment, Pierce cabled Washington for instructions and then made a formal request to Ramon A. Salzar, Minister of Foreign Relations of Nicaragua, stating that Goldtree had written him. Salzar's reply presented Goldtree in an entirely different light, for the latter had not only not told all but had lied about himself. First, he had violated the customs law, for at the time of his arrest, he was trying to smuggle on his person a number of small arms, some pieces of jewelry, and twenty-three rugs, as well as other small items. The Foreign Minister also pointed out that Goldtree had not paid his fine, nor had he availed himself of the courts of Guatemala. Therefore his demands for redress and payment were virtually an insult to the government.

General Young had learned an important lesson—to investigate with great care any complaint made before writing a formal request or protest. Provoked with Goldtree, Minister Young informed him that since he had violated Guatemalan laws, he would have to go into the Guatemalan courts. He promised that he would not make any demands unless the United States goverment directed him to do so. And he knew that under the circumstances the United States would back him.

Hardly had Pierce completed his records on Goldtree when on October 12, the President of Guatemala, General Santos Zelaya, declared himself dictator, dissolved an extra session of Congress, assumed control of the government, and ordered a new election. Minister Young cabled Secretary Gresham and in a letter of the same date explained more fully what had taken place. On October 10, Zelaya had issued a proclamation in which a tax increase of ten per cent in gold had been placed upon all taxable imports. The people of Guatemala City opposed the tax, denying that the president had authority to enforce it, and called for a special session of Congress. When the members met on October 12, they did not have a quorum; so the presi-

dent dissolved the group, took control, and ordered a new election for deputies. Then he placed the different members under
arrest and required them to report daily to the military command. "The president is today dictator, and apparently with
absolute power. The situation is grave. However, there is no
fear of an outbreak," reported General Young to Washington.[16]

A week later Pierce reported that no new development had
occurred. Zelaya had inaugurated some very salutary measures.
He had removed all duties from all livestock imported into the
Republic, as well as the duty on salted meats, "which will render
that article much cheaper than it has been and will be of interest
to most packers in the United States." Pierce stated that the
government was working well and that Guatemala was enjoying
a season of profound peace. In his report of November 2, Pierce
said that the new order of things had been accepted with satisfaction by all of the people of the Republic. He believed that
the president had inaugurated many measures calculated to
lighten the burden of the people.[17]

Affairs were not going well in Honduras, for rumors indicated
that a revolution was threatening. Revolutionists under General
Policarpo Bonilla were organizing in Nicaragua to invade the
country. General Young reported: "It is very difficult to get
reliable information from the Republic, the telegraph wires
being down. But all is not tranquil." The revolution failed and
Bonilla fled to Nicaragua. Finding that Nicaragua's government
did not wish to be involved with the Honduran revolutionists,
Bonilla left for Guatemala on the American ship the *Costa Rica*.
On November 6, at Amapala, some Hondurans fired on the
ship because the captain refused to surrender Bonilla to them.
Fortunately no one was injured and no damage incurred. Minister Young cabled Secretary Gresham three days after the incident stating that he had demanded whether the Honduran government had authorized firing on the *Costa Rica*. Pierce reported
that he was on the U.S.S. *Alliance* where he was awaiting reply;
and added grimly, "Had I authority I would make short work
of the matter." In a telegram to Antonio Lopez, Minister of
Foreign Affairs, General Young protested "against the insult to
the American flag and the illegal act of firing into the American
ship *Costa Rica* on the 6th." Then he added, "I demand a dis-
avowal of this act by your government—an apology for the same;
will your excellency give me an immediate answer to the above?"[18]

The foreign minister immediately offered an apology and disavowed the act, asserting that his government never had the least intention of causing any offense to the government of the United States. Minister Young considered that this answer satisfied the demands he had made; so he accepted it and left the *Alliance* to return to the legation.

His handling of the *Costa Rica* incident made General Young a very popular man in Nicaragua and in the United States. On November 12, Secretary Gresham issued to the public a detailed account of the incident, explaining that the apology made on the part of the Honduran government was entirely satisfactory to the United States, "and it is believed that will end the incident." In reporting the Secretary's announcement the *Atlanta Constitution* captioned the news item with "He's the Man to Do It—When General Pierce Young Demanded an Apology He Got it. Honduras is Now Mighty Sorry."

The General was making a success in the foreign service. He was liked generally in official and non-official capacity. He was warmly welcomed at social functions. He appeared to be maintaining the dignity of his station with courage and with courtesy.

XV

༚ ༚ ༚
༚

The Warwick of the South

AFTER his secretary arrived in Guatemala, Minister Young
went back to the United States on leave. He landed on
January 8 in San Francisco, and from there went on to Washington. After several days in the capital, where he reported
to the Secretary of State on conditions in Central America, he
left for home and arrived on February 2 in Atlanta, where he
was kept busy receiving the hearty welcomings of his host of
friends.

In an interview with newspaper reporters, Pierce emphasized
that Americans, especially business men, did not know very
much about the wonderful opportunities available in Guatemala. He described the large coffee plantations and the production
of fruit, sugar cane, cocoa, and coffee. He believed there was
a great future for Guatemala, and wanted to help Americans
learn the real facts about the country.[1]

After visiting his sister and her family at Walnut Plantation
for a few days, Pierce again returned to his friends in Atlanta.
Early in February he was invited by Walter G. Cooper, Chief
of the Department of Publicity and Promotion, to a meeting
of the civic board which was planning for the Cotton States
and International Exposition to be held in 1895. When called
upon to comment, Pierce stated that he thought the exposition
was a great project, and was pleased that Atlanta planned to
undertake it, "for I know that means success. It will be of vast
value to Atlanta, Georgia, and the entire South." He added
that he believed that it would do more than anything else to
draw into closer commercial relations the United States and the

states of Central and South America. "That commerce naturally belongs to us and we ought to have it. It really belongs to our own southern ports and they should take great interest in the enterprise, as they doubtless will."[2]

When asked if Guatemala, Honduras, and the other Central American states would send representatives, Pierce replied that he was sure they could be counted on, for these governments and the people were enterprising and always alive to anything that would advertise their resources. He believed that upon proper invitation they would take part and their exhibits would form a most interesting feature of the exposition.[3]

While General Young was at home, he heard from one of his staff members in Guatemala who reported an "outbreak" in the office that resulted in the dismissal of a subordinate, W. C. Stuart. He also received another letter from a refugee, F. M. Fruboden, expressing fear that Bonilla, who by this time had succeeded in being elected president of Honduras, was planning to expel "all Americans from Honduras who aided the legitimate, recognized government of Honduras against him." The writer wanted General Young to advise President Cleveland and Secretary Gresham to be slow in recognizing Bonilla's government, even after he was actually elected, until Pierce had returned and fully advised himself of the facts and occurrences of the past few months and the intentions Bonilla had for the future. Fruboden stated that he and his family had fled to Guatemala to escape the cruelty of Bonilla, and added: "Your absence just now from Central America is regretted for someone needs to assert authority rather than a subaltern."

Returning to Washington to see President Cleveland and Secretary of State Gresham, General Young then went to San Francisco, where after a delay of several days, he sailed for Central America on April 18. Back in his office, he found that the turmoil in Honduras was still seething.

Pierce was occupied with many problems. First, he was swamped by various requests from Americans throughout the United States. Many asked Minister Young to check on long lost relatives. Frequently the missing person was someone who fled the United States owing a big debt. Other requests were for information about investment in railroad or steamship lines, or offers to sell heavy cast-iron guns which were outmoded in the United States.

While General Young was on his vacation in Georgia, he

was disturbed about the low market price of cotton and corn. After his return to Guatemala he had a letter on May 25 from Clark Howell, managing editor of the *Atlanta Constitution,* who complained that "Down, down, down, goes cotton, corn, and everything else. The railroads are all in the hands of receivers, and in financial matters are getting worse. I think you are exceedingly lucky in being away safely ensconced behind a ten thousand dollar salary. . . . Our people have about all of this one [national administration] that they want."

He heard discouraging news from his family too. The dry weather had prevented planting and when the rains finally came everything was practically ruined. It was clear to General Young that things were not going well with his sister and her family. Dr. Jones could not collect for his services. Louisa wrote of her husband's inability to pay a loan which he had contracted. "Outside of my own immediate family you are my only relative and to whom else can I go? He thinks of course he will be amply able to meet the debt, but I doubt it. Tom has ever had the most perfect confidence in me, and not under any consideration would I by an act of mine forfeit that confidence, so do not write anything that is not intended for his perusal." Then she added confidentially, "About that Howard bank check, he said by mutual agreement you would send $100 to the bank for me the 1st. of June and as the Van Dyke and Hanley grocery men were pressing him persistently, if I was perfectly willing to let a part of the money go to liquidate that debt, it would greatly relieve him; of course I said yes for the debt was for family supplies. Hence I signed the check." Pierce realized that he would have to be careful in helping his sister for Dr. Jones was sensitive about anyone's aiding his family. After Pierce had rented a house he offered to send for the two oldest girls to visit him; he sent his nephew Tom, Junior, seeds from Guatemala to plant on the farm. General Young also encouraged young Tom and his sisters to be independent and praised his nephew for farming and the two older girls, Carrie and Emmie, for teaching school.

At times General Young pitied his brother-in-law; then there were times when he was discouraged about him. Therefore he was glad to learn from his sister several weeks later that Dr. Jones's health had improved and he was devoting more time to farming, although cotton was still selling cheap. "I sincerely hope this year's crop may reach a million bales and will be worth

2 or 3 cents. We could then be forced to quit growing so much which would eventuate a great benefit to the whole South," Louisa wrote.

By August the finances of the Jones family had improved. Mrs. Jones proudly bragged of the wonderful watermelon and cantaloupe crops and the fresh vegetables with which they were blessed. She also told of her oldest daughter Carrie's new adventure of taking in summer boarders. A few days later Louisa wrote thanking her brother for the fifty-dollar check enclosed in his last letter and asking him not to send any more as they had enough for their present needs. She expressed her gratitude to Pierce for offering to take her daughters, but explained they and Tommy were her life, and she would "die of grief and loneliness," if they left home. His sister warned Pierce not to settle himself "too well in Central America" so that he would not be willing "to live in old Georgia again, and don't disappoint us about the winter visit. I'm looking forward to the time with anticipations of such happiness." When Pierce became sick with rheumatism in August, Louisa was worried, and her husband also expressed his distress and hoped and prayed for a rapid recovery.

Pierce enjoyed and appreciated the letters from his sister's family, for Dr. Jones always gave the national, state, and county political news, and usually included newspaper clippings. The news on August 14 was that the primaries for the Georgia senate and house of representatives had been held. Tom expressed the hope that a tariff bill would be passed by Congress. "While it is not all we desire it will relieve the awful tension the country has suffered for so long and do infinite good," he wrote wishfully. In the fall of 1894, Dr. Jones described the political candidates and explained how strongly he opposed Dr. Felton, who was rumored as a possible candidate for Congress. He was much concerned over the growth of the Populist movement in Georgia and its success in the state election. "God only knows what will become of us! As the Rad[ical]s have a clean majority over all other parties. . . . The populists have made gains everywhere which has made them arrogant and aggressive and will probably elect many of their candidates to county offices."

Another interest of General Young besides politics was the Cotton States and International Exposition. He was glad to learn from his sister in November that Atlanta was stirred up over the exposition and every paper was full of it. Pierce had not been idle. He had persuaded Culver Smith of Atlanta to extend an invitation to the Guatemalan government to send an exhibit, with the hope that forty or fifty natives of Guatemala would be sent to the exposition. Smith explained that they intended to build a native village inside the grounds and there show all of the native games, amusements, dances, and so forth. It was planned that a number of the natives in the village would be constantly at work, making the pottery of the country, the nut-ivory carvings, the calabash work, the egg-shell carvings, and such other things as would prove of interest to the visitors at the fair. The articles made were to be sold as well as others which could be imported. Pierce also extended a formal invitation to President J. M. Barrios of Guatemala to attend the exposition. In his letter he gave many interesting facts as reasons why the republics of Central and South America should bring "handsome exhibits to the exposition to be held during the months of September, October, November, and December, 1895." Pierce added, "To one who is as deeply interested in the reforms and progressive ideas of the republic of Guatemala as his excellency the president, it is needless for me to enumerate the great advantage that may accrue to this republic from a proper and extensive exhibit of its products and its great and growing interests at this international exposition." He was serious about the Exposition, for he had hopes it would bring the South—his South—closer economically to Central America. He believed that the United States did not realize the importance of these countries, and he did everything possible to bring about a better understanding.

Throughout January 1895 General Young visited with the President of Guatemala and his wife and frequently had lunch with them. Although he was unwell, he continued to work at his post. A request for leave was turned down. Instead of improving in health, Pierce began to have trouble with his legs. He wrote in his diary on February 13, 1896, "Leg very painful," and a week later, "I am sick in bed." A few days later he recorded that he suffered severe pains from the "gout" in his legs. However, he continued to perform his diplomatic duties, attend opera, and entertain his friends, including President Barrios and his wife. In February, he collected data about a boundary dispute between Nicaragua and Mexico and sent them to Secretary Gresham.[4] By April, much to his satisfaction, the dispute had been settled amicably.

But Minister Young was having his trouble with Americans in Guatemala City. Several incidents involving physical attacks on United States citizens caused him to demand from President Barrios immediate reparation, and he was able to report that "ample compensation" was made. Much of Pierce's time was spent investigating claims by Americans against Guatemala or answering numerous inquiries of American citizens and industrialists about cheap lands, taxes, climate, coffee business, newspapers, names of lumbermen, and the market for various products, especially ammunition.

General Young complained in his letters to his sister of the untrustworthy servants upon whom he had to rely. He found that he could not trust the native cooks for they would steal and sell the groceries. He entertained his staff often and endeared himself to them by taking them on drives or allowing them frequent visits to Antigua and San Jose. He often loaned money to stranded Americans and frequently paid return fares for them.

Since his health did not improve, Pierce applied again for a leave. It was granted and in June he left for the United States. In Washington he reported in an interview that the United States was popular in Nicaragua; especially in times of trouble with other countries the nation looked to the United States. He thought that Guatemala offered great opportunities to thrifty agriculturists who had a little capital to work on. "Coffee culture is very remunerative, but it cannot be entered upon without large capital, while the production of corn and meat offers splendid opportunities for those of small capital. I have never known corn to sell for less than $2 gold per bushel, and the climate and soil are most admirably suited to such production. Hogs and all kinds of stock bring a high price in the market," he reported enthusiastically. When asked about the population, General Young replied that a great many foreigners were daily coming into Guatemala; the Germans were there in great numbers. He explained that Guatemala City had a population of 80,000 people and was rapidly growing; in fact in the past ten years its population had increased by ten thousand. Pierce assured his interviewers that anyone could travel with safety in Guatemala. No one had any fear of being robbed. "The Mazos are the carriers of the country, and these men are employed to transport on their backs as much as $1,000 in silver, and no one stops to think about any danger of having the money stolen." He concluded, "I think a decided era of progress is on in Central

America, and the republics there are bound to become more and more important."

After a few days in Washington, Pierce hurried to Kingston, Georgia, to the welcoming arms of his sister and her family. But his health did not improve as quickly as he had thought it would in his home climate. He soon realized that he could not get the rest he needed among his sister's busy family. So he went to Lithia Springs, a resort near Atlanta, where he rested several weeks. Then he moved to the Kimball House in Atlanta, where he would be close to his sister and also to his friends. He stayed there until September, commuting frequently to his plantation and to Kingston to see the Jones family.

Pierce returned to his post in Central America in October. He was deeply moved to be met by his staff, and distributed gifts that he had bought for them in the States. Soon after his return he was robbed by a Negro servant and had to go into the local police court. His experience made him have more respect for the local officials and for the courts, which tried to carry out their duties under great difficulty.

Pierce bought a horse and tried riding for recreation, in an effort to improve his health. No marked improvement resulted. Yet he did not allow his illness to interfere with the performance of official duties. One of his closest friends was Mrs. Zelaya, wife of the President. He enjoyed her companionship and frequently attended opera and concerts, rode horseback, and attended bull fights with her. However, he tried to walk as much as possible in order to exercise his feet, which bedeviled him constantly. He admitted in his diary on December 6, "I am very sick," yet the following day he had to go to Honduras in the Renton Case. Edwin F. Uhl, acting secretary of the Department of State, wired General Young on March 19, 1895, stating that a naval investigation had established that Charles W. Renton, an American, had been murdered at Brewers Lagoon, Honduras. Uhl advised Pierce to urge the government of Honduras to take prompt action "lest delay enable guilty parties to escape punishment." When Honduras failed to act after three months, Uhl telegraphed General Young to urge immediate action, and to report progress. The minister telegraphed immediately that President Bonilla assured him that the Honduras government was prosecuting an investigation with diligence and vigor and he hoped soon to have satisfactory results. Two days later Young was able to report that President Bonilla made a thorough investigation with full documentation. On June 25, 1895, Pierce telegraphed Secretary of State Richard Olney that three arrests had been made. Uhl wrote him on July 2 to proceed at once to Tegucigalpa and learn the present status of the case, "and personally impress upon the authorities of Honduras the confident hope" of President Cleveland that the accused murderers be speedily brought to trial and, upon conviction, made to suffer the extreme penalty of the law.[5]

Although Pierce's health was the cause of a great deal of suffering on the long arduous trip to Tegucigalpa he felt the investigation was a major success. On the last day of 1895, he wrote in his diary, "I humbly thank my heavenly Father for all the blessings of this year which have been many." He returned to Guatemala the first week of January.

A letter from Louisa written December 30, 1895, made Pierce homesick. She described the Christmas season at her home, and added that they all wished he could have been with them during the holidays, "but know that you must have had a more pleasant time where you were. . . . We all wish for you all things good, and hope your trip will prove most agreeable and beneficial to you, and your voyage has been perfectly safe with a calm sea. The great exposition closes tomorrow night, and how lonesome Atlanta will be. . . . Mrs. Joseph Thompson's picture is to be on all tickets sold today. She must like notoriety and Mrs. Felton goes on to Washington to conduct the contest for the Sr.'s seat in Congress; what is woman coming to!"

General Young was alarmed to learn in January that Dr. Jones had been sick and unable to work for a month. He realized how desperate the financial situation had become at Kingston when his nephew Tom wrote on January 7 that he had lost his horse in December and would have to buy one before he could do much farming. He asked his uncle to lend him seventy-five or a hundred dollars until fall, saying he was willing to pay eight or ten per cent interest. General Young sent his nephew the money. In addition he sent coffee and various Central American seeds for experimental planting. He took pride in his sister's courage and independence and the affection and esteem with which her children regarded her.

From January through May of 1896, General Young was busy with routine ministerial matters. Since his health did not improve he did not travel far from the capital. Early in May he received approval for a request to return to the United States for a rest.

With his servant George, he sailed for New York on May 23 on the Columbia Liner *Advance,* and landed very tired on June 22. He immediately went to see a physician, and on his advice entered the Presbyterian Hospital as a private patient.

From the hospital he wrote Tom Jones on June 23, "I got off the ship yesterday quite sick, but not too bad to lay me up. After I had been in the ship several days my feet began to swell. I thought it best to just move into a good Hospital for a week before trying to come home. I am very comfortably situated opposite the Park and my boy George is with me; after one week here I expect to come right to your house. You can write me here. I am under the best doctors and nurses in the city of New York. . . . I shall now try to get well of my illness. I shall be very glad to get to you, but I feel it best to be treated in a hospital where everything could be done in the best way. Write to me."

As soon as Dr. Jones received Pierce's letter, on June 29, he replied, "Our hearts reach out to you in loving sympathy for your affliction. We hoped from your first letter that we might welcome you home today, but disappointment takes your place." Then he added, "When your first letter after reaching New York came, my first impulse was to hasten to your side, but circumstances existing at the time prevented. I hope you feel assured that it will afford me the greatest happiness to come and serve you in any and every way upon earth whenever you wish, and hope you will not hesitate an instant." Louisa expressed regret that she and her husband were not well; however, they would come to him at a moment's notice whenever Pierce wished them to do so. "Do not fear about my strength; it is quite sufficient for the journey. Tom has desired to go ever since we heard of your arrival and illness in New York, and is ready to start at any hour." In closing she said, "I pray God you are better this morning and will very soon be able to come to us. . . . God bless and heal you."

On July 2, General Young sent Dr. Jones the following telegram: "I am better today. May wire you to come on in a few days." Dissatisfied with the news from Pierce, Tom wrote Dr. C. Irving Fisher, superintendent of the hospital, inquiring about his brother-in-law's condition. When he did not hear immediately Tom wired Dr. Fisher on July 3 that he was leaving for New York to see about Pierce. In the meantime Dr. Fisher wrote Mrs. Jones, assuring her that General Young's condition was not regarded as critical, "and that he is really much more comfortable than when he came in some ten days ago. He is not confined to his bed, and he hopes before long to make the journey homeward, stopping in Washington on his way."

On the way to New York, Dr. Jones stopped in Atlanta and gave the *News* a brief history of the General's ailment: "His heart has failed to discharge its duty for some time; swelling has set in in his feet and he suffers a great deal. The disease seems to have its effect in other parts of his system." He stated that when he received a letter from the General a few days before he was exceedingly anxious, "for in it he spoke of having trouble in breathing. Knowing the man and his ailment so well, I take this as indicative that dropsy of the heart has set in."[6] Future developments proved the correctness of the doctor's fears.

Dr. Jones arrived in New York on Saturday, July 4, and went at once to the hospital. He found Pierce sitting up and in a jovial mood; in fact, improved to such an extent that he was eager again to take up his journey within a few days to his Southern home. Two days later Louisa was reassured by a letter from her husband that her brother was better. Although he thought Pierce's condition decidedly serious, he was not in immediate danger. The next morning, finding Pierce cheerful and anxious to go home, Dr. Jones wrote his wife, "He has taken a little breakfast this morning sitting in an easy chair—but the trouble is that he sits up more than he should because he breathes easier in that position." The doctor added that despite his serious illness, Pierce's first thoughts were for his family and friends, and he sent his love and best wishes.

On Monday morning his condition rapidly changed for the better. He sent Dr. Jones to see Dr. E. G. Janeway, a consulting physician, and requested permission to leave. But before Dr. Jones returned to the hospital, in the short space of an hour, General Young had a sinking spell "and the spirit of the noble patriot and distinguished diplomat had crossed the Great Beyond."[7]

The *Atlanta Journal* on July 1 carried to the people of Georgia and of the South the first news of Pierce's serious illness. It also gave encouragement that General Young "would be about again in a few days." Therefore Louisa was especially shocked and numbed with grief to receive a telegram from her husband on July 6, that "General Young died very suddenly at eleven-thirty this morning. Cannot leave here for a day or two." Pierce's sudden death at first was unbelievable to the people of Cartersville. Then gloom seemed to settle upon his friends, who found it hard

to realize that the fabulous veteran was gone. An incident showing how greatly beloved the General was by the people occurred
in front of the post office about noon on Wednesday, two days
after his death. "On his fine river plantation near town are many
tenants, who without a single exception, worshipped him. When
the news reached the plantation that the magnanimous landlord had died, operation in farm work instantly ceased. Tenant
asked tenant, could it be true? In a body they hurriedly moved
toward Cartersville. The post office was reached, a copy of the
Atlanta Constitution was secured, and the leader began to read
the sad story. With eagerness they caught every word that fell
from the lips of the reader, who, sorrow stricken, could hardly
articulate. When the sad story had been finished, looking into
each other's tear-bedimmed eyes, they winded their way sorrow-
fully to the depot to find out when the remains would reach
Cartersville."[8]

Newspapers throughout the country carried an account of
Pierce's death, with an account of his life. Some stated that the
news of the death of General Pierce M. B. Young would carry
sorrow to every old soldier. His home town paper described
Pierce as "a most genial nature," saying that "a braver soldier
never drew a sword, and his thousands of friends and admirers
throughout the country will receive the news of his death with
the most profound sorrow."

Probably the *Macon News* best summarized the feelings of a
majority of newspaper editors: "General Young was a courteous
and chivalrous gentleman, a true Georgian and Democrat, a
faithful friend and a man of undaunted courage." The *Cartersville News* headlines were "The Dauntless Young to Rest Beneath
Bartow Sod. The People Sorrow. They mourn the loss of a distinguished citizen. Last Hours of General Young hopeful even up
to an hour of his death. He passes peacefully away."

Louisa was partly consoled in her grief by many telegrams and
letters of condolence from many of Pierce's former Confederate
comrades and friends. Secretary of State Olney wired: "The
President's sincere condolence and my own are offered you by
reason of the death of your brother, General Pierce M. B. Young
at New York yesterday. Upon learning the wishes of his family
the Department will arrange for transportation to place of burial."
The Bartow Camp of Confederate Veterans, upon Louisa's request, made arrangements for the funeral. General Clement A.
Evans, Major General Commander of the Georgia Division

United States Confederate Veterans, issued an order to all veterans in which he praised the gallantry, service, and genial nature of General Young. When the funeral train carrying the body arrived in Atlanta it was met at the depot by Confederate veterans (who acted as an honorary escort to Cartersville), by members of the United Daughters of the Confederacy, and many Atlanta friends. A special train brought Pierce from Atlanta to his home. There it was met by the Masonic fraternity, the Bartow Camp of Confederate Veterans, the fire department, city and county officials, and an "immense crowd of people the like of which had never been seen in Cartersville under a similar occasion."[9]

More than 5,000 friends and representatives from various organizations overflowed the Tabernacle to pay tribute to the distinguished warrior and diplomat. Besides the large choir of more than a hundred voices, and others assembled on the rostrum of the church, special seats were occupied by distinguished Georgians from all walks of life. The visiting speakers paid tribute to the courage, gallantry, geniality, and humility of General Young whose death touched "a cord that vibrated all over the country."[10] They emphasized that courage was the basis of freedom, and that no nation could become great without courageous leaders; such a man was Pierce Young, whose heart was big because he loved his fellow men, and in turn, was loved himself, for he possessed those attributes that ennobled and immortalized him in the hearts of his friends.[11]

Pierce Manning Butler Young might be called the Warwick of the South, since he was more often a supporter of leaders than a leader; he assumed leadership himself only when it appeared necessary and unavoidable. More often he remained in the background—willing for his friends to get full credit. He was a Southern gentleman, a gallant soldier of the Confederacy, a worthy public servant—and a proud and loyal American.

Notes

CHAPTER I

1. D. D. Wallace, *The History of South Carolina* (New York: The American Historical Society, Inc., 1934), II, 424.

CHAPTER IV

1. Morris Schaff, *The Spirit of Old West Point, 1858-1862* (Boston: Houghton Mifflin and Company, 1907), p. 149.
2. *Ibid.*, 165-66.
3. Frederick Whittaker, *A Popular Life of General George A. Custer* (New York: Sheldon & Co., 1876), pp. 36-46.

CHAPTER V

1. (Extract from) Special Orders, No. 30, P. M. B. Young Collection, Walnut Plantation.
2. (Extract from) Special Orders, No. 162, P. M. B. Young Collection.
3. *Atlanta Constitution*, March 19, 1893.
4. *Ibid.*
5. *Atlanta Constitution*, March 12, 1893.
6. *Ibid.*
7. *Atlanta Constitution*, March 19, 1893.
8. *The War of the Rebellion, A Compilation of the Official Records of the Union and Confederate Armies* (Washington: Government Printing Office, 1898), 11, Pt. 2, pp. 957-58. (Hereafter cited O R).
9. 11 O R Pt. 3, p. 660.
10. Unidentified, undated newspaper clipping, P. M. B. Young Collection.
11. *Atlanta Constitution*, March 12, 1893.
12. 27 O R Pt. 2, pp. 732-33.
13. *Ibid.*, 727-28.
14. *Ibid.*, 721-23, 679-85.
15. *Ibid.*
16. *Ibid.*, 312.

CHAPTER VI

1. 29 O R Pt. 1, p. 444.
2. *Ibid.*, 446.
3. *Ibid.*, 446-47.
4. *Ibid.*, 452.

5. 29 O R Pt. 2, p. 788.

6. *Ibid.*, 862-63.

7. Letter, April 2, 1864, P. M. B. Young Collection.

8. 36 O R Pt. 1, pp. 1, 872, 899.

9. Undated clipping from *Augusta Chronicle*, in scrapbook, P. M. B. Young Collection.

10. 42 O R Pt. 2, p. 656.

11. *New York Times*, quoted in *Atlanta Constitution*, August 8, 1896.

12. 42 O R Pt. 2, p. 1279.

13. 42 O R Pt. 1, pp. 634-36.

14. 42 O R Pt. 3, p. 1228.

15. 44 O R Pt. 3, p. 902.

16. 42 O R Pt. 3, p. 781.

17. *Ibid.*, 866.

18. Unidentified, undated clippings in scrapbook, P. M. B. Young Collection.

19. 42 O R Pt. 3, p. 1255.

20. 44 O R Pt. 3, p. 933.

21. Unidentified, undated clipping from scrapbook, P. M. B. Young Collection.

22. Clipping, *Augusta Chronicle*, April (no day given), 1897, scrapbook, P. M. B. Young Collection.

23. 47 O R Pt. 2, p. 1112 (Special Order 32).

24. Private papers and letters, P. M. B. Young Collection.

CHAPTER VII

1. I. W. Avery, *The History of the State of Georgia from 1850 to 1881, Embracing Three Important Epochs: The Decade Before the War of 1861-5; The War; The Period of Reconstruction, With Portraits of the Leading Public Men of This Era* (New York: Brown & Derby, Publishers, 1881), p. 335.

2. *Congressional Globe*, July 27, 1868, p. 4499.

3. Avery, *op. cit.*, 389-90.

CHAPTER VIII

1. *Congressional Globe*, Third Sess., 40th Cong., 1868-1869, Part I, H. R. No. 1515, Dec. 14, 1868.

2. *Congressional Globe*, Third Sess., 40th Cong., 1868-1869, Part II, Feb. 10, 1869, p. 1059.

3. *Ibid.*, Appendix, 230-31.

4. Undated clipping, scrapbook, P. M. B. Young Collection.

5. Undated clipping, scrapbook, P. M. B. Young Collection.

6. *Congressional Globe*, First Sess., 41st Cong., 1869, March 5, 1869, p. 16.

7. *Washington Evening Star*, Sept. 21, 1869.

8. *Congressional Globe*, Third Sess., 41st Cong., 1870-1871, Part I, Jan. 16, 1871, pp. 524, 527, 530.

9. *Ibid.*, Jan. 24, 1871, p. 703.

10. *Ibid.*, Jan. 24, 1871, p. 705.

11. *Ibid.*, Third Sess., 41st Cong., 1870-1871, Part II, pp. 951, 952, 1147.

12. *Ibid.*, 1186.

13. *Congressional Globe*, First Sess., 42nd Cong., 1871, Part I, p. 176.

14. *Acts and Resolutions of the United States of America Passed at the Forty-second Congress, December 2, 1872-March 3, 1873*, p. 48.

15. *Congressional Globe*, First Sess., 42nd Cong., 1871, Part I, March 22, 1871, p. 228.

16. *Ibid.*, Part II, Appendix, pp. 155-57.

CHAPTER IX

1. Letter in Hambleton Collection, Emory University Library.

2. *Cartersville Standard and Express*, Aug. 22, 1872.

3. *Ibid.*, Sept. 12, 1872.

4. *Atlanta Daily Constitution*, Nov. 7, 1872.

5. Mrs. W. H. Felton, *My Memoirs of Georgia Politics* (Atlanta: Index Printing Co., 1911), pp. 8-9.

6. *Cartersville Daily Herald,* July 22, 1874.
7. *Rome Courier,* April 26, 1874.
8. *Ibid.*
9. Unidentified, undated clipping, P. M. B. Young Collection.
10. *Rome Courier,* April 26, 1874.
11. *Cartersville Daily Herald,* July 22, 1874.
12. *Rome Courier,* Oct. 13, 1874.
13. *Atlanta Constitution,* Oct. 20, 1874.
14. *Rome Courier,* Oct. 28, 1874.
15. Avery, *op. cit.,* 513.
16. Quoted in the *Savannah Daily Advertiser,* March 7, 1875. This clipping was sent to Pierce by E. A. Silva, late sergeant major of Jeff Davis Legion who wrote, "Evidently, upon its face the impression is instantly made, no man wrote it."

CHAPTER X

1. *Boston Daily Globe,* June 17, 1875.
2. Undated clipping, P. M. B. Young Collection.
3. Correspondence of L. N. Trammell and Senator Thomas M. Norwood, Dec. 1875-Dec. 1877, in Emory University Library.

CHAPTER XI

1. *Cartersville Free Press,* Jan. 15, 1880.
2. *Atlanta Daily Constitution,* June 10, 1880.
3. *Atlanta Daily Constitution,* June 26, 1880.
4. *Atlanta Daily Constitution,* July 16, 1880.
5. *Ibid.*
6. *Atlanta Daily Constitution,* July 29, 1880.
7. *Ibid.,* Aug. 5, 1880.
8. *Ibid.,* Aug. 8, 1880.
9. *Ibid.,* Aug. 6, 1880.
10. *Ibid.,* Aug. 11, 1880.
11. *Ibid.*
12. *Ibid.*
13. *Atlanta Daily Constitution,* Aug. 12, 1880.
14. *Columbus Daily Times,* Aug. 14, 1880.
15. *Atlanta Daily Constitution,* Aug. 27, 1880.
16. *Ibid.,* Sept. 8, 9, 1880.
17. *Ibid.,* Oct. 9, 1880. Avery states 54,345 votes, p. 601.
18. *Columbus Daily Times,* Aug. 25, 1880.
19. Felton, *op. cit.,* 325.

CHAPTER XII

1. *Atlanta Constitution,* Jan. 5, 1886.
2. *Cartersville Courant-American,* Nov. 1, 1888.
3. *Ibid.*
4. *Ibid.*
5. *Augusta Chronicle,* Jan. 7, 1886.
6. *Ibid.*
7. *Atlanta Constitution,* Jan. 5, 1886.
8. Letter in P. M. B. Young Collection.
9. *Cartersville Courant,* July 29, 1886.
10. *Atlanta Constitution,* Nov. 11, 1886.

CHAPTER XIII

1. *Atlanta Constitution,* Oct. 11, 1887.
2. *Ibid.,* Oct. 19, 1887.
3. *Columbus Enquirer-Sun,* May 10, 1888.
4. *Cartersville Courant-American,* April 20, 1888.
5. *Augusta Chronicle,* June 17, 1888.
6. Unidentified, undated newspaper clipping, P. M. B. Young Collection.
7. *Cartersville Courant-American,* May 16, 1889.
8. *Atlanta Constitution,* Dec. 7, 1889.
9. *Ibid.,* Nov. 11, 1889.
10. *Ibid.*

CHAPTER XIV

1. *Atlanta Constitution,* March 9, 1893.
2. Letter in P. M. B. Young Collection.
3. *Atlanta Constitution,* March 22, 1893.
4. *Ibid.,* March 31, 1893.
5. *Brunswick Advertiser,* April 5, 1893.
6. *Atlanta Constitution,* March 31, 1893.
7. Unidentified, undated clipping, scrapbook, P. M. B. Young Collection.
8. *Atlanta Constitution,* June 29, 1893.
9. *Ibid.,* July 8, 1893.
10. *Ibid.*
11. *General Records of the Department of State,* Record Group 59, Appointment Papers of P. M. B. Young and Selected Diplomatic Despatches, Central America, Vol. 36, 1893-1894.
12. *Ibid.*
13. *Ibid.*
14. He was overthrown in December 1893 by Policarpo Bonilla.
15. Letters in P. M. B. Young Collection.
16. *General Records of The Department of State.* General Zelaya had led a successful revolt in April and June 1893 against President Sacaza.
17. *Ibid.*
18. *Ibid.*

CHAPTER XV

1. Unidentified clipping, dated Feb. 2, 1894, scrapbook, P. M. B. Young Collection.
2. Unidentified, undated clipping, scrapbook, P. M. B. Young Collection.
3. *Ibid.*
4. *General Records of The Department of State.*
5. *Papers Relating to The Foreign Relations of The United States with The Annual Message of The President, Transmitted to Congress, December 2, 1895* (Washington: Government Printing Office, 1896), Part II, pp. 882-935.
6. *Cartersville News,* July 10, 1896.
7. *Ibid.*
8. *Ibid.*
9. *Cartersville Courant-American,* July 9, 1896.
10. *Ibid.*
11. *Ibid.*

Selected Bibliography

The Annual Cyclopedia 1894. New York: D. Appleton and Company, 1895, XIX.

Avery, I. W., *The History of the State of Georgia from 1850 to 1881, Embracing Three Important Epochs: The Decade Before the War of 1861-5; The War; The Period of Reconstruction, with Portraits of the Leading Public Men of this Era*. New York: Brown & Derby, 1881.

Basso, Hamilton, *Beauregard, the Great Creole*. New York: Charles Scribner's Sons, 1933.

Bonner, J. C. and Lucien E. Roberts (eds.), *Studies in Georgia History and Government*. Athens: University of Georgia Press, 1940.

Borcke, Heros von, *Memoirs of the Confederate War for Independence*. 2 Vols. Edinburgh: Blackwood, 1866.

Brooks, Robert P., *History of Georgia*. Boston: Atkinson, Mentzer & Company, 1913.

Brown, Joseph M., *The Mountain Campaigns in Georgia; or, War Scenes on the W. & A.* Buffalo, N. Y., Art-Printing Works of Matthews, Northrop & Co., 1886.

Bryan, Thomas Conn, *Confederate Georgia*. Athens: University of Georgia Press, 1953.

Burge, Mrs. Dolly Sumner (Lunt), *A Woman's Wartime Journal; An Account of the Passage Over a Georgia Plantation of Sherman's Army on the March to the Sea, as Recorded in the Diary of Dolly Sumner Lunt (Mrs. Thomas Burge)*. New York: The Century Co., 1918.

Candler, Allen D., and Clement A. Evans (eds.), *Georgia; Comprising Sketches of Counties, Towns, Events, Institutions, and Persons, Arranged in Cyclopedia Form*. 3 Vols. Atlanta: State Historical Association, 1906.

Cartland, Fernando G., *Southern Heroes; or The Friends in War Time*. Cambridge: Riverside Press, 1895.

Chanal, Francois V. A. de, *The American Army in the War of Secession*. Leavenworth, Kan.: G. A. Spooner, 1894.

Clark, Walter (ed.), *Histories of the Several Regiments and Battalions from North Carolina, in the Great War 1861-65. Written by Members of the Respective Commands*. 5 Vols. Goldsboro, N. C.: Nash Brothers, 1901.

Cooper, Walter G., *The Story of Georgia*. 4 Vols. New York: The American Historical Society, Inc., 1938.

Coulter, E. Merton, *A Short History of Georgia*. Chapel Hill: University of North Carolina Press, 1947.

Cox, Jacob Dolson, *Military Reminiscences of the Civil War*. 2 Vols. New York: Charles Scribner's Sons, 1900.

Crafts, William Augustus, *The Southern Rebellion: Being a History of the United States from the Commencement of President Buchanan's Administration through the War for the Suppression of the Rebellion. Prepared from Official Documents and Other Authentic Sources*. 2 Vols. Boston S. Walker, 1867.

Cunyus, Lucy Josephine, *The History of Bartow County, Formerly Cass*. Bartow County, Georgia: Tribune Publishing Co., Inc., 1933.

Davis, Jefferson, *The Rise and Fall of the Confederate Government*. 2 Vols. New York: D. Appleton and Co., 1881.

————————, *A Short History of the Confederate States of America*. New York: Belford Co., 1890.

Day, Samuel Phillips, *Down South; or, An Englishman's Experience at the Seat of the American War*. 2 Vols. London: Hurst and Blackett, 1862.

Dowdey, Clifford, *Experiment in Rebellion*. Garden City, N. Y.: Doubleday & Company, Inc., 1946.

————————, *The Land They Fought For; The Story of the South as the Confederacy, 1832-1865*. Garden City, N. Y.: Doubleday & Company, Inc., 1955.

Draper, John William, *History of the American Civil War*. 3 Vols. New York: Harper & Brothers, 1868.

Dugat, Gentry, *Life of Henry W. Grady*. Edinburg, Tex.: The Valley Printery, 1927.

Dunbar, Alice, *The Political Life of John Brown Gordon, 1865-1880*. Emory University, Ga., 1939 (M.A. Thesis).

Dupuy, Richard Ernest and Trevor N. Dupuy, *The Compact History of the Civil War. With Battlefield Maps Designed by T. N. Dupuy and C. G. Dupuy*. New York: Hawthorn Books, 1960.

Eaton, Clement, *A History of the Southern Confederacy*. New York: The Macmillan Co., 1954.

Eckenrode, Hamilton James, *Jefferson Davis, President of the South*. New York: The Macmillan Co., 1923.

Eggleston, George Cary, *The History of the Confederate War; Its Causes and Its Conduct; a Narrative and Critical History*. 2 Vols. New York: Sturgis & Walton Company, 1910.

Evans, Clement A. (ed.), *Confederate Military History; A Library of Confederate States History. Written by Distinguished Men of the South*. 12 Vols. Atlanta, Ga.: Confederate Publishing Company, 1899.

Evans, L. B., *All About Georgia, Two Hundred Years of Romance and Reality; a Bicentennial Tribute*. New York: American Book Company, 1933.

Felton, Mrs. W. H., *My Memoirs of Georgia Politics*. Atlanta: The Index Printing Company, 1911.

Fielder, Herbert, *A Sketch of the Life and Times and Speeches of Joseph E. Brown*. Springfield, Mass.: Press of Springfield Printing Company, 1883.

Folsom, James M., *Heroes and Martyrs of Georgia. Georgia's Record in the Revolution of 1861*. Macon, Ga.: Burke, Boykin & Company, 1864.

Ford, Henry Jones, *The Cleveland Era, A Chronicle of the New Order in Politics*. New Haven: Yale University Press, 1921.

Forman, Sidney, *West Point; A History of the United States Military Academy*. New York: Columbia University Press, 1950.

Freeman, Douglas S., *R. E. Lee, A Biography*. 4 Vols. New York: Charles Scribner's Sons, 1934.

––––––––––, *Lee's Lieutenants, A Study in Command*. 3 Vols. New York: Charles Scribner's Sons, 1942.

––––––––––, *The South to Posterity; an Introduction to the Writings of Confederate History*. New York: Charles Scribner's Sons, 1939.

Garrett, Franklin M., *Atlanta and Environs, a Chronicle of Its People and Events*. 3 Vols. New York: Lewis Historical Publishing Company, Inc., 1954.

General Records of the Department of State, Record Group 59 Appointment Papers of P. M. B. Young and Selected Diplomatic Despatches Central America, Vol. 36, 1893-94.

Gilmer, George R., *Sketches of Some of the First Settlers of Upper Georgia, of the Cherokees, and the Author*. New York: D. Appleton & Company, 1855.

Gordon, John B., *Reminiscences of the Civil War*. New York: Charles Scribner's Sons, 1903.

Grady, Henry W., *The New South*. New York: R. Bonner's Sons, 1890.

Headley, Joel Tyler, *The Great Rebellion; a History of the Civil War in the United States*. 2 Vols. Hartford, Conn.: American Publishing Company, 1865.

Hensel, William U., *Life and Public Services of Grover Cleveland, Twenty-Second President of the United States and Democratic*

Nominee for Re-election, 1888. Philadelphia: Hubbard Brothers, 1888.

Hill, Louise B., *Joseph E. Brown and the Confederacy.* Chapel Hill: University of North Carolina Press, 1939.

Howe, Daniel Wait, *Civil War Times, 1861-1865.* Indianapolis: The Bowen-Merrill Company, 1902.

Howell, Clark, *History of Georgia.* 4 Vols. Chicago: The S. J. Clarke Publishing Co., 1926.

Johnson, Amanda, *Georgia as Colony and State.* Atlanta, Ga.: Walter W. Brown Publishing Co., 1938.

Johnson, Zachary T., *The Political Policies of Howell Cobb.* Nashville, Tenn.: George Peabody College for Teachers, 1929 (Ph.D. Thesis).

Johnston, Richard M. and William Hand Browne, *Life of Alexander H. Stephens.* Philadelphia: J. B. Lippincott & Co., 1878.

Jones, Charles C., *Georgians During the War Between the States (An Address Delivered Before the Confederate Survivors' Association in Augusta, Ga., April 26, 1889).* Augusta, Ga.: Chronicle Press Co., 1889.

――――――, *Military Operations in Georgia During the War Between the States (An Address Delivered Before the Confederate Survivors' Association in Augusta, Ga., April 26, 1893).* Augusta, Ga.: Chronicle Job Printing Company, 1893.

Jones, Charles E., *Georgia in the War, 1861-65.* Atlanta, Ga.: Foote & Davies, 1909.

Knight, Lucian L., *Alexander H. Stephens, The Sage of Liberty Hall, Georgia's Great Commoner.* Athens, Ga.: The McGregor Co., 1930.

――――――, *A Standard History of Georgia and Georgians.* 6 Vols. Chicago: The Lewis Historical Publishing Company, 1917.

Kurtz, Wilbur G., *Historic Atlanta, A Brief Story of Atlanta and Its Landmarks.* Atlanta, Ga.: The Conger Printing Company, 1929.

Martin, Isabella D. and Myrta L. Avary (eds.), *A Diary from Dixie, as Written by Mary Boykin Chestnut, Wife of James Chestnut, Jr., United States Senator from South Carolina, 1859-1861, and Afterwards an Aide to Jefferson Davis and a Brigadier-General in the Confederate Army.* New York: D. Appleton and Company, 1914.

Maurice, Sir Frederick Barton, *Statesmen and Soldiers of the Civil War; A Study of the Conduct of War.* Boston: Little, Brown, and Company, 1926.

McCabe, James D., Jr., *Life and Campaigns of General Robert E. Lee.* Atlanta, Ga.: National Publishing Company, 1866.

McClellan, Henry B., *The Life and Campaigns of Major-General J. E. B. Stuart, Commander of the Cavalry of the Army of Northern Virginia.* Boston: Houghton, Mifflin and Company, 1855.

McElroy, Robert McNutt, *Grover Cleveland, The Man and the States-*

man; an Authorized Biography. 2 Vols. New York: Harper & Brothers, 1925.

McMaster, John Bach, *A History of the People of the United States During Lincoln's Administration.* New York: D. Appleton and Co., 1927.

Meade, George Gordon (ed.), *The Life and Letters of George Gordon Meade, Major General United States Army.* 2 Vols. New York: Charles Scribner's Sons, 1913.

Meriwether, Mrs. Elizabeth (Avery) (pseud: George Edmonds), *Facts and Falsehoods Concerning the War on the South, 1861-1865.* Memphis, Tenn.: A. R. Taylor & Co., 1904.

Merrill, Horace Samuel (Oscar Handlin, ed.), *Bourbon Leader: Grover Cleveland and the Democratic Party.* Boston: Little, Brown, 1957.

Moore, James, *A Complete History of the Great Rebellion; or, The Civil War in the United States, 1861-1865.* Philadelphia: Quaker City Publishing House, 1867.

Nevins, Allan, *Grover Cleveland: A Study in Courage.* New York: Dodd, Mead & Company, 1933.

——————, *The War for the Union.* 2 Vols. New York: Charles Scribner's Sons, 1959.

Nichols, George W., *The Sanctuary: A Story of the Civil War.* New York: Harper & Brothers, 1866.

Nixon, Raymond B., *Henry W. Grady, Spokesman of the New South.* New York: A. A. Knopf, 1943.

Northen, William J. (ed.), *Men of Mark in Georgia; A Complete and Elaborate History of the State from its Settlement to the Present Time, Chiefly Told in Biographies and Autobiographies of the Most Eminent Men of Each Period in Georgia's Progress and Development.* 6 Vols. Atlanta: A. B. Caldwell, 1907.

Norton, Frank H., *The Life of Alexander H. Stephens.* New York: J. B. Alden, 1883.

Parker, George Frederick, *Recollections of Grover Cleveland.* New York: The Century Co., 1909.

Patton, Sadie, *Sketches of Polk County History.* Asheville, N. C.: The Miller Printing Company, 1950.

Phisterer, Frederick, *Statistical Record of the Armies of the United States.* New York: Charles Scribner's Sons, 1883.

Poore, Ben Perley, *Perley's Reminiscences of Sixty Years in the National Metropolis.* 2 Vols. Philadelphia: Hubbard Brothers, Publishers, 1886.

Regulations of the Georgia Military Institute, Marietta, Georgia, January 1850.

Russell, Sir William H., *My Diary North and South.* New York: O. S. Felt, 1863.

Schaff, Morris, *The Spirit of Old West Point, 1858-1862.* Boston: Houghton, Mifflin and Company, 1907.

Stine, James H., *History of the Army of the Potomac*. Philadelphia: J. B. Rodgers Printing Company, 1892.

Swinton, William, *Campaigns of the Army of the Potomac; a Critical History of Operations in Virginia, Maryland and Pennsylvania from the Commencement to the Close of the War, 1861-65*. New York: Charles Scribner's Sons, 1882.

Tankersley, Allen P., *John B. Gordon: A Study in Gallantry*. Atlanta, Ga.: Whitehall Press, 1955.

Temple, Mrs. Sarah Blackwell (Gober), *The First Hundred Years; A Short History of Cobb County, in Georgia*. Atlanta, Ga.: Walter W. Brown Publishing Company, 1935.

Thomason, John W., *Jeb Stuart*. New York: Charles Scribner's Sons, 1930.

Wallace, David D., *The History of South Carolina*. 4 Vols. New York: The American Historical Society, Inc., 1934.

The War of the Rebellion, A Compilation of the Official Records of the Union and Confederate Armies. 53 Vols. Washington Government Printing Office, 1898.

Whittaker, Frederick, *A Popular Life of Gen. George A. Custer*. New York: Sheldon & Company, 1876.

Whyte, James H., *The Uncivil War; Washington During the Reconstruction, 1865-1878*. New York: Twayne Publishers, 1958.

Wise, George, *Campaigns and Battles of the Army of Northern Virginia*. New York: The Neale Publishing Company, 1916.

Woodward, C. Vann, *Tom Watson, Agrarian Rebel*. New York: The Macmillan Co., 1938.

Woolley, Edwin C., *The Reconstruction of Georgia*. New York: Columbia University Press, 1901.

NEWSPAPERS

Atlanta Constitution, 1868-1896
Atlanta Daily Herald, 1872-1876
Atlanta Journal, 1883-1896
Augusta Chronicle, 1870-1890
Boston Daily Globe, 1872-1891
Brunswick Advertiser, 1875-1890
Cartersville Courant, 1885-1886
Cartersville Express, 1870-1875
Cartersville American, 1886-1896
Cartersville News, 1895-1896
Cartersville Standard, 1870-1896
Columbus Daily Enquirer, 1858-1873
Columbus Ledger, 1886-1890
(Augusta) *Constitutionalist*, 1865-1876
(Cartersville) *Free Press*, 1878-1883
Macon News, 1884-1890

Macon Daily Telegraph and Messenger, 1870-1884
New York Tribune, 1870-1890
Rome Daily Bulletin, 1869-1887
Rome Commercial, 1865-1876
Rome Daily Courier, 1879-1887
Rome Daily Tribune, 1887-1890
Savannah Daily Advertiser, 1868-1875
Savannah Morning News, 1870-1888
 (Milledgeville) *Union Recorder,* 1872-1880
Washington Post, 1877-1896

Index